Shipped but Not Sold

Perspectives on the Global Past

Anand A. Yang and Kieko Matteson

SERIES EDITORS

Shipped but Not Sold

Material Culture and the Social Protocols of Trade during Yemen's Age of Coffee

Nancy Um

University of Hawai'i Press
Honolulu

Color images were made possible by a generous contribution from the Harpur College of Arts and Sciences Dean's Office at Binghamton University.

Paperback edition 2022

Printed in the United States of America

Library of Congress Cataloging-in-Publication Data

Names: Um, Nancy, author.
Title: Shipped but not sold : material culture and the social protocols of trade during Yemen's age of coffee / Nancy Um.
Other titles: Perspectives on the global past.
Description: Honolulu : University of Hawai'i Press, [2017] | Series: Perspectives on the global past | Includes bibliographical references and index.
Identifiers: LCCN 2016044210 | ISBN 9780824866402 (cloth ; alk. paper)
Subjects: LCSH: Ceremonial exchange—Yemen (Republic)—History—18th century. | Merchants—Yemen (Republic)—History—18th century. | Yemen (Republic)—Commerce—History—18th century.
Classification: LCC GN449.8 .U4 2017 | DDC 394/.4—dc23
LC record available at https://lccn.loc.gov/2016044210

ISBN: 9780824893927 (paperback)

University of Hawai'i Press books are printed on acid-free paper and meet the guidelines for permanence and durability of the Council on Library Resources.

Contents

List of Illustrations

Figures

Plates

Following page 82.

Acknowledgments

While I was conducting archival research for my PhD dissertation almost twenty years ago, I noticed that the Dutch and English East India Company records from Yemen reflected a consistent preoccupation with ceremonial activities staged for merchants and gift exchange. Because I was primarily interested in architecture and urban form at that time, these references were unwelcome distractions to the goal of my study, so I paid little attention to them. Moreover, these cyclical receptions and gift encounters were sometimes described in the context of long, repetitive, and tedious disputes that, quite frankly, seemed petty and overdrawn. Many years later, when I returned to the Dutch archives, I came to understand that these disputes were primarily oriented around material goods and that they were extremely relevant rather than peripheral to the study of long-distance trade in Yemen. Many in-depth conversations with colleagues from different fields who are committed to various theoretical orientations helped me to engage in new ways of reading and thinking about sources, some of which I had been working with for many years. The paragraphs below constitute an effort to acknowledge the generous and lively but also challenging voices that are present, in some way or another, in the pages that follow.

I am fortunate to have landed in the vibrant Art History Department at Binghamton University, which has been, in every way, a perfect intellectual home for me. My colleagues at Binghamton have heard parts of this project in various forms and have commented generously and intelligently on them. Thanks are due to all of them for offering support throughout this process and providing specific suggestions for reading, but also for their inspiring collective vision of an expanded field of art history. Andrew Walkling went even further in offering help with early modern English orthography and conventions, while cheerfully fielding questions about seventeenth- and eighteenth-century Britain. Years ago Pam Smart lent me a stack of books, many of which appear in my bibliography, particularly those on exchange theory and notions of value. She deserves special mention for entertaining the tentative anthropological inclinations of an art historian with exceptional kindness and enduring support. Other colleagues on campus, such as Mary

Youssef, Kent Schull, John Chaffee, John Cheng, Nancy Appelbaum, Melissa Zinkin, Doug Holmes, Kathleen Sterling, Sébastien Lacombe, Lisa Yun, Ricardo Laremont, and Jon Karp, have offered opinions, support, and advice along the way. The wonderful graduate students I have worked with in recent years have set my work off in new and unexpected directions, particularly those in two recent seminars, Art in the Age of Discoveries in fall 2014 and The Art of Embassy in spring 2015. Special thanks go to my recent advisees, Hala Auji, Paulina Banas, Anwar Ibrahim, Deniz Karakaş, Laine Little, Lena Mei, and Zohreh Soltani, who always inspire me to work harder. Special thanks are due to Zohreh, who took time away from her own work to generously assist with the compilation of this index.

Most of this book was written while looking out at the Pacific Ocean from a beautifully appointed office at the Getty Research Institute in 2013–2014. That the Getty would sponsor a scholar's theme based on maritime interaction and visual culture was a great boon to my work. Thomas Gaehtgens and Alexa Sekyra offered an engaging program during that year, and the GRI staff, especially Peter Bonfitto, helped to foster an ideal environment for intensive research and focused contemplation. My colleagues at the Getty were wonderful companions in the lecture hall and around the seminar table but also by the pool and at Monday dinners. Thanks are due to all of my fellow scholars from Connecting Seas, but especially Corinna Riva, Carl Knappett, Meha Priyadarshini, Chanchal Dadlani, Christine Göttler, Vanessa Crosby, Alex Knodell, Hannah Baader, Kristina Kleutghen, Galia Halperin, Gert van Wijngaarden, Lihong Liu, and Suzanne Blier. Daniela Bleichmar must be singled out for the incisive comments she offered throughout the year, which raised the level of our discussions, but also for her warmth and friendship.

Audiences that heard me speak at the Townsend Center at UC Berkeley, Binghamton University, UC Merced, the annual meeting of the Middle East Studies Association, the European University Institute in Florence, the Eighteenth-Century Interdisciplinary Salon at Washington University, and the Getty encouraged me to open up my perspectives in important ways. Many generous friends and colleagues commented on particular aspects of the project or provided advice along the way, such as Jeff Cody, Gail Feigenbaum, Brian Considine, Richard Guy, Sylvia Houghteling, Prita Meier, Dana Leibsohn, Meredith Martin, Amanda Phillips, Sinem Arcak Casale, Sussan Babaie, Philip Stern, Kerry Ward, Naindeep Chann, Steven Topik, and Polly Roberts. Santhi Kavuri-Bauer, Wendy Shaw, David Simonowitz, and Heghnar Watenpaugh have given much-needed support through the years. Mohammad Gharipour has offered more encouragement and endorsement than I could ever deserve.

Resources at the National Archives in The Hague and the India Office Records at the British Library made this study possible. I thank the many librarians and archivists who helped me obtain documents in their reading rooms and remotely. Frank Kanhai was particularly generous and supportive. Staff members of the interlibrary loan offices at the Binghamton University Libraries and the Getty Research Institute worked tirelessly to obtain difficult sources and to track down obscure references. Various libraries and collections provided images and the permission to publish them, such as the John Hay Library, Brown University; the Royal Geographical Society (with IBG), London; the Musée Bartholdi, Colmar, France; the British Library; the British Museum; the American Numismatic Society; the New York Public Library; the National Museum of Denmark; the Stichting VOC-Schip Amsterdam; the Groninger Museum; the Moscow Kremlin Museums; and the Cleveland Public Library. I am especially grateful to those collections that have provided high-quality digital images and publication rights to them without restriction: the Rijksmuseum, Amsterdam; the Walters Art Museum; the Wellcome Library, London; the Victoria and Albert Museum; and the J. Paul Getty Museum, Los Angeles. They set a compelling model for the future of visual collections in the public domain.

In chapters 2 and 4, I revisit arguments made in articles I have published previously: "Order in the 'Arbitrary': The Distribution, Content, and Temporal Cycles of English Merchant Tribute in Eighteenth-Century Yemen," *Journal of Early Modern History* 18:3 (2014): 227–253; "Foreign Doctors at the Imam's Court: Medical Diplomacy in Yemen's Coffee Era," in "Transcultural Networks in the Indian Ocean, 16th–18th centuries: Europeans and Indian Ocean Societies in Interaction," edited by Su Fang Ng, a special issue of *Genre: Forms of Discourse and Culture* 48:2 (July 2015): 261–288; and "Chairs, Writing Tables, and Chests: Indian Ocean Furniture and the Postures of Commercial Documentation in Yemen, 1700–1750," in "Early Modern Objects in Motion," edited by D. Bleichmar and M. Martin, a special issue of *Art History* 38:4 (September 2015): 718–731. I thank Brill, Duke University Press, and Wiley-Blackwell for allowing me to draw on and amend that body of previous work.

The American Institute for Yemeni Studies, the Getty Research Institute, and the Harpur College Dean's Office at Binghamton University provided generous financial support for a project that required a great deal of travel, periods of release from teaching, and significant costs for permissions and color image reproduction. At the University of Hawai'i Press, I am truly grateful to Michael Duckworth, who has had unwavering faith in my work for many years. I thank Masako Ikeda for her interest in material culture, her willingness to take on my project, and her generous spirit. I could not have asked for a better editor.

Robert, Eliot, and Oliver have put up with this book for a long time, but also, with their patience and because of the happiness they inspire, have helped it to come to fruition. While making sure that I was never hungry, Robert has taught me that it is never worth the energy to worry about things that are out of your control. I cannot imagine a life without his support and companionship. Eliot and Oliver have taught me that it is always better to play a game of Monopoly, catch a frog outside (sorry, frogs!), or re-create the destruction of the first Death Star than it is to write another sentence, read another article, or edit another line. They are my treasures and my joy. Without my sister, Janet, I would be lost in the world.

But, in the end, this book is dedicated to my dear parents, who never needed to read Marcel Mauss to know that the cycle of gift exchange locks individuals into enduring relationships that also entail binding social responsibilities. Growing up, I really hated this unsentimental view of the world of gifts, which took all of the fun out of the act of receiving. Christmases and birthdays were the most extreme occasions for guilt. I never thought that this cynical disposition would eventually inspire me to think deeply about gifts and their various social meanings, thus serving as the basis for a scholarly book about the politics of exchange and all of its material contingencies in far-away Yemen, on the edge of the Indian Ocean. Having my parents right here with me as I send off this manuscript is a gift in the purest sense of the word, and one that cannot be enumerated or returned.

Note on Spelling, Conventions, and Dates

The spellings of names and places vary considerably in the documents consulted for this study, which were written in Arabic, Dutch, English, French, and German. In some cases, multiple spellings are used for the same name even in a single record or on a given manuscript page. As such, the task of keeping spelling consistent and recognizable has been difficult. The standards listed below represent my attempt to render this diverse material legible and coherent for a wide audience of readers.

Names of people and places in Yemen and Arabic terms have been assimilated to a standard, but simplified, Arabic transliteration system based on the one used in the *International Journal of Middle East Studies* unless there is an accepted alternate spelling in English, such as "Mocha" and "Sanaa." Special symbols, such as dots under consonants and lines over vowels, are omitted, but the ʻayn and hamza are marked. However, it is important to note that many of the names of Yemen's officials and traders, in addition to some more general terms, derive from the accounts of European observers who struggled to convey unfamiliar sounds in writing. Some are quite easy to decipher, but others remain uncertain. The latter are left in their original spelling and are delineated with quotation marks. Names, terms, and quotes drawn from VOC documents have not been assimilated to modern Dutch orthography. Names of cities in India are written as they would have been in the eighteenth century, for instance "Bombay" rather than "Mumbai" and "Cannanore" rather than "Kannur."

For the names of Indian trade textiles I generally use the spellings offered in the glossary of Irwin and Schwartz, *Indo-European Textiles*, which remains the most comprehensive compendium of these varieties. Thus they are usually delivered in their Anglicized forms even if they were sold by Indian, Dutch, or French merchants or if the cognates in Persian or other Indian languages are known. I therefore use cossae instead of *khasa* and soosie rather than *susi*. The body of water that is located between modern Iran and the Arabian Peninsula is referred to simply as "the Gulf." I call the institution that was generally known as the English or British East India Company, and also the United Company of Merchants of England Trading to the East Indies, the EIC throughout this text, and the people associated with it "the English," for the sake of consistency. When dates are derived from Arabic sources, they are presented as the *hijri* date followed by the Gregorian calendar date, separated by a slash, as in 1113/1701–1702.

Introduction

> The circulation of objects, especially across the edges of societies, civilizations, and trading regimes, is not merely a physical process but is also a movement and displacement of competing conceptions of things, a jostle of transaction forms. Global economies do not control the meanings of the commodities that their profits turn upon, even if the appropriation of these goods in the form of gifts, commodities, or prestige invaluables inevitably entangles receivers in wider relations that are not easily shrugged off.
>
> —Nicholas Thomas, *Entangled Objects*

Arabian stallions. Bottles of fragrant rosewater. Slivers of aromatic agarwood from Southeast Asia. Gilded porcelain coffee cups from China and Japan. Tufted Persian velvet in red, green, and blue. Translucent turban wrappers of Bengali muslin. Shimmering pieces of heavy satin from Gujarat. Bales of coffee beans grown in the mountains of Yemen. Sacks of cloves, cinnamon, mace, and nutmeg. Vials of spiced oils. Yardage of English broadcloth. Chests filled with silver pieces of eight. Chairs and tables crafted of tropical hardwoods. Casks of arrack distilled from rice and sugarcane on the island of Java.

This diverse list of colorful products includes commodities that were offered or sought in the markets of India and connected ports on the Red Sea and the Gulf around the year 1700. It also resembles a ship's manifest enumerating cargos that were shuttled around the region at the same time. Yet these items have been singled out here, not for their value as commodities to be bought or sold in the early modern marketplaces of the western Indian Ocean, but rather because they were "promiscuous objects" that also played ceremonial, social, and utilitarian roles in an intensely commercial society that was oriented toward the sea in early eighteenth-century Yemen. There these items were offered, displayed, exchanged, consumed, or utilized by major international merchants and local trade officials in a number of socially exclusive practices that affirmed their identity, status, and commercial obligations and also sustained the livelihood of their business ventures. This study looks at what happened to these goods, both local and imported objects, when they were diverted from the marketplace for a set of directives that were seemingly quite nontransactional.

Early Modern Commodities in and out of the Marketplace

It is increasingly popular to tell the story of single types or classes of commodities that developed a global purview in the early modern era. For instance, a comestible product such as coffee inspired a wide-reaching and relatively new audience by the end of the seventeenth century, when Europeans had picked up the habit from their neighbors in Arab lands and the eastern Mediterranean.[1] By the middle of the eighteenth century, the coffee plant was cultivated in both the Eastern and Western hemispheres, thus becoming global in its production as well as its consumption. Manufactured items, such as Asian porcelain, fostered new markets during the same period, while also inspiring many imitations worldwide.[2] Brightly patterned printed cotton textiles from India introduced a wave of sartorial novelty in Europe and spurred agricultural and industrial innovations that crossed world regions.[3]

Yet in the bazaars of Yemen, these items were far more than mere commodities. In addition to the commercial demand they inspired, they were also displayed, consumed, worn, or used in ceremonies of entry staged for major merchants who arrived at the jetty of the Red Sea port of Mocha. Some constituted the main fodder for commercial gifts that European merchants offered to local trade officials in Yemen's ports and emporia, even to the imam. Others were essential utensils brought by merchants to sustain their business endeavors on the Arabian Peninsula. As commodities, gifts, objects of display, everyday instruments, and highly potent signs, many of these goods operated in and circulated between linked commercial spheres and registers of exchange. Taking inspiration from the recent surge in historical work on global consumption that has effectively opened the door for a close consideration of the material dimensions of daily life, this study locates a whole host of Indian Ocean commodities in dense webs of social meaning among a diverse community of mobile merchants on the southern Arabian Peninsula from 1700 to 1740.[4]

Although today it is cast as remote and isolated, in the age when ships served as the dominant mode of long-distance travel, Yemen sat at the center of multiple intersecting oceanic networks, wedged at the meeting point of the Red and Arabian seas but also linked to the Mediterranean and the Indian Ocean. While the goods mentioned above were clearly subject to the global demand that activated their movement across oceans, in Yemen their meanings were not circumscribed to their commodity status, nor were they ever stable. I contend that the meaning and value of mobile and highly sought-after commodities may be better understood when their movement is suspended (at least momentarily) and they are located in specific rather than general geographic circumstances, with the interest of highlighting the intricate relationships that early modern merchants sustained with various classes of objects, locally derived and imported.

Yemen's Age of Coffee

During the seventeenth and eighteenth centuries, Yemen sat at the center of an increasingly caffeinated world. As such, much of its early modern history can be narrated through its engagement with the coffee plant, bean, and drink. Although *Coffea arabica* is native to the Horn of Africa, the hot, dark, brewed beverage familiar to us today was first consumed in Yemen in the early fifteenth century. The bush was also first cultivated actively there, thus furnishing a major local product of trade for the Ottomans, who occupied the region from 1538 to 1636 and are credited with establishing Yemen's coffee industry.[5] Coffee plants were farmed in the mountains, and the beans were shipped over land and by sea to eager consumers in the northern markets of Jidda, Cairo, and Istanbul, but also to the east, particularly Iran.[6] The Ottoman governors on Yemen's coast were the first to greet European company merchants who arrived in Mocha, a port that had been developed for trade and naval activity in the early sixteenth century.[7] The English came in 1609 and the Dutch in 1616, but neither in search of coffee, which they then knew little about. Rather they sought a stake in the western Indian Ocean trade, with the goal of filling the vacuum left by the weakening of Portuguese maritime power.

The Ottomans were also responsible for tying together, under the sultan's name, Yemen's north and south, regions that had been politically split for centuries, generally along the lines of the Shiʿi Zaydi highlands and the Sunni coastal lowlands. However, Ottoman ambitions outgrew the stability of their regime. In 1636 the Qasimi imams, of a local Zaydi family, ousted them, while also adopting from them a largely unified Yemen that they oversaw from the mountain highlands. The Qasimis have received little notice by modern historians of the Middle East, and when they are mentioned, they are usually sketched as relatively insular.[8] Yet records of the Indian Ocean trade show that the Qasimi imams of Yemen were deeply invested in global exchange and maintained close contact with foreign merchants.

If Yemen's age of coffee began under Ottoman rule, it came to fruition and full productivity under the Qasimis, who installed a centralized coffee emporium in the lowland town of Bayt al-Faqih some time in the middle of the seventeenth century (Figure 0.1). Merchants from Jidda and their local

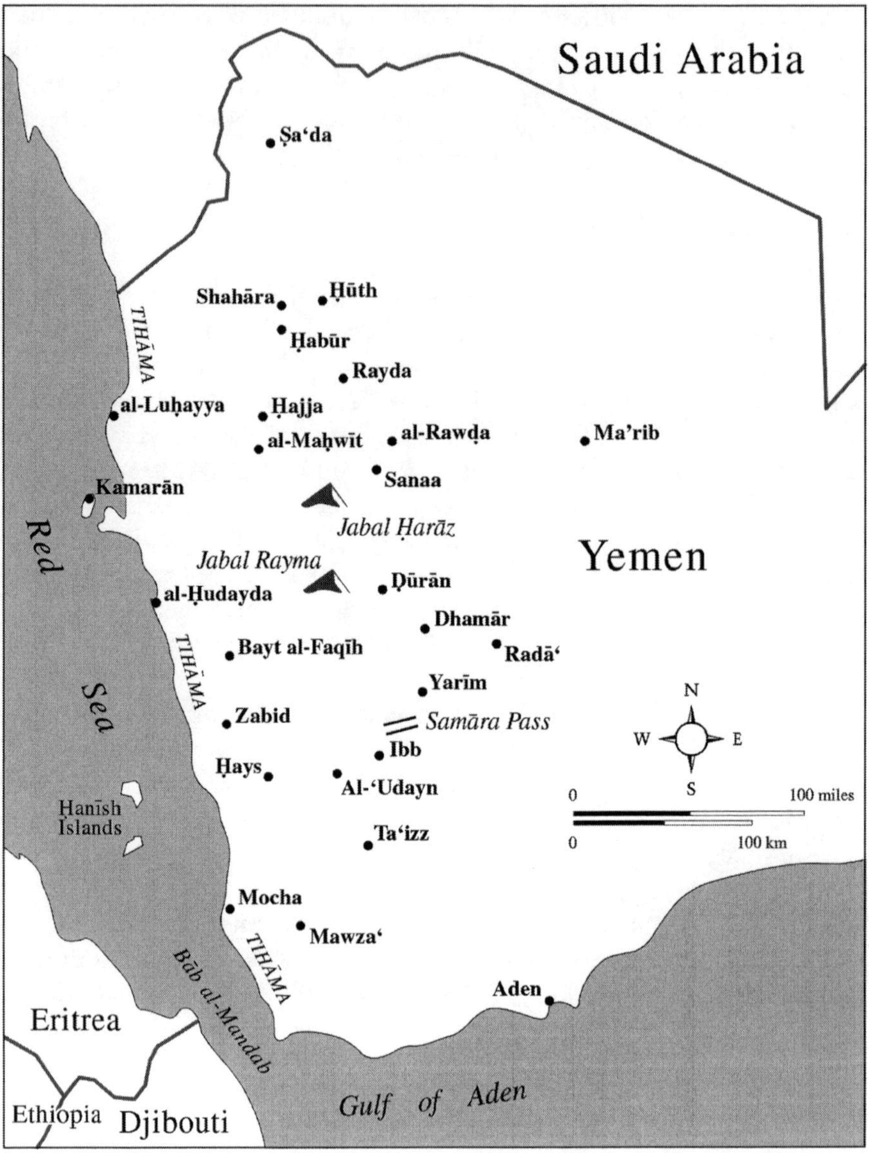

Figure 0.1. Map of Yemen. Drawn by Barry Levely.

agents frequented this market, in addition to Gulf traders who arrived from ports such as Basra in modern-day Iraq, Kung on the Persian coast, and Musqat in Oman. In the late seventeenth century, coffee also came to dominate English and Dutch interests in the Yemen trade. The French and Ostenders, who arrived in Yemen in 1709 and 1719, respectively, followed soon after.[9] Bayt al-Faqih was not the only coffee market in Yemen, but it was certainly the largest and the most international, with all of the above-mentioned merchants renting houses there for the duration of the coffee intake season. For this reason, Kristof Glamann, a VOC (Vereenigde Oost-Indische Compagnie, Dutch East India Company) historian, called Bayt al-Faqih the "centre of a trade of a world-embracing character," animated by merchants from the north and the south, who shipped via Red Sea, Mediterranean, and Indian Ocean channels.[10] The period from 1700 to 1740, which marks a high point in demand there as well as punctuating the end of Yemen's near monopoly on the bean, is the focus of the current study.

Competitors began to challenge Yemen's singular status as the world's major coffee purveyor as early as 1725, when the Dutch finally harnessed the quality and yield of the plant, with which they had experimented for many years on the island of Java.[11] The next year marked the first time coffee grown in Southeast Asia outweighed the Yemeni bales sold in Amsterdam. French colonial cultivation efforts succeeded soon afterward. In the 1730s coffee grown on the Caribbean island of Martinique and shipped through Marseille began appearing in the markets of the eastern Mediterranean, thus reversing the long-standing east-to-west flow of the bean.[12] Small quantities of coffee are still exported from Yemen, but the region relinquished its nearly exclusive role as a global coffee provider by the middle of the eighteenth century.

As important as coffee is to Yemen's trade history, one must recognize that it was one of many commodities to pass through local ports and emporia during this era. In fact, some of Yemen's major merchants, such as Mulla Muhammad 'Ali, the famous shipowner from Gujarat, did not deal in coffee at all but rather focused on selling Indian textiles in Yemen, with the goal of procuring Central American silver for the mints of the subcontinent. So coffee serves as an important but not exclusive commodity of focus as well as constituting an overarching contextual backdrop of this study because of the increasing European interest in it. Although Europeans' demand for coffee did not exceed that of Muslim merchants from both the Mediterranean and the Gulf regions in this period, the Western presence in Yemen's coffee market is important because of the copious records it yielded. In fact, the voluminous European documentation makes this era one of the best recorded in Yemen's premodern history.[13]

This book relies upon these materials, now housed in archives in The Hague and London, but with the understanding that Europeans were never the most numerous or active merchants in Yemen, only its most dedicated observers. Their records also narrate more than the history of the overseas trade. They provide precious perspectives on local events, some of which were wholly or partially overlooked by Yemen's historians. The few Europeans who had the opportunity to visit the highlands, such as the French surgeon Barbier in 1712, left unique descriptions of Imam al-Mahdi Muhammad's (r. 1686–1718) everyday routines and his inquisitive interest in the nature of the French monarchy. It is also through European eyes that we can add to our understanding of some of the political upheavals that originated in Yemen's interior and then trickled down to the coast. The Dutch, for instance, provide a day-by-day account of the extended 1727–1728 struggle for the imamate between two competing candidates, al-Mansur Husayn (r. 1727–1748), son of the previous imam, and al-Nasir Muhammad bin Ishaq (d. 1754), who was seen by many as more suitable for the position. Although these two rivals were based in the Yemeni highlands, they sent representatives to vie for the lucrative ports and the lowlands as strategic lynchpins in their struggle. The Dutch records of the 1728 siege of Mocha thus add to a historical narrative that has been told only from the perspective of the mountains.

Other key events directly involved the Europeans as participants and not just observers. For instance, in 1719, after prodding from the Ottomans, Imam al-Mutawakkil Qasim (r. 1718–1727) installed a ban on European coffee purchases at Bayt al-Faqih.[14] This ban was highly ineffective and in place for only a short period of time, but it indicates that Europeans could be a source of anxiety for other coffee merchants who were active in Yemen, namely those shipping for Cairo and the wider Ottoman world. In 1737 the French sent three warships to Yemen with the claim that the governor of Mocha, Faqih Ahmad Khazindar, had violated their trade agreement.[15] They ended up firing on the port, damaging the city's Great Mosque, and seized the southern fort in order to get their outstanding debts repaid. This attack was remembered and recounted in the city for decades to come and was often cited by later travellers to Mocha. Although largely one-sided, these narratives of observation, engagement, encounter, and conflict serve as key sites for the examination of the early modern cross-cultural experience in the western Indian Ocean.

Hierarchies of Trade Administration

Three successive imams, al-Mahdi Muhammad, his nephew al-Mutawakkil Qasim, and the latter's son al-Mansur Husayn, were engaged players in the

Indian Ocean trade during Yemen's age of coffee. Despite the fact that he rarely left his mountain seat, the imam was deeply aware of events that took place in the lowlands and across bodies of water in connected ports. In fact, he owned a pair of ships that docked at Mocha and dispatched them yearly across the Indian Ocean to the Gujarati port of Surat. Communications between the coast and the imam's capital were maintained consistently through messengers and letters, although the journey took at least eight days. Overseas merchants in Yemen maintained close contact with the imam, occasionally visiting the court in person but more frequently through written correspondence. The large sample of translated letters in the Dutch National Archives attests to the vibrancy and consistency of these connections from the perspective of one of Yemen's foreign merchant groups. The Dutch and the English, in particular, appealed directly to the imam to settle commercial disputes, for instance to get long-standing debts incurred by other merchants paid, or even for minor domestic claims, such as a disagreement about a rental contract with a landlord in Mocha. Merchants based on the coast also sent the imam lavish gifts, sometimes annually, as I describe in chapters 2 and 3.

By contrast, overseas merchants dealt directly with a number of provincial officials on a daily basis. The imam appointed these administrators, particularly the governors of the ports and Bayt al-Faqih. Although we can not account for the full purview of their governing responsibilities, we can gather from the sources that they were expected to collect taxes and duties from their district, which were supposed to be funneled directly to the highlands. They were also concerned with local security, charged with ordering the troops stationed in their cities, and maintaining the upkeep of urban fortifications. Shaykh Salih al-Huraybi (d. 1723) held the post of Mocha's governor in the early years of the eighteenth century under Imam al-Mahdi, who also named him *wazir* (minister at court). After leaving Mocha, he oversaw Bayt al-Faqih and thus occupied some of the most lucrative administrative posts in all of Yemen during the period under consideration. His successor in Mocha, Amir Rizq, was formerly a *nakhudha* (ship captain) who led Imam al-Mahdi's ships on their yearly voyages to India. Undoubtedly his awareness of maritime affairs merited him the promotion to coastal governor under the following imam, al-Mutawakkil, in 1718. His son, 'Ali bin Amir Rizq, followed in his father's footsteps, taking the Mocha post after his death in 1721. One of the most illustrious governors of Mocha, Faqih Ahmad Khazindar, held the position twice, first in the 1720s under Imam al-Mutawakkil and then again in the 1730s under al-Mansur. The European merchants of Mocha constantly complained about his unjust policies and avaricious methods, which were cited as reasons for the 1737 French bombardment of the port, after which he was permanently removed.

Many lower-ranking officials were also involved in the trade, although their exact duties are not entirely clear from the records.[16] For instance, the *amir al-bahr* was the overseer of port affairs who would maintain a watch over the seashore and identify new ships as they appeared in the harbor. Presumably he would also have held responsibility over the fishermen, boat owners, and other members of the maritime populace. The chief *sarraf* (money-exchanger) of Mocha was also a key figure in the trade; he took responsibility for the collection of duties and taxes from merchants at the conclusion of each trading season. Two major merchants, Hasan Hasusa and Muhammad Yasin, who was originally from Basra but died in Mocha, held this post in the early eighteenth century. The imam maintained a *wakil* (commercial agent) at the port as well. This agent conducted trade on the imam's behalf, while also engaging in his own independent commercial enterprises. Qasim al-Turbati, a long-standing resident and merchant of Mocha who often traded with the Europeans in the city, held this position during the 1730s.

The Social Construction of Yemen's Overseas Merchants

The names of these local merchants who also held official positions—Muhammad Yasin, Hasan Hasusa, and Qasim al-Turbati—appear as main characters in the pages that follow. I also identify major merchants from India as key players in Yemen's overseas trade, such as Mulla 'Abd al-Ghafur and his grandson successor, Mulla Muhammad 'Ali, shipowners from the port of Surat; Sidi Yaqut Khan, the admiral of the Mughal Navy, based at Danda-Rajpuri, south of Bombay; and the Mappila Muslim Ali Raja of Cannanore on the Malabar coast. European company merchants, namely the Dutch, English, and French, were also prominent figures in Mocha's trading world.[17] These merchants have been singled out of a much larger and lesser-known group as members of Mocha's major overseas merchant class, a category I refer to consistently and strategically in this study.

While relying upon the designation "major overseas merchant" as an organizing concept, my larger goal is to clarify the limits and parameters of this proposed grouping. In general, the possible measures one can use to gauge merchant status, such as relative trade volume, are unavailable or unevenly accessible for the western Indian Ocean context. Even Arabic terminology employs only vague terms to differentiate various classes of commercial actors. Historically, the *tajir* (pl. *tujjar*, merchant) was a wholesaler whose trade extended outside of local markets and who dealt in a relatively large volume of goods.[18] Thus the term *tajir* serves to distinguish a major trader from a *ba'i'*, a retailer in the bazaar, in terms of his scope and scale of enterprise. It also sets apart the *tajir* from a travelling peddler, of the type that might sell assorted wares periodically, while undertaking the pilgrimage, for instance. Yet scholars of trade lack more precise language to differentiate various subgroups of traders in terms of financial scale and social standing within this widely cast grouping of the *tajir.* In the absence of readily available terms, many historians have resorted to relatively generic descriptive language to gauge and convey merchant status. For instance, while being remarkably attentive to the nature of merchant identities and the social dynamics of trade, André Raymond refers to the al-Sharaybi family of coffee merchants in eighteenth-century Cairo as "great merchants" (*grands tujjar*); Jessica Goldberg describes those featured in the letters of the Cairo Geniza as the "middling sort"; and Gagan Sood designates a diverse group of early modern Indian Ocean actors as "merchants of substance."[19]

Unfortunately, available sources are of little help in attaining more precision about the relative status of the *tajir,* particularly for Yemen. Merchants are rarely mentioned in local Arabic texts, and when they are their commercial activities are often subordinated to their pious profiles.[20] In one rare instance, a resident of Mocha referred to the Surati shipowner 'Abd al-Ghafur in hyperbolic terms as "the king of merchants" (*malik al-tujjar*), which signals the high esteem in which his activities were held in Yemen but does not provide further specification.[21] On the other hand, we have copious data about the dealings of the European company traders who were active there, which allows us to track their transactions with a great deal of accuracy. These records, comprising company archives and travel narratives, offer certain pieces of information about their Asian and local counterparts, but they are usually fragmented, uneven, and available only for the parts of their enterprises that concerned European interests.

A few examples demonstrate that social status and financial standing were not necessarily dependent categories among the overseas merchant class, which Goldberg suggests was the case with the merchants of the medieval Cairo Geniza as well.[22] For instance, Qasim al-Turbati was described as Mocha's leading merchant for many years even after he incurred major losses from an Arabian Sea shipwreck in 1716.[23] At the time, VOC merchants surmised that this calamity would cost him dearly, estimating the hefty loss of 16,000 to 20,000 Spanish reals. Their assessments appear to have been correct. After that unfortunate occurrence, he began to accrue significant debts to both the English East India Company (EIC) and the VOC, which remained unpaid until his death in 1737. Yet his social and political standing was apparently unaffected by this blow to his financial status. Throughout the 1720s and 1730s, he continued to maintain a close relationship with the imam of Yemen, serving in appointed positions in

Mocha. He was second to the governor in the 1720s and the imam's *wakil* in the 1730s. He wielded the influence of these privileged posts and the support of local officials in order to maintain his shaky business, even as he continued to build up debt and as his aggrieved lenders tried in vain to discredit his reputation.[24] His case reflects the extent to which connections to Yemen's imam and his provincial administrators could override the financial dissolution of one's commercial enterprise.

In sharp contrast, one can consider the case of Mocha's Baniyan merchants, Hindu and Jain traders from the Kathiawar Peninsula in Gujarat. Operating in southern Arabia, in the Gulf, and along the eastern coast of Africa, members of this mobile trading group were key players in the world of overseas commerce and occupied many different positions in regard to it. They are best known as brokers to major traders, including the Europeans, but they also engaged directly in wholesale activities. Moreover their brokerage work usually entailed other tasks and skills, such as translation and banking, which merited many the title of *sarraf.* In 1719 the Dutch cited three of Mocha's chief Baniyans as the city's highest volume traders, in addition to three other Muslim merchants: al-Turbati, Muhammad Yasin, and a certain Hajji Muhammad, who was described as a Turk.[25] Yet the Baniyans, who were considered to be *dhimmi*s (protected minorities) only by an extremely gracious understanding of Islamic law,[26] were socially marginalized and politically vulnerable throughout Yemen. Records from Mocha and other cities where they operated reveal that they were often pressed to surrender their profits to the local treasury through various measures of coercion that sometimes entailed the use of force.[27] In this case, their trading volume and impact on overseas commerce far outstripped their social and political clout in the city.

These examples suggest the difficulties in calibrating how economic standing, trade volume, and social status line up within and among the merchant classes historically in Yemen. They also suggest that the most prominent, visible, and politically connected merchants of Yemen were not always the most financially stable. For these reasons, I take up merchant class as a social category rather than one that can be determined by quantifiable means alone, thus following the call of historian Natasha Glaisyer and others "towards broadening the agenda of economic history."[28] In the case of eighteenth-century Yemen, we can discern a diverse yet small group of long-distance maritime traders whose cargo arrived on high-capacity ocean-going vessels each year according to the rhythms of the global wind cycle, who owned or rented large, multistory houses that were located along Mocha's coastline, who maintained close contact with the imam and his many provincial officials, and who engaged in a set of shared yet exclusive social practices and protocols that constitute the subject of this study. These merchants operated in far-flung networks that extended across the Arabian Sea rather than along shorter distances within the bounded Red Sea or Gulf region and occupied a place of privilege in Yemen's trading society. It may be said that they were the upper social echelon of the overseas merchant class based in Mocha in the first half of the eighteenth century.

Yet this category of Yemen's major overseas merchants may not be circumscribed by a single place of origin or identity. Instead it cuts across the various groups that traded in Yemen. Notably, those Arabic verses that described ʿAbd al-Ghafur as the "king of merchants" did not indicate that he was a Sunni Bohra who lived in India and rarely or perhaps never visited Yemen's shores, thus suggesting a lack of differentiation between Indian merchants and their local counterparts that may be surprising to modern readers.[29] Additionally, merchants associated with the Dutch, English, and French East India companies, and some private ones, should be counted among this privileged class of local traders and those based in India. By locating them on a shared social plane with major Asian and local merchants, I react particularly to the long-standing perception among historians that Europeans were a disruptive or marginalized presence in Indian Ocean markets. As a conceptual model, the work of Sood spurs me on; he has argued effectively that we need to understand convergences within the tightly interconnected Islamicate Eurasian sphere rather than allow later definitions of nation and continent to mold our understanding of early modern identities.[30]

In the case of Mocha, these high-volume European wholesalers occupied a shared status with major Asian and local wholesalers. Moreover they often struggled to make sense of local protocols for trade and thus sometimes mimicked the conventions, modes of consumption, and social rites of their Indian counterparts in Yemen. But in other cases, they implemented their own unique customs and modes of operating. A close consideration of their selective adoption of locally dominant social and cultural practices provides an avenue for us to further interrogate the extent to which Europeans assimilated to or served as shaping forces in Indian Ocean markets before the high age of empire, an enduring question in the study of early modern European commercial expansion.

In order to better describe the category of the major overseas merchant, I draw comparisons between this group and the *dhimmi*s, religious minority communities that were governed by the Pact of ʿUmar, an agreement that required Muslim authorities to provide protection for them based on their adherence to certain regulations regarding behavior and activity. In eighteenth-century Yemen, *ahl al-dhimma* (protected minorities) comprised the Baniyans but also the sizeable and long-established Jewish community. It should be noted, however, that the seventeenth and eighteenth centuries represented a period of tumultuous upheavals for both, and particularly the latter, as widespread messianic movements emboldened Jewish communities across the Islamic world. In Yemen these led to heated confrontations with the Zaydi imam that were regarded as outright rebellion and a violation of their enduring relationship.[31] In response, Yemen's Jewish community was exiled temporarily to the lowland town of Mawzaʿ in 1679; the imam intended ultimately to expel them from Yemen entirely. Although many eventually returned to their original respective home cities around Yemen after a yearlong deportation, some died in exile, all experienced loss and hardship, and their status was irrevocably changed after that cataclysmic experience.

As Bernard Haykel has shown, these turbulent events occurred during a time of intense debates among Zaydi religious scholars in the Yemeni highlands, who were increasingly coming under the influence of Sunnis and Sunni-oriented thinkers.[32] Those who leaned toward Sunni interpretation argued that religious minorities should not be permitted to live anywhere on the Arabian Peninsula, whereas the Zaydis took a much more delimited and tolerant stance on this issue. Although neither *dhimmi* group witnessed another large-scale expulsion attempt, the result of these intra-Muslim doctrinal differences and disputes was that both the Baniyans and the Jews witnessed extreme shifts in their status in the eighteenth century, swinging between periods of persecution and hostility and the granting of certain privileges by the imam.[33] While the Jews were not heavily involved in the international trade during this time, the commercially active Baniyans, who were granted their *dhimmi* status only in the mid-seventeenth century, serve as a useful contrast to the major overseas merchants. The Baniyans played an essential role in the success of Yemen's long-distance trade and, like the Europeans, received certain trade privileges that exceeded the expectations of their *dhimmi* status. Yet both groups were perennially perceived as outsiders, even after many years of residence and activity in Yemen's ports and emporia.

Learning from Trade Diaspora Communities

Shipped but Not Sold emerges from and responds to a rising interest in premodern merchant groups whose trading networks extended over widespread geographies. The most productive work in this realm has highlighted "trade diaspora" communities, such as Francesca Trivellato's study of the Sephardic merchants of seventeenth-century Livorno, Sebouh Aslanian's research on the Armenian traders of New Julfa during the same period, and Goldberg's reconsideration of the Jewish merchants of the medieval Cairo Geniza.[34] This body of work is valuable precisely because it looks at the organizational mechanics of trade, concentrating on how commercial activities were conducted among a group of dispersed merchants across long distances during times when travel was arduous and modes of communication were slow and sometimes unreliable.

Based on meticulous readings of understudied or misunderstood archival materials, Trivellato, Aslanian, and Goldberg explore the social organization of these trading groups with the understanding that a single merchant's success often hinged upon the efforts of many agents, partners, and officials in multiple locations. They show that financial transactions encompassed only one part of the commercial enterprise by sketching premodern trade as a social rather than purely economic endeavor that was fundamentally underpinned by diverse interactions and exchanges within and across seemingly closed groups. I follow upon their lucid instruction by looking at the social world of the long-distance trade in Yemen and suggesting that a sense of belonging was constituted, at least in part, through material objects that were exchanged, consumed, used, or displayed prominently by the major overseas merchant class.

These earlier studies are important also for offering the perspective that the enterprises of overseas merchants were relatively fragile, even those of leading traders. Similarly in Yemen, merchant status was often contingent upon faraway social and political realities and subject to the vagaries of sea travel, as in the case of al-Turbati. Trivellato, Aslanian, and Goldberg effectively call into question the notion that family, ethnic, and religious networks were independently self-sustaining and thus advocate the need to look closely at how the social fabric of the long-distance trade was nurtured and developed. By denaturalizing the assumed robustness of merchant relations, especially within relatively tight-knit yet geographically dispersed communities, and calling into question any implicit sense of trust that bound them together, their work allows us to understand that merchants were constantly in the process of crafting and honing their identities, cultivating relationships with agents, partners, and officials, and negotiating their delicate legacies over expansive distances and across diverse cultural, religious, and political spheres.

These lessons are crucial to understanding the maritime trade in the Indian Ocean, particularly after the arrival of Europeans, who introduced new commercial codes that joined rather than replaced much longer established regional codes. Moreover, while looking within the bounds of a single community, Trivellato's work especially sheds light on early modern merchant interactions that cut across a wide spectrum of groups, as was the case in eighteenth-century Yemen, with its ties that stretched from London and Amsterdam to Surat and Batavia (Jakarta) and thus required multiple means and objects of mediation to communicate across social, cultural, and linguistic boundaries.

The Material Practices, Protocols, and Routines of Trade

We may understand this diverse grouping of Yemen's major overseas merchants not only by the scope of their trade activity, the overlapping maritime routes they travelled, and their shared social standing, but also by the privileges they received, the common activities they participated in, and the reoccurring objects they utilized within them. As the following chapters show, their exclusive status was conferred and confirmed yearly through their involvement in repetitive rites and routines that, as I argue, were closely associated with the cycles of maritime trade. Participation in these rites was restricted to certain merchants at the invitation of or with approval by local authorities and officials. By taking part, these merchants were set apart from the brokers, low-level merchants, and retailers in Mocha, but also from the nameless masses of the maritime proletariat. So although European merchants often cast certain rites, such as the requirement to bestow annual gifts to local trade officials, as burdens, they were actually privileges of the local trade system to which only a limited membership was invited.

The trade records of the EIC and VOC devote a certain amount of energy to the description of these practices, particularly the lavish ceremonies that were staged for merchants who arrived on Yemen's shores each year to trade, the gifts that were expected of all major merchants each season and also accompanied most written inquiries and official visits, and the small and often impromptu receptions that took place within merchants' houses and always entailed rites of welcome, such as the sprinkling of rosewater and the offering of coffee. While attesting to the pervasive need to engage in such practices in order to assimilate to local norms and expectations, our European narrators just as readily dismiss many of them with the assumption that lavish ceremonies were indicative of the excesses of Eastern governance and that requisite gifts reflected the corrupt system of trade dominated by Oriental despots. Predictably, many modern scholars have followed the tone and tenor of these sources by generally ignoring or sidelining these practices in more recent studies of maritime commerce. On the whole, with their deep and structural reliance on economic measures of interpretation, Indian Ocean historians have been uninterested in the social life of trade, understanding commerce within the narrowest possible light of its transactional processes and restricted to those exchanges that resulted in a tangible loss or profit.

As sketched here, the cycles of trade began as soon as merchants appeared in the harbor of the port and not from the instance of their first commercial transaction. Moreover, much of the wider social activity that merchants engaged in, such as ceremonial receptions and the practices of merchant tribute, may be counted as steps in the extended commercial process and the associated aspects of long-distance shipping. Along with many everyday tasks, such as record keeping and letter writing, these various rites and routines must be considered the actual substance of commercial activity rather than its peripheral excess.

This initiative to look at the social and material activities of long-distance merchants draws upon a long-standing historical interest in abstract concepts of trust and reputation as key to the structure of cross-cultural trade. Inspired by or in reaction to the pioneering work of economist Avner Greif, recent historians, such as Trivellato, Aslanian, Goldberg, and others, have made a case for looking at how trust was constituted and sustained in and across various commercial contexts.[35] Yet Greif and those who followed him have looked primarily at the behavioral aspects of merchant conduct to examine how traders viewed their commercial partners and agents and how they all presented themselves in the far-flung spheres within which they operated. As such, the material, physical, and tangible dimensions of what Greif called "the reputation mechanism" have not been explored seriously.[36] I suggest emphatically that material objects, many of which mirrored the ones held in Yemen's warehouses and the cargo holds of ships docked in Mocha's harbor, also played a role in the maintenance of merchant relations as legible and weighty social markers.[37] As Greif and others have shown, one's reputation was never set in stone but required constant renewal and was subject to reevaluation over time. This prevailing instability, along with the cyclical nature of the maritime trade, allocated an important place to material objects as essential tools in the yearly assertion and confirmation of a merchant's standing and reliability, which were not determined entirely by "intangible attributes."[38]

As a crucial model, historians of the Dutch overseas empire, particularly the Cape, have been attentive to the roles that material objects played in representing social hierarchies in inherently diverse trading communities. In fact, practices of consumption were so extreme among the Dutch in their Asian capital of Batavia that they inspired the establishment of a number of sumptuary codes regarding dress and display in the mid-seventeenth century.[39] As a pioneer in this regard, historian Robert Ross has looked closely at how clothing, housing, carriages, the seating program within the church, and ceremonies staged at weddings and baptisms were calibrated and modulated as crucial and highly visible sites when and where social status was represented in Cape Town under the VOC and then the British. He posits a fundamental intersection among material display, social standing, and evolving concepts of respectability.[40] Gerald Groenewald goes even further by showing how material culture, consumption practices, and the protocols of display were key to the development of "social capital" among a rising group of merchants in eighteenth-century Cape Town.[41] Both highlight the importance of material objects as major constituents of merchant identity in port cities and maritime trading societies, with their mixed and itinerant populations. Even so, both portray horses, jewels, and houses as reflections of identities already formed, relatively static symbols of respectability, or examples of bald ostentation. While bolstered by these provocations, I attribute a much more dynamic role to objects as key tools of the trade that aided in the ongoing processes of commercial activity and engagement rather than simply reflecting the endpoint of its financial proceeds.

Port cities and emporia in Yemen were complex sites where multiple languages were spoken, several currencies were used, and various calendars were employed. With this backdrop, merchants and trade officials used material objects conspicuously as important communicative tools and visually legible signs. Rather than seeing them as inert recipients of meaning or static status markers, I suggest that these goods were active mediators of the cross-cultural encounter, structuring the nature of commercial exchange and sustaining merchant relations in a rapidly transforming and increasingly diverse Indian Ocean world.

Thinking about Exchange

By looking at commodities within the overlapping realms of gift, display, and consumption practices, I follow a long line of scholars who have explored the dynamic world of commodities, gifts, and exchange. Although this lineage has been amply traced by anthropologists, and to a certain extent art historians, before me, these salient ideas have not yet been fully engaged for the study of goods in the early modern Indian Ocean.[42] Of key importance is anthropologist Arjun Appadurai, who argues that "things" must be suspended within a dynamic understanding of the conditions of exchange.[43] Pushing back against the iconic legacy of Marcel Mauss, Appadurai undermines the conception of gifts and commodities as exclusive categories of objects, offering the alternative of thinking about both as temporal stages that objects could move in and out of fluidly. In the commercial environment of eighteenth-century Yemen, certain goods were exceedingly pliable in their roles as commodities, gifts, and objects of display and consumption. These mobile goods were exchanged or utilized at particular moments within the trade encounter, thus punctuating its significant stages and requisite imperatives. These aspects of timing and temporality, which were articulated initially by Pierre Bourdieu,[44] are particularly crucial to an understanding of the processes of the western Indian Ocean trade, which was governed by the strict tempo of the global wind cycle that brought major overseas vessels into the city from January to April and facilitated their departure in August and September each year.

According to anthropologist Annette Weiner in regard to Oceanic societies, "the work necessary to produce social identities in things and people is a tremendous burden."[45] This burden is even weightier in a diverse merchant community in which most participants bring their own sets of assumptions and understandings about the meaning and value of the goods they trade and carry. Her focus on women as social actors and the inalienable objects they held sway over may seem to have little to do with the profit-oriented and extremely male-dominated commercial world of the Indian Ocean. Yet with the underlying assumption that no system of exchange is independent or fully self-sustaining, Weiner shows how networks of giving and taking, but also keeping and preserving, fundamentally informed each other. This sensitivity to different but often simultaneous registers of exchange helps us to understand the pressures placed on items that were shipped but not sold, essentially the objects that were reserved from trade in this deeply commercial society that was engineered precisely to move goods quickly and vigorously in the interest of profit. Weiner's legacy pushes us to look seriously at how various modes of exchange worked in parallel operation with the wholesale trade, in this case those of gift exchange, diplomatic engagement, and the local network of informal favors.

Thomas takes these notions even further, suggesting that "objects might be introduced into a particular situation as commodities or gifts and transmitted into a particular domain of exchange in another form," thus insisting that we look closely at the ways items are bestowed and the variability of their meanings within mutable yet clearly linked contexts of exchange.[46] Following his directives, one can see that certain items, such as those imports that Yemen's merchants deployed widely in social rites, were indeed more "promiscuous" than others, appearing both in and out of the wholesale and retail marketplaces, but they were also sometimes held back from them for the purposes of gift exchange or ceremonial display and presentation. Thomas provides a platform for asking how the gift form of an object may have derived or diverged from its commodity state, whose agendas it may have served, and how that gift may be read in different ways by the giver and the receiver. Although Thomas is fully invested in the colonial context, his framework is still extremely useful to the student of early modern (and noncolonial) Yemen. There, objects that moved through and between these registers actively accumulated complex and multiple social meanings, which could be deployed quite differently among the various groups that participated in the overseas trade. Thomas has argued forcefully that we must look at each exchange as regionally specific, with the understanding that European-introduced commodities in the Pacific did not unequivocally convey colonial agendas but could be read and appropriated by their users according to a deeply particular local logic.[47] The objects featured in the following pages were charged social signs that were legible to merchants from around the globe, but they also attained a localized set of uses, meanings, and significance within the social and material entanglements of Yemen's ports and emporia. Following Thomas' lead, I explore the "full range of transaction forms" that these goods participated in.[48]

Sources

Many different types of objects travelled across long distances to arrive on Yemen's shores or left the region by way of the jetty of Mocha. Some were valuable items made of high-quality materials and manufactured with specialized technical knowledge, such as silk textiles, Asian porcelain, and ebony chairs. Others were quite ordinary, including reams of paper, quills, scales, and wax candles. Yet relatively few illustrations of these objects appear in this book, although some contemporary pictorial sources and comparable items are deployed as visual tools of reconstruction. This imbalance of image and text is the result of the poor survival rate of historic material culture in Yemen and more generally around the Indian Ocean. For that reason, we must derive our understanding of these goods from textual references or comparative material rather than from an extended corpus of extant objects.

So, like many other studies on the early modern Indian Ocean, this one relies upon the voluminous archival materials left by the European East India companies, namely the EIC and VOC. These records include many different types of writings: logbooks of everyday activities at the port of Mocha and the coffee emporium at Bayt al-Faqih; letters written by merchants in Yemen to those in other trading ports, particularly to offices in Bombay and Batavia; translations of missives sent to the imam and his provincial officials; ledgers of prices and purchases; and charts detailing local company expenditures and gift registers. These records have formed the foundational cornerstones of Indian Ocean history, with their copious data about the trade. In this case, they have also structured the chronological limits of this study, particularly the VOC *dagregisters* (daily logbooks), which constitute an almost continuous record from 1701 to 1740, when Dutch merchants were posted at the port with relative consistency.

EIC and VOC sources are particularly valuable because local records in Arabic are almost silent about the workings of commerce in the region. In fact, most of the historical records of Yemen were written far from the coasts and thus tend to focus on the intrigues of the highland court or inland happenings. When Arab chroniclers and biographers mention the coastal trade, it is usually in the context of a specific conflict, such as the French bombing of the port of Mocha in 1737.[49] Yet these brief accounts must be brought into dialogue with the much more voluminous European sources. By doing so we can derive an understanding of a diverse and dynamic maritime trading world that responded to both internal and external stimuli, while also providing more than one perspective on events that are narrated primarily by Europeans.

Although these European sources have constituted the core material for the study of the wider Indian Ocean trade, it is universally recognized that they pose significant challenges as historical documents. The VOC and EIC records for Yemen are not neutral accounts of trade activity that may be exploited unconditionally for data. To the contrary, they are fundamentally underpinned by the perspective that the local system of trade was rampantly unchecked and that Arabian Peninsula governance was implicitly corrupt. Moreover these records were not meant for the eyes of inquisitive modern historians but were penned as reports to home offices for the scrutiny of supervisors who were always concerned that far-away employees could mishandle company funds or abuse their trade privileges. For that reason, one must read these documents carefully and along with other types of sources in order to tease out their dominant, although sometimes inscrutable subjective positions and fundamental biases, as well as to highlight the patently defensive posture they embody.

So I call upon EIC and VOC sources regularly, but rarely in isolation. Rather I read them in productive tension with related sources, whether from other European merchants and travellers or Arab writers. However, my motivation to work across English, Dutch, French, and Arabic sources does not emerge from the simple desire to discount certain conflicting facts, figures, narratives, or interpretations on the basis of majority agreement. Rather they are combined to underscore and understand the implicit structure and logic of the sources at hand, and hence to use them more effectively. I follow the approach to documents that underpins historian Sanjay Subrahmanyam's notion of "connected histories," which can be achieved only by reading across a variety of sources closely to penetrate the "fine grain of events" without privileging any single voice.[50]

I also follow on the impulses of the anthropologist Ann Stoler, who, like me, spent much time in the reading room of the National Archives in The Hague and suggests that archival documents have "itineraries of their own."[51] By assimilating her directive to conceive of "archiving-as-process" rather than "archives-as-things,"[52] I use the documents of the EIC and VOC with the understanding that their writers were compelled to flatten the experience of trade into the restrictive space and predetermined format of the company document or letter, but that these tightly conceived systems of documentation also disclose subtle ruptures and fissures that must be examined closely. As Atlantic historian Toby Ditz has proposed, commercial letters, when read discursively, reveal "the matrix of social relations within which the writing takes place" and thus can be useful to scholars beyond the structured lists of prices, products, and ship names that they offer.[53]

Organization of the Book

Chapter 1 begins at the moment of arrival in the harbor of Mocha, delving into the ceremonial receptions that the local administration of the port staged to welcome high-profile merchants when they arrived from their extended sea journeys. Described in detail by some European observers, these ceremonies involved drummers, musicians, flags, and parades of decorated horses as well as the appearance of the city's notables splendidly dressed in imported textiles to welcome new arrivals at Mocha's jetty. Afterward the ships' authorities were brought to the governor's house for a formal reception with coffee, the burning of incense, and the sprinkling of rosewater. The *nakhudha*s (ship captains) from western India received quite elaborate ceremonies and made the most demands regarding the size and nature of their receptions, sometimes refusing to come on land until their requests were met. Inspired by historian Paula Sanders' meticulous work on processions in the Fatimid city of Cairo, I explore these visually dynamic ceremonies and the material objects that were deployed in them.[54] The merchants' expectations about these ceremonies sometimes led to disputes, which could be quite heated but also provide compelling evidence that welcome rituals were not just empty, extravagant displays of pomp. Rather they constituted a requisite stage of commercial initiation when the local maritime administration, in addition to other merchants, vetted and sized up new arrivals. Material objects, such as flags, sumptuous robes, Arabian horses, various items of reception, and architectural spaces, played a key role in this process of selection and the conferral of local approval.

All major overseas merchants were obligated to offer gifts to local officials in order to establish or sustain their trading rights in Yemen. Yet most

European observers cast the local preoccupation with such offerings as an example of the insatiable appetite that fickle Oriental despots had for trinkets. Drawing on VOC and EIC gift registers, I contend in chapter 2 that these material exchanges must be understood as meaningful and necessary aspects of merchant protocol that overlapped with the processes of trade in a highly structured manner and that the gifts bestowed by European merchants in Yemen may not be collapsed indistinguishably with other types of offerings, such as diplomatic bestowals, imperial gifts, and acts of pious charity, which were markedly more unique in character and have received a considerable amount of recent attention from historians and art historians. By contrast, merchant gifts were remarkably formulaic in nature and were relatively routine items that overlapped with Indian Ocean commodities in uneven ways, thus drawing their power and meaning from their association with extended commercial geographies. Some were even brought into the realm of local ceremonial by the imam. This close perusal of European commercial gift practices also reveals that these merchants became quite adept at the local grammar of giving, even if they decried its legitimacy in their letters to home offices.

While chapter 2 focuses on the content of European gifts, which are copiously documented in VOC and EIC registers, chapter 3 turns to the gift practices of the major merchants from India who traded in Yemen. Unlike their European counterparts, some major Indian merchants delivered their yearly gifts to Yemen's imam at the beginning of the trade season, expected reciprocal offerings in return, and sent off their bestowals (the contents of which were often kept secret) with a great deal of ceremony. As such, Asian gifting practices, which have a much longer but more fragmented history than those of the Europeans, shed considerable light on local expectations for merchant tribute as well as the tight relationships that Yemeni officials sustained with Indian entrepreneurs. I also argue that the presentations surrounding yearly gifts, which were visually impressive, exceeded the value of the gifts themselves, inscribed within a language of public display. These bestowals were consumed not only by their intended recipients but also by those who observed their conveyance and passage, which were awe-inspiring in their size and scope.

Chapter 4 delves into the objects that English and Dutch merchants imported from Bombay, Batavia, London, and Amsterdam for their daily use. These were transported as pieces of cargo destined for the Arabian Peninsula, but unlike the majority of imported goods, they were diverted from the cycle of commercial exchange after arriving at their destination and used to sustain the European merchant enterprise in Yemen. Imported scales, basic writing materials, and the company seal were essential for their trade and suggest a pervasive suspicion of local measures and modes of accounting. Medicine from abroad and copious supplies of alcohol were more liminal. Rather than simply differentiating European from local lifestyles, these imported items were doled out as gifts to local officials or administered to gain commercial favor in this site of relative isolation for European traders. Indian manufactured furnishings circulated as hybrid objects that allowed Europeans to maintain their conventional dining, seating, and documentary customs but were wholly unmatched to the floor-oriented construction of Yemeni buildings. When considered along with the cargo that was transported to be sold at the port, these objects were far more than utilitarian goods. In fact, they allow us to reflect on the dynamic and multifaceted character of the import, which was intended for the purposes of exchange and to sustain the very structure of the overseas trade enterprise.

Scope of the Study

It is perhaps more fashionable now to think in terms of wide bodies of water rather than circumscribed land masses. Even so, my readers will not find a comprehensive study of the Indian Ocean trade, its volume, products, and major events. Yet some of the content of the following chapters will seem familiar to those who have read sources and studies on other Indian Ocean, Asian, or Arab ports: elaborate ceremonies staged for new arrivals, quibbles and debates over the content and distribution of requisite gifts, and complaints about the hardships of living in a foreign and remote port. However, rather than making bold assertions that pertain to a broad context, I focus on Yemen while offering a modest provocation to others working on related sites around a vast linked geography of ports, emporia, and islands to ask similar questions in order to bring the wider maritime region into focus in a multisited manner.

To that end, I draw comparative information from varied sites, such as the Mediterranean cities frequented by the merchants of the Cairo Geniza, the coastal emporia of India, the Dutch colonial cities of Batavia and Cape Town, the kingdom of Ayutthaya in Thailand, and Tokugawa Japan. However, comparison is not used as a tool to make larger arguments about the wider Arab world, the vast Indian Ocean, or the early modern era in general. Rather I use comparison in order to make interpretive points sharper and to gain critical leverage on the Yemeni case. Grounded firmly in current debates in early modern Arab studies, European expansion, and Indian Ocean history, this book operates as what Trivellato has called "global history on a small scale," which looks closely at the structural mechanics of cross-cultural encounters that were rooted in a single place, albeit one that was tightly connected to other locations around the globe.[55]

Although European company merchants, namely of the EIC and VOC, figure prominently in the following pages, I wholly reject the format of a company history. My goal is to read across sources for a materially attentive and socially inclined understanding of the Yemen trade. Thus Dutch narrators are asked to provide insight on the activities of local merchants, and English sources are used to better understand the motivations of their French counterparts. While company policies and trade strategies are important, I strive to locate each merchant within the commercial world of eighteenth-century Yemen and to avoid wide-sweeping generalizations that aim for similarities rather than subtleties and particularities.

ONE

Rites of Entry at the Maritime Threshold

Beginning each year in January, galleys, brigantines, and *ghurab*s (two- or three-masted ships used in the Arabian Sea, popularized in English as grabs) would arrive at the Red Sea port of Mocha from India, Europe, and Southeast Asia. Elaborate ceremonies were staged to welcome the authorities of those vessels that were owned by the city's major overseas merchants. They included local Arab traders who were either from Yemen or were long established there, Muslim shipowners from India, and Europeans associated with the Dutch, English, and French East India companies. Even Yemen's imam, who lived in the mountain interior, owned ships that he sent to Surat yearly. His two vessels were celebrated proudly upon their annual return to Yemen's coast.

ARRIVAL AT MOCHA

One of the most descriptive accounts of these ceremonies was offered by the French supercargo Godefroy de la Merveille of *Le Curieux,* which arrived at the port from Brest in January 1709.[1] This pioneering mission, subrogated by the French Compagnie des Indes, was dispatched with the hopes of initiating a trading relationship with the Qasimis and providing the French direct access to the region's coffee. When *Le Curieux,* along with the two other ships in its convoy, cast their anchors, the forts around the city sent up flags, as did the VOC trading establishment on shore, "in order to do us honor," according to La Merveille. After exchanging salutes, the governor of Mocha sent a boat with a flag and streamer waving to *Le Curieux.* There were three people on board. The first was the *amir al-bahr* (the administrator of port affairs), dressed in a robe of pleated green fabric with long hanging sleeves over a yellow striped underrobe. With him was Vira, a Baniyan broker who spoke Portuguese. It was noted that Vira wore a white robe with a beautifully embroidered belt and a multicolored silk scarf on his shoulder. There was also a Dutch merchant who spoke French well and was "cloath'd after the Turkish manner." The captain told the *amir al-bahr* about their journey and then expressed his interest in obtaining local trading privileges, for which they presented letters addressed to the governor of Mocha, Salih bin 'Ali al-Huraybi.

These missives were brought to shore, and al-Huraybi sent back a polite response in Arabic, which was accompanied by a letter in Latin from the two Franciscan missionaries who resided in Mocha and some refreshments for the crew. The next day one of the Franciscans came on board La Merveille's ship. The captain asked him to arrange the first French audience with the governor that day. The Franciscan proposed that they wait until the next day, "having a Design that we shou'd make a publick Entry, as being the first *French* Officers that had arriv'd in his Government; but we pray'd him to dispense with that Ceremony." So La Merveille and Captain de Champloret of *Le Diligent* appeared at Mocha's jetty "accompany'd by some of our Officers in proper Habits, and with a Retinue very neatly dress'd," but without advance notice.

Even so, a large reception awaited them when they entered the city through Bab al-Sahil (the Sea Gate). There they found twelve horses that were "well-equip'd," around two hundred soldiers, and musicians holding kettledrums. The *amir al-bahr* was there to greet and escort them to the governor's palace, followed by a large group of city inhabitants. Although they refused to remove their shoes before proceeding into the house, a customary practice in Yemen, they were granted entrance. There the governor, who was seated upon "two Carpets embroider'd with Gold, leaning upon Cushions of the same Stuff," greeted them politely. Al-Huraybi agreed to send their request to trade to Imam al-Mahdi Muhammad, who lived in the hilltop town of al-Mawahib near Dhamar, a journey of around eight days from the coast. They were then served coffee and concluded the audience. After leaving the palace, they went to the house of Vira, where they spent a few days before returning to their own house.

This description was drawn from one of La Merveille's letters that was published in Jean de la Roque's *Voyage to Arabia Felix,* a book that features firsthand accounts written by the merchants who made this inaugural journey to Yemen in 1708 to 1710 in addition to the one directly following, in 1711 to 1713.[2] La Merveille's account provides a sense of the complexity of the cross-cultural encounter in the early modern western Indian Ocean, which was never a simple East-meets-West scenario but rather involved various intermediaries, in this case Dutch merchants, Indian brokers, and Italian missionaries, all conversing and writing in different languages, which were not necessarily their own.

This record is instrumental in understanding local ceremonies of entry because after many years of appearing at the port, the French and other observers came to consider these rites too common to be described in full.[3] Modern Indian Ocean historians too have simply dismissed such ceremonies as trivial affairs compared to the economic exchanges that followed, which have received considerably more interest as topics worthy of historical investigation. In this chapter, I take ceremony seriously, thus pushing back against the idea that, "to the reasoning eye, ceremony was contentless form designed to mask the mechanisms of power and awe the unenlightened mind," which James Hevia has effectively critiqued in regard to the Qing Dynasty.[4]

Indeed other accounts, even shorter and more fragmentary, reveal that these meetings in Mocha's harbor could be much more vexed, contentious, and impactful than La Merveille's narrative reveals. For instance, on February 10, 1730, the *Fateh Jang* docked at Mocha from Gujarat.[5] The vessel was owned by the shipping magnate Mulla Muhammad 'Ali, one of the major merchants of Surat, whose family had sent ships yearly to the Red Sea for decades. Its captain (*nakhudha*) was Muhammad Husayn, the son of the shipowner. The term *nakhudha,* which was used across the Indian Ocean, is often translated as "ship captain," but it is important to specify that the *nakhudha* did not possess technical skills of seafaring. A pilot was on board to direct the ship across the sea. The *nakhudha* served as the ship's leading authority and was also entrusted with the business affairs of the shipowner upon arrival at the destination point. Essentially the *nakhudha* served as the overseas proxy for the merchant himself.

In this case, our observers were not those aboard the Gujarati vessel but the VOC merchants of Mocha, who kept copious records of various happenings at the port and serve as valuable narrators of local events. On February 12, they tell us, Muhammad Husayn's broker sought out the governor to inform him that this *nakhudha* required five cannon shots upon entry and that he should send an extra retinue of soldiers, horses, flags, and other ornaments to meet him outside the city gate. Moreover the *nakhudha*'s baggage should pass into the city uninspected. Yet as Muhammad Husayn sailed on a small lighter boat from his ship to Mocha's jetty, only three cannons were fired, and the reception that awaited him on shore had been prepared according to the governor's own discretion, along with the mandate that his goods would be checked. Rather than accepting this disappointing welcome, Muhammad Husayn circumvented his arrival at the jetty and entered the city through an alternate gate to the north of the city. Then, on land, he avoided the inspection of his goods by leaving his bales on the large field in front of his house. After being prodded by two major local merchants, Qasim al-Turbati and Muhammad Yasin, the governor, Faqih Ahmad Khazindar, finally sent his son with apologies to the *nakhudha.* The governor then went to inspect the goods in person that afternoon. The Dutch observers note with great interest that among them were golden soosies (striped or checkered fabrics of silk or cotton and silk blend), "bodidaars" (presumably another type of Indian fabric, likely from Gujarat), shawls, and fine pieces of cloth.

Similarly, a few months later, on May 11, the Dutch mention that a three-masted ship owned by Sidi Yaqut Khan II (also known as Sidi Surur II), the ruler of Janjira, had arrived at Mocha. Located south of Bombay, the state of Janjira had come under Mughal rule periodically but was mostly autonomous since the Sidis established control in the early seventeenth century.[6] The Sidis, who were originally from Africa, served as admirals of the Mughal Navy, but little is known about their trading activity. The Dutch write that this ship came from Surat with many textiles in its cargo. Two days later, on May 13, the Sidi *nakhudha,* whose name was 'Anbar, was received in the customary manner.[7] "The Captain of the Soldiers and the Amir al-Bahr, along with a group of military and four or five horses, drums, and pipes, according to tradition, went out of the gate and outside to escort this *nakhudha* into the city." However, apparently "this ceremonial retinue was not adequate to the *nakhudha,* nor complete, because the Imam's preference was not apparent, so he resolved to go back on board immediately." In this case, Governor Khazindar rectified his mistake more publicly, for the next day the *nakhudha* came into the city "with the Imam's preference and a splendid retinue."[8]

When we compare these two brief VOC observations to La Merveille's much lengthier firsthand narrative, we can confirm that these ceremonies were by no means engineered specifically for the Europeans who arrived at Mocha. To the contrary, the major merchants from India, in addition to the *nakhudha*s of the royal Mughal ships and those of the Qasimi imam, expected a full and appropriately scaled welcome when they appeared at the port and were unwilling to accept a diminished reception at the jetty.[9] The VOC accounts also provide the sense that these early moments of contact between those on land and those at sea were not episodes of unequivocal welcome and open hospitality, as was portrayed in 1709, but could be tense moments of evaluation, when those on land sized up those who arrived in the harbor and those coming in from the sea enumerated the circumstances of their reception. The tenuous nature of this encounter was made clear in 1737, when the French arrived in three warships disguised under different flags with the intention of forcing the port administration to accede to their demands. When the governor's boats were sent out to these ships with refreshments, his representatives were taken hostage.[10] Clearly there was more at stake in these initial encounters in Mocha's harbor than simple politesse.

The two later accounts also confirm that the number of salutes, soldiers, horses, and musicians that were offered at the port upon entry were not always consistent. For instance, the *nakhudha* 'Anbar had been initially offered only four or five horses, whereas the French had been welcomed with twelve. Additionally, the French had received five cannon shots when they arrived in the harbor in 1709, as opposed to the three that Muhammad Husayn was granted when he set out for the jetty in 1730. It also appears that the governor calibrated these various elements based on his appraisal of the ship but could be convinced to offer a more generous presentation if prodded, as he did for 'Anbar. These ceremonies were also carefully planned along the urban armature of the city. Members of the welcoming party waited strategically either inside or outside of the Sea Gate, and certain *nakhudha*s, such as Muhammad Husayn and 'Anbar, watched closely to see how far out of the city the party would advance to greet them as they came into the port.

We can also see that the newly arrived French, while having received a particularly lavish welcome, seemed to have had the fewest expectations about it, to the extent that they were willing to forgo the ceremony altogether. By contrast, 'Anbar refused to come ashore until an adequate reception was offered, and Muhammad Husayn skillfully avoided his diminished reception at the jetty of Mocha by choosing an alternate route of entry into the city. It would be reductive to attribute the French position to unfamiliarity with local affairs just because they were European. Of course, both *nakhudha*s were from India and neither could be considered local to Yemen. Rather their relative lack of interest in their reception seemed to stem from the fact that the French were on their inaugural mission to Mocha and thus had few expectations about their port entry. Muhammad Husayn's family members were major players in the western Indian Ocean trade, having sent ships to the Red Sea for decades. Although this may have been the *nakhudha*'s first visit to the port, which may have been why his broker was so eager to assure an appropriate entry, he had clearly been briefed on what kind of welcome was due to him as the family's representative. Sidi Yaqut Khan's vessels had appeared there since at least the year before.[11] It is also important to note that Governor Khazindar had been appointed just days before Muhammad Husayn's February 1730 entry.[12] Although he had served as Mocha's governor once before, in his second term he may have been trying to innovate port protocols by scaling down these ceremonies of reception, a scheme that was quite unprecedented and that these two arrivals squarely rejected.[13]

It is clear that those who were aware of the port's rites and routines, whether from Europe or Asia, were generally more attuned to the power and utility of these ceremonial receptions. As an example, in 1722, when the governor-elect of Bombay William Phipps stopped in Mocha on his way to take his high-ranking position, an unusually lavish ceremony was staged to recognize his arrival. The English residents noted with great delight:

> We thought it expedient for Y^{r} Hon^{ors} Credit as well as to strike an Awe of that Governm^{t} into these People that he should be received with more Marks of Distinction than other European Chiefs that only come to reside here. Accordingly he landed the 14th June and as he past by in the Boat was saluted from the Imaums Ships and all the Moors Ships in ye Road, he was received at his Landing by the Second, ye Chief Merchants of the Place, and Nocquedahs of all the Ships, the Govern^{r} receiving him at the Door of an inner room in his House, at which time the Forts Platform, and Musquetry fired, and from thence he was conducted to the Factory by the Second & c^{a} that received him at the Waterside.[14]

The same letter continues by noting that Phipps' reception was equivalent to that reserved for ambassadors and observing with great pleasure that the new French chief had not been received in this elaborate manner. Although they were focused primarily on outdoing the other Europeans in town, by noting the scale of the chief's reception, the precise locations where the city's notables greeted him, and the exact timing of cannon shots, the EIC merchants echo the concerns of the *nakhudha*s. Together they recognized that these ceremonies were much more than empty displays of pomp and extravagance and fully acknowledged the subtle indications that were suggested by the scale and spatial and acoustic calibration of each entry rite.[15]

Those who had traded at the port for any extended period of time would surely have also noticed that the majority of those who appeared at Mocha's jetty did not receive such a lavish welcome. For instance, the local Red Sea and Gulf seafarers who arrived on small vessels known as *jilba*s and trankeys (boats used in the Gulf region) throughout the year were excluded from this type of reception. Baniyans, who were major figures in the overseas trade but often socially marginalized, were even charged to enter the city, as in 1734, when members of their community had to pay 20 Spanish reals each upon arrival.[16] The common peddlers who appeared with pilgrimage ships eventually heading for Mecca and the members of the general maritime proletariat were not granted such a greeting. As such, the ceremonies offered at Mocha's jetty were acts of social ordering when hierarchies within the overseas trading and travelling class became fixed in visually conspicuous ways. So those who were received with these ceremonies were immediately recognized upon entry as major high-volume, long-distance traders, an exclusive status at the port of Mocha. Moreover the hundreds of soldiers and residents who gathered to observe their entry duly executed their role as witnesses, thus endorsing the expressed hierarchy of this social order.

The Material Culture of Commercial Initiation

While the 1709 French account differs starkly from the later VOC and EIC accounts in their perception of these ceremonies and their importance, they do share an overarching preoccupation with their material elements and visual aspects. It is clear that a wide corpus of "things" was put into play to stage such rites: cannons and flags, the sumptuous robes and textiles that were worn or displayed, horses decorated with elaborate fittings sometimes made of silver and gold, musical instruments, and pieces of imported porcelain that were used to serve coffee or sprinkle rosewater. Although we lack actual images of these ceremonies and extant examples of the objects that were deployed in them, it is possible to delve into the material and sensory culture of these rites. The three accounts that have just been presented provide a useful springboard from which to work.

Without question, the ceremonies that began at Mocha's jetty were similar to the types of pageantry and displays that were staged in many other contexts, both in the East and the West, ancient and more recent, which also involved the mobilization of masses of soldiers, musicians, horses, and flags. Indeed these "generalized . . . symbols of authority" were deployed widely across the region for public events. They were aptly described by Sanders as the "gestures, salutes, and acts of homage dictated by protocol [that] were the building blocks of ceremonies. . . . These highly disciplined and prescribed acts composed an idiom that was used by all Islamic dynasties."[17] In early modern Yemen, these familiar items were also utilized as icons of honor in contexts that were neither coastal nor commercial, for instance in the celebrations that were staged to ring in Eid al-Adha or to welcome the arrival of an important ambassador.[18] As Bernard Haykel has written, the eighteenth century marked a noted rise in such forms of display and ceremonial pageantry in Yemen, drawing directly from Ottoman ritual precedents.[19] Similarly lavish programs were also held in other ports to welcome incoming ships, such as those staged at Cape Town when the VOC fleet arrived from Batavia each year on its inward journey to the Dutch Republic.[20]

While recognizing that these ceremonies seem to be relatively generic, I make the vital case that the objects used in them must be considered within the specific maritime commercial context in which they were wielded, displayed, and bestowed, thus recognizing the "historically particular character of the form of appropriation."[21] Objects, especially prime imported and local commodities, were complex signs in the world of the long-distance cross-cultural trade, often oscillating within shifting systems of value and significance. But they could also be suspended within dynamic local social matrices, articulated within a specific urban context, and subject to stark social reversals in everyday life. Thus they obtained their efficacy as signs from their malleability as social markers.

FLAGS

Mocha residents usually expected the appearance of a major oceangoing boat before it even arrived in the harbor. When an overseas vessel was sighted at Bab al-Mandab, the opening of the Red Sea, a messenger was dispatched to Mocha to inform those at the port of its imminent arrival. After it entered the harbor, the vessel's flag was used to make the initial identification of the crew and its origin point. Atlantic historian Markus Rediker has emphasized that a "dazzling array of flags, colors, standards, jacks, pennants, ensigns, and banners, especially those signifying nation and empire, were the most important means of communication among seafaring craft of all kinds."[22] Observers from Mocha's shoreline sometimes spoke of their inability to make out a flag in the distance, thus suggesting how closely they scrutinized these colors from the shore as clues to any new arrival.[23]

Even so, small boats always followed to confirm the initial identification, as we saw with the French. This was because flags were not always trustworthy as identifying maritime markers, particularly during this era, which Rediker has cast as the "golden age of piracy." As the same author has ably shown, while flags were used as identifying symbols, pirates were famous for deploying them variably and strategically.[24] For instance, Hubert Hugo, who attacked Mocha in the 1660s, was likely French but often flew English colors.[25] The Jolly Roger, with its various menacing forms, was not a flag of identification but rather hoisted only at the very moment of confrontation, as an inducement to the crew of the overtaken vessel to give up without a fight.[26] It is clear that the infamous banner was only one of many flags that pirates would use at sea. To quote Rediker again, "Every pirate ship worth its salt had a complete set of national flags, all the better with which to confuse prospective prizes and even naval vessels that might wish to chase them."[27] Thus, for pirates and rovers, flags were temporally contingent markers subject to selection rather than fixed signs of identity.

But even outside the world of piracy, the practice of flying false flags was quite widespread.[28] According to Roque, the three vessels that came into Mocha's harbor in 1709 displayed white flags, likely the merchant banner of St. Malo, which carried a voided black cross in the center, a red quarter at the top left, and the remaining quarters in white with ermine backgrounds.[29]

However, they had flown an EIC flag, which bore narrow red and white stripes and a Union Jack in the corner, through parts of their journey around the African coast.[30] One of their three ships was actually a Dutch vessel from Middleburg that they had seized en route around Ascension Island in the Atlantic.[31] When it arrived at Mocha, *Le Grand Vainqueur*, as it was then known, carried its newly acquired French colors that effectively masked its previous identity, which would have been expressed in a tricolor striped flag with the VOC insignia in the center.[32] In 1737, when the French arrived in Mocha with their three warships, each displayed a different flag—English, French, and Dutch—to avoid raising initial suspicions about their intentions. Rather than being stable markers of identity, flags could be manipulated on the masts of maritime vessels in active ways depending on where one was sailing and with what purpose. As much as flags were crucial tools of identification at sea, they were temporally variable and undependable as indicators. One could never be certain of the crew's identity or mission until they were contacted directly, making the initial stage of the maritime encounter particularly ambiguous and dangerous.

While flags were wholly mutable signs when hoisted on the mast of a mobile vessel, they played a much different role when planted on a stable flagpole in the space of the port city. As viewed by La Merveille in 1709, the Qasimis used a pointed red flag with a saltire cross bearing the white sword of Dhu'l-fiqar and three crescents.[33] A version of this flag, but without the cross or crescents, is pictured clearly in a later watercolor, dated 1832 (Plate 1). The sword with a curved and split tip is a particularly potent Shiʿi symbol and thus would have served to identify the local Zaydi regime, in contrast to Sunni maritime powers that would have been present in the Red Sea and western Indian Ocean at this time, such as the Ottomans or the Mughals. Hoisted upon the northern and southern forts of Mocha, which were built on spits of land that jutted out from the coast, this waving symbol would welcome ships into the crescent-shaped harbor, as it had for La Merveille, while a third flag was usually raised on the battery at the Sea Gate, marking the landward point of access to the city, as Rupert Kirk shows. This configuration of three strategically placed flags is represented in the image that accompanies the French account of their 1737 attack (Figure 1.1).[34]

In addition to the Qasimi flag, figure 1.1 portrays those of the three main European companies at the port, the Dutch, English, and French, as relatively naturalized parts of the local landscape of Mocha. But this rendering also demonstrates, albeit subtly, that the different parties that administered and traded in the city used flags in varied ways. As described earlier, public structures, in addition to the imam's ships, were marked with the red and white Qasimi ensign. Dutch, English, and French merchants

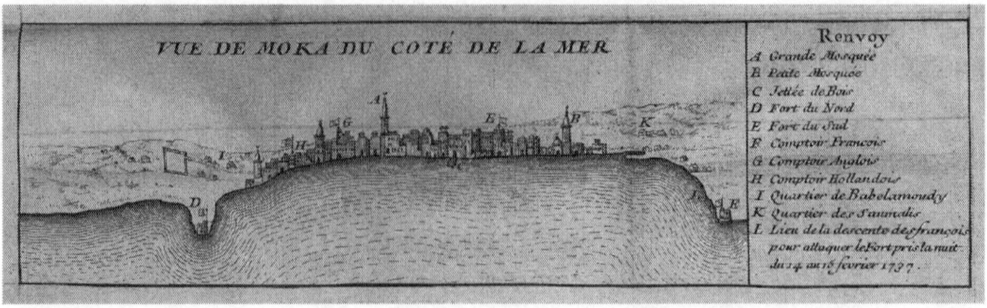

Figure 1.1. View of Mocha from the harbor, published in Pierre François Guyot Desfontaines, *Relation de l'expédition de Moka en l'année 1737 sous les ordres de M. de la Garde-Jazier, de Saint-Malo* (Paris: Imprimerie Joseph Bullot, 1739). Courtesy of the Cleveland Public Library.

hoisted their company flags upon their ships and used the same markers to identify their houses, which also served as their trading establishments in Mocha.[35] Yet, as figure 1.1 demonstrates, Europeans were apparently the only ones who found it appropriate to fly a flag from a residential commercial establishment in this port city. We never see representations of flags on other houses, not that of the governor nor those of other merchants, and flags are never mentioned as being on the residences of any other group, even in passing.[36] It appears that local merchants and those based in India found flags to be fitting signs for ships, as maritime insignia, but did not employ them on land. It is possible that they viewed this right as singularly suitable for landed ruling authorities. For this reason, European flags were uniquely conspicuous as viewed from the sea, especially because the European houses were located right along the shoreline, as figure 1.1 shows clearly.

In fact, the right to fly colors above a land-based residence in Mocha was by no means a natural license granted to all port city residents. Rather it was a commercial privilege, stipulated clearly in trade agreements that were forged between Europeans and the local administration. The French agreement of 1709 identified the right to "set up the Flag on the House where they lodge" as the third article.[37] And like all privileges, this one could be subject to change, alteration, and revocation. According to VOC records, on January 22, 1723, through the governor as intermediary, Imam al-Mutawakkil Qasim informed the three companies, Dutch, English, and French, that they would no longer be allowed to wave their flags from their Mocha residences and that the English could no longer beat their drum in Yemen.[38] The French responded vehemently that it was their right to wave their flag, and the Dutch resolved to write to the imam about the issue. Although Yemeni authorities did not pursue this issue further (it seems to have simply disappeared from the VOC records after that point), it is clear that the flag and the drum exceeded the meaning of a rote identifier or a passive symbol.

The Dutch specify clearly that this seemingly arbitrary and unexpected demand did not originate with the imam but was instigated by an Ottoman envoy who had just visited the court in Sanaa. This was not the first time the Ottomans had tried to persuade Yemen's imam to curtail the rights and privileges of European merchants in Mocha.[39] The Ottomans resented that the Qasimis had so readily allowed Europeans direct access to coffee beans in Yemen, with the contention that their influx of silver had diminished the supply of coffee while also raising the price of the bean. Of course, it was the Ottomans who first spearheaded coffee cultivation in Yemen, when they occupied the region from 1538 to 1636. As historian Jane Hathaway has suggested, after their expulsion they lamented that they had once been the beneficiaries of the revenue that was then flowing from Ottoman lands directly into the Qasimi treasury. This was indeed a considerable sum because the majority of beans at Bayt al-Faqih were destined for Cairo and further Ottoman distribution.[40] These concerns reached a peak in the early 1720s, but by 1726 the Ottomans had all but given up on efforts to stem this economic competition.[41]

The Ottomans had other grounds upon which to deem the European presence in Yemen objectionable. Following the Hanafi school of law, the Ottomans held that non-Muslims should not be allowed to live anywhere on the Arabian Peninsula, an opinion that contrasted with the more tolerant Zaydi position on this particular issue.[42] According to Haykel, the point became especially heated within Yemeni circles at this time in which Sunni legal stances were gaining increasing traction. Because the Hanafi stance on European residence in Yemen dovetailed conveniently with the overriding Ottoman concerns about their economic influence at Bayt al-Faqih, the two positions became closely intertwined in the first quarter of the eighteenth century. In this context of intra-Muslim debate, flags were much more than simple markers. They also visibly advertised the presence of trading groups that some onlookers deemed contentious. In eighteenth-century Mocha, flags, particularly European flags, were thus tied up in issues of wide-reaching geopolitical, religious, and economic concern.

The heavy symbolic weight of the European flag was made emphatically clear again in 1739, when the Dutch decided to pull their long-established factory from Mocha. At that time, VOC representatives were sent to the port to settle their accounts and remove the remaining belongings from the house they had rented for many years. Although they cancelled their rental contract, they did not "dare take the flagpole."[43] The *chaush* (captain of the soldiers) at that time, Amir Sulayman, warned that if they tried to remove it, it might inspire a negative response from the local population, which would ultimately hinder their departure. But the Dutch made sure to clarify to the governor that the remaining flagpole should not be taken as a sign of their continuing economic presence at the port. These exchanges suggest that a flagpole, even without a flag flying from it, was an important sign of the long-standing commercial relationship that had been sustained between the Dutch and the local administration for over fifty years, since their extended residence in Mocha began. It also adds to the impression that flagpoles were not found on houses other than those of the European trading companies.

Flags were crucial but unreliable markers that were hoisted liberally during ceremonies of commercial initiation. But they also carried a different meaning at sea than on land. At sea they were mutable and variable and could not be trusted. On land they signaled the identity of the owner more dependably, but also reflected an exclusive commercial privilege. Moreover the singular presence of European flags on houses in Mocha became an issue of cross-cultural contestation and served to distinguish European practices from those of other major merchants at the port.

Clothing

In 1709 Governor al-Huraybi of Mocha sent three individuals to the French ship as a welcoming party. In La Merveille's description of this encounter he paused to show considerable interest in the costume of these three people, the first he encountered in Mocha. It is clear that their clothing and the textiles from which they were fashioned immediately caught the eye of the French captain. His interest in the visual attributes of their costume implies that, certainly for the French, dress and textiles were important mediators of the cross-cultural encounter that helped these new arrivals make sense of the unfamiliar surroundings.

In contrast to flags, which rarely merited detailed descriptions in texts, the attributes of local costumes appear in a few useful sources. Later visitors to Yemen, such as Carsten Niebuhr and his colleagues on the Danish expedition of 1763 and Louis de Grandpré, who travelled there in 1790, devote a certain amount of energy to depicting local dress in writing and images. Their prints help us to better understand the way dress operated when deployed as a sign at the maritime threshold. We can use the 1709 welcoming party as a point of departure because it represents some of the diverse constituents involved in Mocha's overseas trade: the *amir al-bahr*, a local official appointed by Yemen's imam, a Baniyan who, with his compatriots, ran the brokerage of the overseas trade in Mocha and other Yemeni cities, and a servant of the VOC, the major European company installed at the port at that time.

When Niebuhr and his party travelled to Sanaa to visit Imam al-Mahdi 'Abbas, they were given gifts of clothing of the type worn by Yemeni highland notables.[44] After Niebuhr returned to Copenhagen, he was pictured wearing this garb (Figure 1.2). The engraving gives a sense of the layering of the *amir al-bahr*'s long full garments, which were described as a splendid green overrobe and a striped yellow robe below.[45] Indeed, the costume represented fits La Merveille's description closely, and many port officials at this time were in fact notables from the north. The Baniyan Vira was attired quite differently, in a white gown that was cinched at the waist with an embroidered belt and a multicolored silk scarf over his shoulder. A later image shows the possible configuration of Vira's long belted garment, although the more specific details of the belt and scarf that are pictured do not match the costume La Merveille described (Figure 1.3).

Even based only on these short textual descriptions, we can come to the conclusion that both individuals wore imported cloth, which was by no means unusual in early modern Yemen, as I discuss in chapter 2. The fabric of the *amir al-bahr*'s green overrobe may have been from Europe, Persia, or China, and the striped garment beneath was likely from Aleppo in Syria.[46] Vira's white robe was likely of cotton, and the belt was probably an embroidered muslin *patka* (sash), both from India.[47] Because of their high quality, the nature of their decoration, their status as imports, and their crisp distinctive colors, these textiles and robes were clearly legible as high-value commodities to the French captain, who noted their fine caliber but made no suggestions about their place of origin. Every ship that arrived in Mocha from overseas carried textiles, and the French ship in 1709, in addition to Muhammad Husayn's and 'Anbar's ships in 1730, were no exception. So the sumptuous and visually conspicuous textiles worn by the *amir al-bahr* and Vira were not necessarily singularized as precious artifacts,[48] but they were likely understood as representative of a type of commodity that could find an eager market at the port. As such, these goods served to entice the trade sensibilities of our French captain. Donned by his welcoming party, they suggested that such rich goods would find an eager local market and, by extension, that the French should come on shore and unload their own textiles immediately.

But dress also carried other functions at the moment of first contact at Mocha. Like a flag at sea, clothing was one tool used to identify new arrivals, allowing for one to distinguish poor peddlers from important merchants and locals from foreigners. This function was extremely important in a cosmopolitan commercial society in which merchants were always sizing up

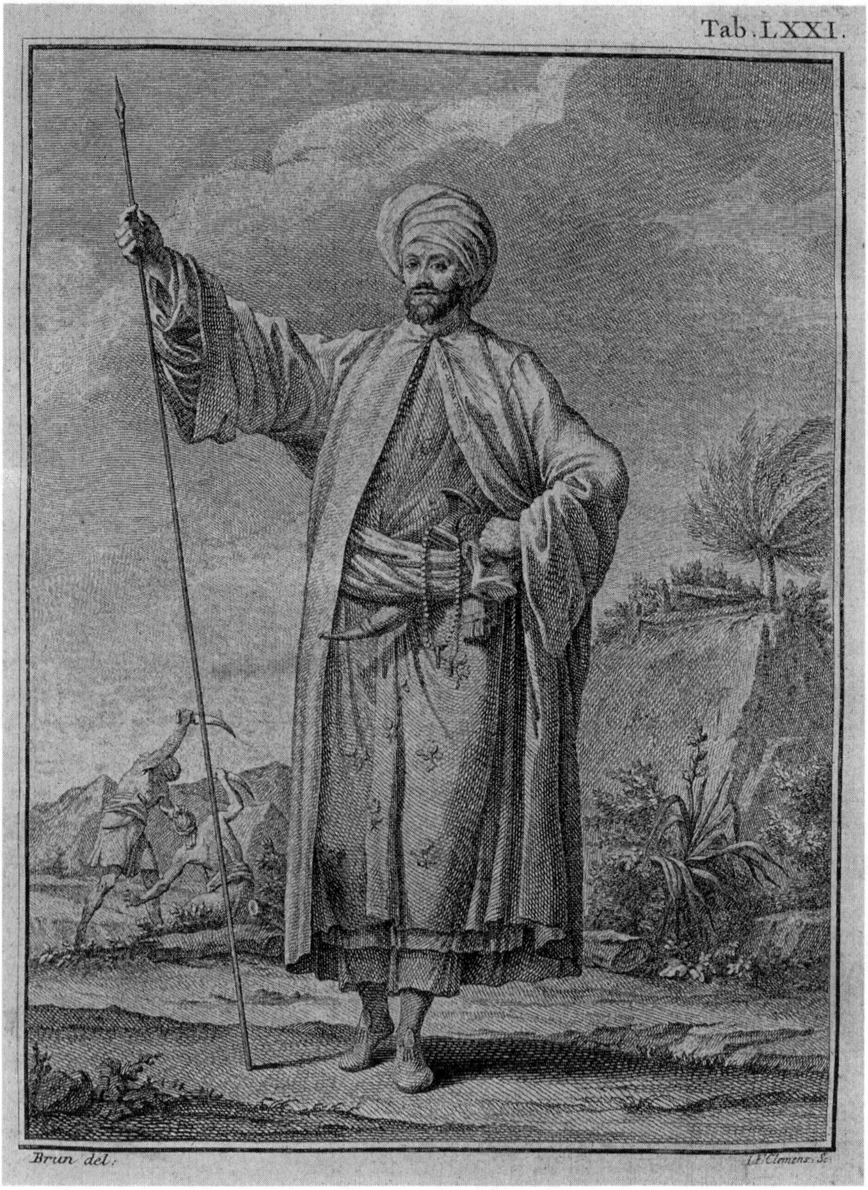

Figure 1.2. "The dress of Arab notables in Yemen," published in Carsten Niebuhr, *Reisebeschreibung nach Arabien* (Copenhagen: Nicolaus Möller, 1774), 1: pl. 71. Courtesy of the John Hay Library, Brown University Library.

their potential trading partners, literally from their first appearance at the port. Yet, like a flag, costume should be understood as a particularly unwieldy tool in that endeavor.

The Baniyans and their sartorial habits in Yemen serve as a potent example. As we know from both textual and visual sources, Baniyans might wear the long robe that was described by La Merveille in 1709 and pictured by Grandpré in 1790 (Figure 1.3), but they more often wore a very different type of untailored dress, as depicted by Georg Wilhelm Baurenfeind, the artist who accompanied Niebuhr in 1763 (Figure 1.4).[49] A white loincloth was wrapped around the lower body and cinched with a silver belt. Another cloth was draped over the shoulders, leaving the chest bare. It appears that Vira chose to wear the more sumptuous long robe for his encounter with the French in Mocha's harbor in 1709, rather than this much simpler and sparser draped garment.[50] Indeed Grandpré's later image confirms that dress was never a natural extension of identity but was often selected and staged particularly for cross-cultural presentation. As apparent in the image's caption, the Baniyan Courji donned his distinct long and robed regalia, referred to as his "full dress," for special occasions, such as the rendering of his portrait by this European observer in 1790.[51] Likewise, in 1709, the French made efforts to present themselves appropriately, in their "proper Habits," when they came on shore.[52]

It is no surprise that the Baniyans would have various types of garb to choose from based on the occasion. But it is necessary to underline that, as *dhimmi*s, they were subject to sumptuary laws regarding dress. For instance, in the mid-eighteenth century, Imam al-Mahdi 'Abbas required the Baniyans to wear red garments and headgear as a sign of identification and humility, new regulations that were spurred on by ongoing debates about *dhimmi*s and the lawfulness of their residence in Yemen, as mentioned earlier.[53] Although the colored dress appears to have been discarded eventually, the tinted headgear was maintained, as demonstrated in Grandpré's 1790 image (Figure 1.3). Rather than simply confirming the tenuous status and periodic oppression of local minority groups, sumptuary regulations that mandated dress underline the notion that members of minority groups could adopt the clothing of dominant groups with relative ease, such that costume had to be legislated and controlled in order to uphold its uniformity and sustain a visual index of religious difference.[54] The regulations also reflect underlying anxiety about the possible failure of sartorial markers, which could allow for members of a minority group to blend into the mainstream unnoticed.

Along these lines, one must take up the third member of the boat that was sent by al-Huraybi in 1709, the Dutch man who wore a Turkish robe. Although the French spoke about him quite briefly, VOC sources from this

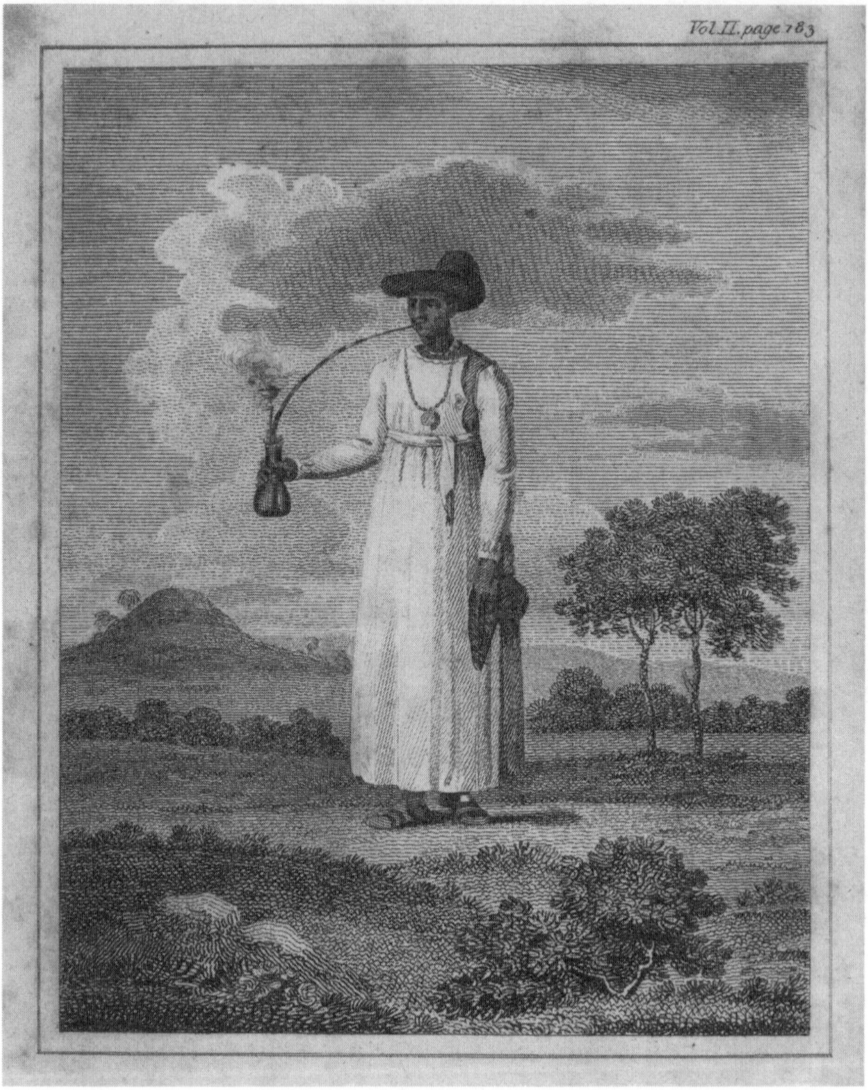

Figure 1.3. "Courji, a Baniyan chief of the French agents at Mocha, in full dress and decorated with a medal of Louis XVI," published in Louis de Grandpré, *A Voyage in the Indian Ocean and to Bengal, Undertaken in the Years 1789 and 1790* (London: G. and J. Robinson, 1803), 2:183. Courtesy of the New York Public Library.

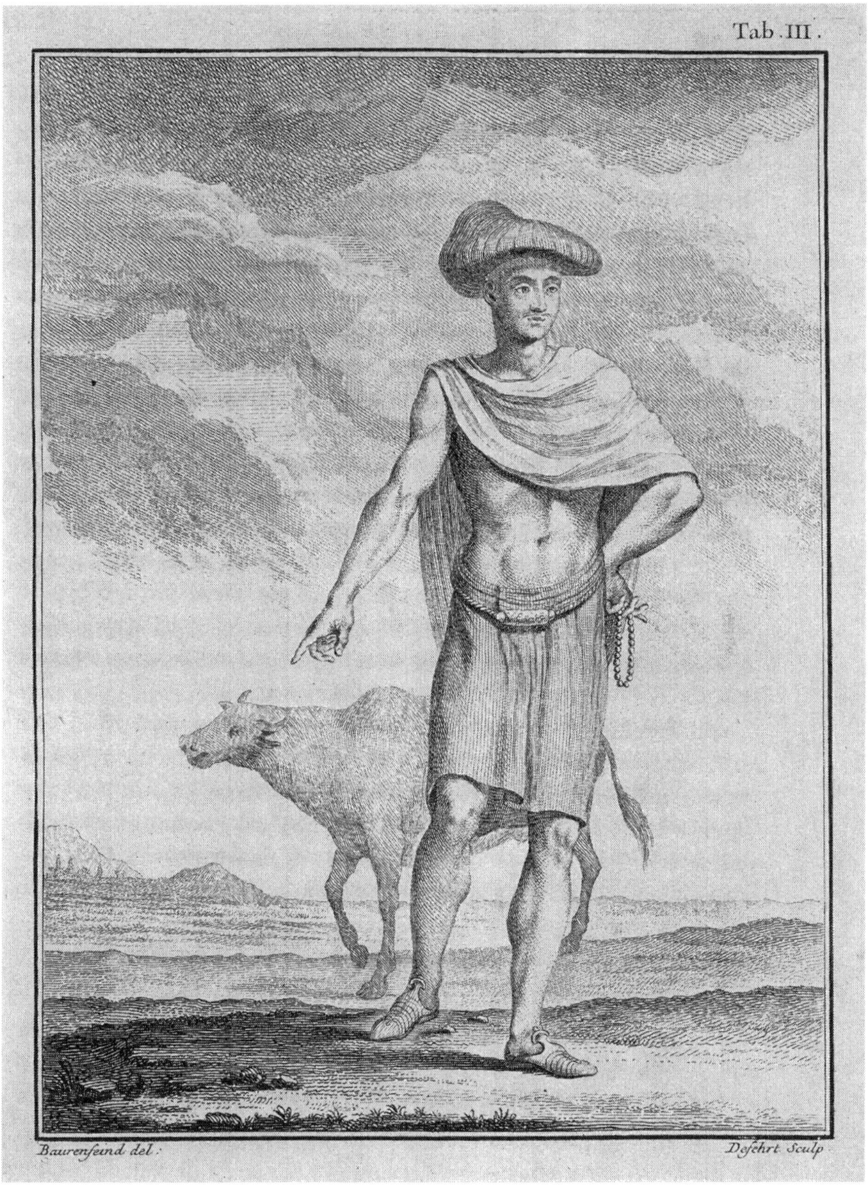

Figure 1.4. "The clothing of Baniyans in Mocha," published in Carsten Niebuhr, *Beschreibung von Arabien* (Copenhagen: Nicolaus Möller, 1772), pl. 3. Courtesy of the John Hay Library, Brown University Library.

time tell us considerably more from the perspective of those on shore. The Dutch recount that after the three ships came into the harbor, their flags were immediately recognized as French. Still, Mocha's governor doubted their identity based solely on their colors, emphasizing the implicit unreliability of flags as maritime markers. So he asked the Dutch to send a translator to the boat along with his representatives. The chief Joan Josua Ketelaar selected a rifleman named Laurens Christoffel Beling, who spoke French well. He instructed Beling to remove his regular clothing and put on a long robe. He also gave "strict orders" that Beling speak only Arabic, Turkish, and French, thus assuming the role of a "Greek Christian," presumably from the eastern Mediterranean.[55] It is not known whether Beling followed that directive, for the French captain eventually came to know exactly who the translator was, although it is possible that he discovered Beling's true identity only after coming on shore. Regardless, the tone of this exchange exemplifies the sense of mistrust and fear that underpinned all initial encounters in the harbor. This set of directives is also instructive in showing that as much as clothing served as a crucial tool of identification at the maritime threshold, it could just as easily be manipulated to obtain different identities, and not just those that were purely Eastern or Western, European or Arab, Muslim or Christian, but also various liminal permutations of these affiliations. As Ann Jones and Peter Stallybrass have demonstrated, clothes could "materialize identities for onlooker and wearer alike," but because they are also "detachable . . . they can move from body to body. That is precisely their danger and their value: they are bearers of identity, ritual, and social memory, even as they confuse social categories."[56]

In the case of Mocha's ceremonies of entry, clothing was not a natural marker of a fixed identity but was deployed conspicuously and consciously to mediate the cross-cultural encounter. It could entice prospective merchants to trade or drive perceptions of local merchants and even be used to conceal identities. It gained its potency as a sign from its shifting indexicality within these dynamic systems of exchange, display, and recognition. As historian Valentin Groebner explains, clothes could serve "both as scrupulously examined billboards of identification and as ciphers of disguise and dissimulation."[57]

Horses

Either outside of the Sea Gate or within it, a large gathering of city inhabitants, soldiers, musicians, decorated horses, and flag bearers awaited the French in 1709 and 'Anbar and Muhammad Husayn in 1730. Of these various elements, horses require focused interest. Much more than a simple

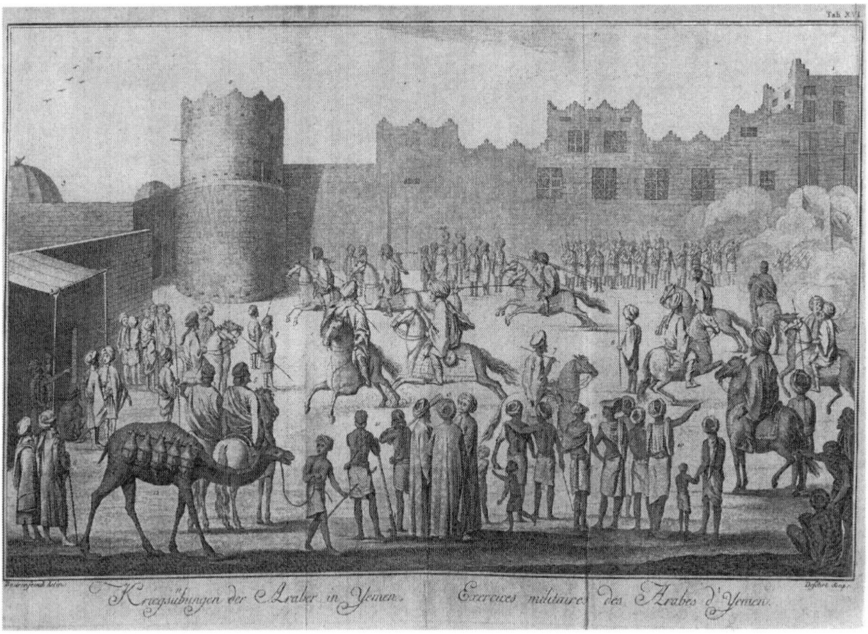

Figure 1.5. "Military exercises of the Arabs in Yemen," with three members of the Danish expedition in the lower center, two Baniyans to their right, and the governor of al-Luhayya in the center, published in Carsten Niebuhr, *Beschreibung von Arabien* (Copenhagen: Nicolaus Möller, 1772), pl. 16. Courtesy of the Cleveland Public Library.

mode of transportation, the meaning of horses went far beyond their functional use. Following the "animal turn" in historical studies, particularly the relevant work of Alan Mikhail, Sandra Swart, and Donna Landry, I examine the horse as an animal that was used, wielded, and exchanged in modes that were encoded with social value rather than as a "natural" feature that populated the landscape.[58]

In Yemen the privilege of riding was accorded only to some, and the act of mounting and dismounting served as a public mode for fixing social hierarchies. Another image from Niebuhr's 1763 expedition depicts military exercises that were witnessed in al-Luhayya, a port to the north of Mocha. In it, one can see an array of types, differentiated by the artist Baurenfeind through their varied modes of dress (Figure 1.5). The image provides a sense of the cultural diversity of Red Sea ports, with Yemenis from the highlands and lowlands, Jews, Baniyans, and those of African descent, such as al-Luhayya's governor Amir Farhan, who appears on horseback. While dress was one tool that onlookers used to distinguish between and among these various groups, access to mounted transit was another mode of differentiation. In this scene, only a few are shown riding, while others are mounted but stationary. The large majority watch the exercises on foot.

In the context of the Yemeni commercial encounter, Arabian horses should also be understood as long-standing items of export.[59] By the early eighteenth century, Arabian breeds could be procured from a number of different sites around North Africa and the eastern Mediterranean, such as Egypt and Syria. Purebred Arabians were sought-after commodities in Mocha and frequently exported from the Red Sea coast, conveyed by Asian and European vessels to the east and west.[60] Over just a few days in August 1731, three ships passed by Mocha from the northern port of Jidda, one English and two Gujarati, carrying a total of two hundred horses as cargo.[61] This was also the time when Arabian horses were brought to England to breed thoroughbreds for racing, which, according to Landry, "revolutionized not only English racing but early modern culture more broadly."[62] Like the textiles I described earlier, horses appeared at the outset in ceremonies of commercial initiation in order to provoke the instincts and aspirations of major merchants from afar, whetting their appetite and encouraging them to begin trading immediately.

In the case of entry rites at Mocha, the distance between the jetty and the destination point was so short that it did not require mounted transportation. When the Dutch arrived at the port in 1701, the *amir al-bahr* was there to greet them with ten beautiful horses they rode briefly to the governor's house. After the audience concluded, these animals conveyed them to the house they had rented in the city.[63] Four years later, when they returned to the port, they declined to ride the horses that were presented to them, claiming that the journey was too short to bother.[64]

But these entry ceremonies must be set apart from everyday practice. As Swart writes of the Cape, "The body of the horse was . . . both a symbol of power and perhaps because of it, a site of struggle."[65] Among the overseas merchant class, rights to horses and mounted transit were by no means standard. Muslim merchants, such as the *nakhudha* Muhammad Husayn, could ride liberally within the city of Mocha. By contrast, *dhimmi*s, which included Baniyan merchants, were not allowed to ride horses within city limits. Technically they could ride donkeys, but they had to dismount when they passed by a Muslim of high standing. Europeans occupied a more liminal status because they were not governed as *dhimmi*s, like the Baniyans, who were both Hindu and Jain, but rather according to the articles of their trade agreements. Although they were allowed to ride horses, this privilege was rigidly controlled. On May 22, 1724, the governor of Mocha informed the Europeans that they could ride on either horses or donkeys in front of their houses and exit the city using only the gate that was located closest to them.[66] They were instructed specifically to avoid riding around the bazaar or through Bab al-Shadhili, the city's eastern gate, which was associated with Mocha's patron saint, ʿAli b. ʿUmar al-Shadhili.[67] They were also ordered not to ride in front of the governor's house; doing so would be in defiance of the governor and the notables of the city.

Although this spontaneous edict from the governor appears to have been a clarification of a previous restriction rather than newly imposed, its spatial specificity is worth expanding upon.[68] The three long-standing European houses were located along the shoreline at the edges of the walled city. The Dutch and the English houses were clustered near the northern gate, Bab al-ʿAmudi, and the French house was adjacent to the southern gate, Bab al-Sandal (Figure 1.6). The imam's command specifically limited their mounted movement to short passages in each direction out of the enclosed precinct. By extension, they were told explicitly to avoid the major landmarks of the city: its *suq* (market), the governor's house, and Bab al-Shadhili, the city gate that led to the highlands and the inland coffee emporium, Bayt al-Faqih. Essentially Europeans were forbidden from travelling on horseback along the city's sacred and commercial thoroughfare, which cut from the east to the west and tied the sea to the mountains. This axis was also the main entry into the city from the jetty. Unlike the edict regarding flags, which was quickly forgotten, this one appears to have been sustained for many years. In January 1735, according to the Dutch, the French merchant Monsieur "La Greene" was reprimanded for riding in front of the governor's house. He claimed he did not know about this rule, which suggests that it may have lapsed for a time, but clearly it had not been entirely forgotten or overridden over the years.[69]

In sharp contrast to these restricted daily movements, during yearly ceremonies of entry Europeans were freely and publicly given the right to travel on horseback along the very route they were forbidden to use throughout the rest of the year. Horses could serve as powerful icons that signified local approval, even momentarily, during ceremonial rites, precisely because their access was more often withheld and strictly controlled. Outside of the ceremonies of entry, access to mounted transit could be granted selectively to recognize a favor or to bestow a particular honor upon a foreign visitor. As an example, in February 1737, when the VOC resident Willem van den Bergh helped the local administration negotiate with the French after their attack on the city, the governor sent him a horse to ride to the palace. No doubt this privilege was granted in order to thank and honor the resident, but also to differentiate the Dutch from the French, who had menaced the city.[70] Additionally, in 1763 the governor of Mocha called for Dr. Cramer of the Danish expedition to treat his injured foot. He sent the doctor a mule to travel upon and invited him to traverse the area in front of his residence mounted, which

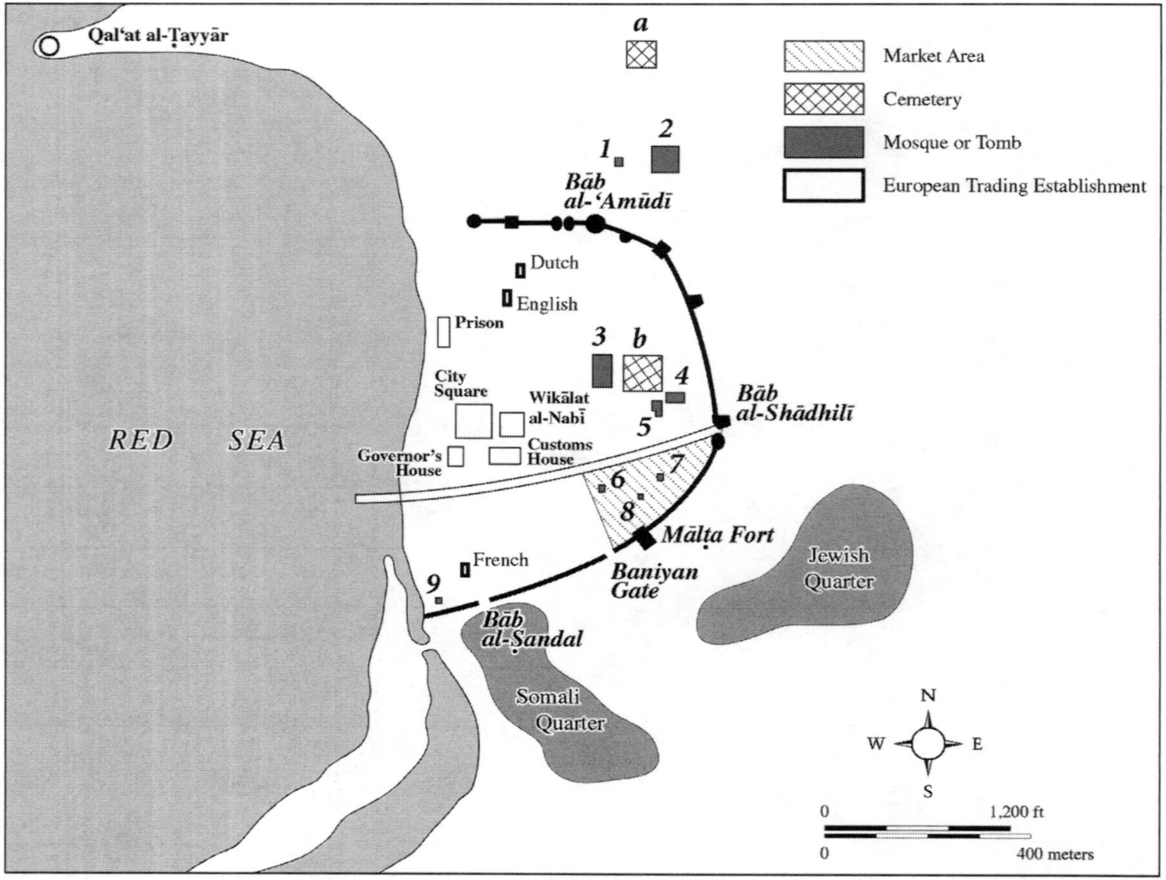

Figure 1.6. Map of Mocha, reconstructed by the author. Great Mosque (3), Mosque of al-Shadhili (4), Tomb of al-Shadhili (5), European cemetery (a). Drawn by Barry Levely.

Niebuhr noted as a special exemption.[71] The status of horses and mounted transportation was further complicated by the fact that the imam of Yemen and his officials often gave horses from their stables as gifts to merchants, including Europeans, as I discuss in chapter 3. Yet the European recipient was restricted from using these gifts freely throughout most of the trade season.

Horses were not simple static markers of honor; they gained their potency as signs in ceremonial rites of entry into Mocha precisely because of the social reversals they enacted. They moved fluidly between and within commodity and gift systems, while also serving as both a privilege and a restriction, highlighting differences among foreign merchants, Muslim, Hindu, Jain, and Christian.

The Offering of Stimulants and Aromatics

At the governor's house, La Merveille was given coffee, but he does not describe how it was tendered. Fortunately, many other accounts provide details about these rites of receiving and dispatching guests, which were not restricted to the governor's palace but were replicated in well-to-do private houses around Mocha and other Yemeni cities. These rites were staged repeatedly to mark everyday social interactions among the city's elite, as well as to seal commercial negotiations that took place in the domestic sphere.

Niebuhr provides the most methodical breakdown of this common ceremony. Upon entering a house one would be seated in the reception room and then offered a pipe filled with tobacco, some sweets, and a cup of coffee, as well as an embroidered napkin to place over the knees.[72] At the end of the visit, right before departing, a servant would sprinkle rosewater and provide incense to scent one's beard. As generic as these ceremonies seemed to all of those who participated in them on a daily basis, and may appear even to the anthropologist of modern Yemen, it is important to note that these offerings and the vessels in which they were presented aligned with the commodities that were central to Yemen's early modern trade on a local, regional, and wider global scale and thus had particular resonances in commercial initiation rituals at the port of Mocha.[73]

Of course, coffee was Yemen's most important export at this time, although its central place in the global market was being challenged formidably precisely during this era. But the coffee that was served at the governor's palace upon entry, and also in local homes, was not the dark brown beverage derived from the roasted bean that we might expect. Sometimes referred to in European sources as "the Sultana's coffee," this was *qishr*, brewed from the husk of the coffee bean and not its more precious flesh.[74] Still consumed in Yemen today, *qishr* derives from a natural waste product of the local coffee trade. This drink, which attains only a pale brown color and a less bitter taste, maintained its status as Yemen's hot beverage of choice, even while the drink made of coffee beans (*bunn*) prevailed elsewhere.[75] When served upon entry at the governor's palace, a cup of hot *qishr* pointed to the prime local availability of this highly sought-after product, but also implicitly evidenced the process by which the botanical good was transformed into a commodity for sale. In essence, *qishr*, a local beverage distinct from its darker, more widespread, and highly caffeinated counterpart, allowed the drinker to contemplate coffee in its pre-export state, thus pointing to Yemen's unique access to this product.

In rites of welcome, a cup of *qishr* was consistently paired with tobacco, which, by contrast, was usually imported to Yemen from India or Iran.[76] Tobacco was first mentioned in local Arabic sources in the sixteenth century. Although its use was initially contested in the southern Arabian Peninsula, mainly in the highlands, it was eventually cultivated in Yemen.[77] In Mocha, tobacco had garnered an eager local audience by the eighteenth century and could be found widely in the *suq*.[78] In this way, these ceremonies brought together coffee, or rather *qishr*, a byproduct of a local stimulant that was being globalized at the time but had been quite controversial among previous generations, with another contested substance, tobacco, which was in the process of being localized.[79] Together they point to the broad-reaching movements and acculturations that undergirded Mocha's early modern overseas trade.

The aromatics that were offered upon exiting the governor's house were also major commodities of the Arabian Sea and Indian Ocean trade. As anthropologist Dinah Jung has shown for the regions of Aden and Lahaj in southern Yemen, the availability and preference for certain perfumes represents "centuries-long intercontinental connections," observations that may also be extended across Yemen more generally.[80] Along with dates, copper vessels, and black cloth and robes, rosewater was brought to Yemen primarily from the Gulf but was often distilled originally in Iran.[81] This trade was supported by large numbers of trankeys that came from Basra in Iraq, Matrah in Oman, and Kung on the Persian coast throughout the year. The incense derived from agarwood or aloeswood, *'ud* in Arabic, was brought from mainland Southeast Asia on westbound ships, including those of the Dutch.[82] This costly aromatic, which was obtained from the resinous heartwood that forms when certain evergreen trees, such as the *Aquillaria*, become infected with a type of mold, played a major role in social interactions around Yemen. It is important to note that local types of incense, namely frankincense and myrrh, which had been avidly sought in Arabia since antiquity, were not the key constituents of these aromatic suites, spurned perhaps because of their enduring associations with Christian liturgy.[83]

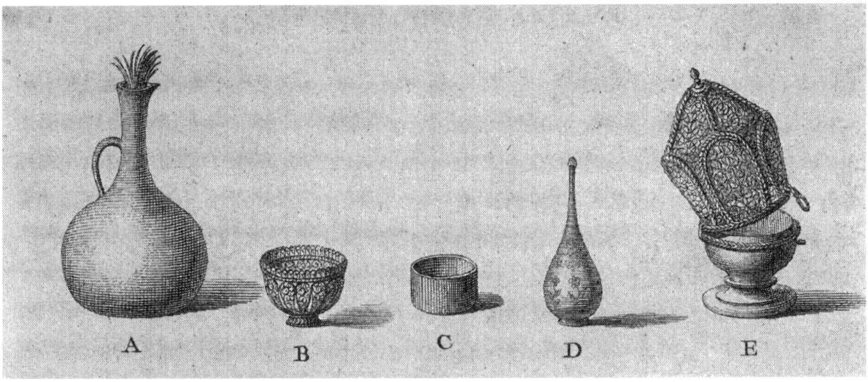

Figure 1.7. Vessels used to serve and drink coffee (A, B, and C), to sprinkle rosewater (D), and to burn incense (E), published in Carsten Niebuhr, *Beschreibung von Arabien* (Copenhagen: Nicolaus Möller, 1772), pl. 1. Courtesy of the John Hay Library, Brown University Library.

Imported aromatics from the Indian Ocean, such as rosewater and *'ud*, in liquid and airborne forms, were deployed much more centrally in Mocha's domestic ceremonies during this time.

According to Niebuhr and pictured in his account, a whole cadre of objects, foreign and local, was used to present these various substances to guests.[84] The *qishr* was tendered in a clay bottle with a globular base and thin neck that was made locally. The one pictured by Niebuhr and marked A on figure 1.7 represents a classic unglazed type that archaeologist Edward Keall refers to as Yemen's "traditional coffee pot."[85] Stalks were customarily placed in its opening to prevent the coffee grounds from spilling out when pouring the hot liquid.[86] For drinking, the elites used small cups from China without handles, sometimes paired with saucers of porcelain, silver, or brass. Although Niebuhr does not specify, the cups he refers to were surely made of porcelain and could have also come from Japan or Southeast Asia.[87] Remnants of characteristic Chinese blue and white underglaze painted cups have turned up in a 1993 site survey from Mocha.[88] In addition, fragments of monochrome brown cups, sometimes called "café au lait" in color, were found. These were likely of the Batavia type that was made in China but carried frequently by the Dutch in the eighteenth century.[89] VOC records confirm that these Asian-made objects, in addition to porcelain cups with gilding from China and Japan, were readily available for sale in Mocha's bazaar, although their cost was likely prohibitive for many Yemeni consumers.[90] The silver and brass *untertassen* (under cups) that Niebuhr labeled B in figure 1.7 were not flat, wide saucers, but rather the rounded *zarf* (cupholder) that was used widely around the Ottoman world and adjacent areas at this time as a sleeve to protect the drinker's fingers from the heat of the substance within. These metal accessories could have been made locally, perhaps by Mocha's Baniyan metalworkers.

According to Niebuhr, ordinary people used simpler earthenware vessels for coffee consumption. These cups were probably of the Haysi type, a domestic ware that developed in response to the need for new coffee utensils in Yemen in the sixteenth century.[91] The 1993 site survey of Mocha turned up shards from a Haysi cup in pinkish clay glazed in brown and olive green.[92] Similar modern versions from the Red Sea coast are fashioned with ridges and set on high bases (Plate 2). These, however, are much more elaborate than the undecorated, straight-sided one pictured by Niebuhr and marked C on figure 1.7.

The aromatics also required specialized dispensers, which were both imported and locally made. The rosewater was offered in a bottle with a round base and a long thin neck to control the flow of the liquid. The one pictured by Niebuhr and marked D on figure 1.7 appears to have been made of porcelain, perhaps enamel painted with floral designs, and was likely from China, which commonly provisioned the Islamic world with these types of dispensers in the eighteenth century.[93] Yet Niebuhr explains that in Yemen porcelain rosewater sprinklers were covered with silver, likely referring to the tapered metal nozzles that were often added (Plate 3). Although Niebuhr informs us that silver incense burners were in use as well, the one he pictures is wooden with a hood of reed openwork (marked E on figure 1.7).[94] This image must have been rendered in Copenhagen based on the two strikingly similar examples that he brought back from the expedition, still in the Danish national collection. Both sit on low wooden bases painted in red, with plaited hoods fastened by reed bands (Plate 4). Although the small ceramic or metal inserts, upon which the charcoal would have been placed, have since been lost, one can easily imagine the wisps of smoke wafting up through the perforations in these braided panels.[95]

When lined up together, as they are displayed in the engraving offered by Niebuhr, one can see how imported porcelain wares from Asia and silver vessels were used alongside their counterparts in coarser materials, such as earthenware, wood, and reed. Together and in the context of rites of ceremonial reception, these imported and local products played various roles as vessels of delivery and tools of consumption of these domestic and foreign stimulants and aromatics. While it is tempting to focus on the striking place of the imported wares, such as Asian ceramics, which signal vibrant external trade connections, it is important to underline that local products were used frequently in assemblage with those that came from other places.[96]

At the ceremonies of welcome that were staged at the governor's house, coffee and tobacco were consumed through the mouth and imported aromatics were taken in through the nose. It is fitting that in Arabic both drinking and smoking are indicated by the word *sharaba,* "to drink," thus these paired activities are enduringly linked etymologically. As with the textiles and horses, arriving merchants would have directly correlated these goods to their commodity identities, thus confirming the availability of such local products for sale at the port as well as the strong local demand for those that were imported. Coffee was indexed prominently as an object of desire, albeit in a state that was radically different from its export preparation. Displayed in a parallel assemblage of native and foreign wares, these local and imported goods presented a dynamic locus of circulation and consumption for stimulants and aromatics in the western Indian Ocean.

Houses

After the audience at the governor's house in 1709, the French captains went to the house of Vira, the Baniyan broker, because they did not yet have their own dwelling. Within a few days they rented a house. Elsewhere I have demonstrated that the merchant's house in Mocha served as a central site where major traders conducted all of their negotiations rather than using public structures.[97] Thus the merchant's house far exceeded the capacity of a residence and also encompassed the various functions of a trading establishment and a warehouse. For this reason, all members of the major merchant class had to own or rent a house in order to conduct the basic functions of wholesale commercial exchange. Even the Baniyans, who did not enjoy all of the social privileges of major merchants in the city, were allowed to rent and own houses in Mocha, which they used in the same way—as residences, trade establishments, and warehouses.[98]

But the right to rent or own and reside in a private house in Mocha was a commercial privilege available only to an exclusive set of seafarers and travellers. This exclusivity is articulated most clearly for the Europeans because they required written trade agreements with the local government, which are well preserved. Major local and Indian merchants did not rely upon written contracts to certify their trade privileges, as their right to trade at the port was never contested or denied. Even so, certain European trade agreements detail the practices of a wider class of major overseas traders in Mocha, for some stipulations that are spelled out quite plainly for the Europeans, such as those pertaining to the house, also pertained to their counterparts from India.

In fact, the large part of maritime travellers that arrived at Mocha was denied the privilege to own or rent a house on shore, even if they could afford to do so. The second article of the French 1709 trade agreement stipulated, "Their Shallops may load and unload from Sun rise to Sun set, but their Men must always pass the Night on board their Ships," signaling that the French crewmembers were not welcome to sleep on shore.[99] Yet because European sailors often tired of staying aboard their vessels after long sea journeys, some would inevitably violate this stipulation and attempt to come on land after dark to visit the small taverns run by Jews to the south of Mocha. Some of these sailors were caught and duly punished.[100] When the skipper and the bookkeeper of the VOC ship the *Noorderquartier* tried to rent a house on shore in 1725, they were quickly informed that this was not allowed. The governor complained to the senior VOC merchants that these crewmen did not know the "customs of Mocha."[101] Only when European crewmen were sick, which was common after long periods at sea, were they permitted to sleep on shore. In these cases, EIC and VOC merchants could rent houses to serve as temporary makeshift hospitals, undoubtedly with permission from the governor.[102] It is not surprising that the local administration would want to keep large numbers of potentially rowdy sailors on board their ships in the dark evening hours, when it was more difficult to monitor the city's population. This surveillance also worked in the other direction. In 1724 the English chief factor ended up sleeping aboard the EIC ship docked in the harbor for one night, for which Mocha's governor reprimanded him.[103]

Most Asian and regional trading boats carried many transit passengers in addition to merchants and their goods. These passengers, who were generally Muslim, did come on land and usually slept in the *khan* (temporary housing facility) in Mocha.[104] The *khan* was a simple lodging space with only provisional accommodations, which was unsuitable for elite merchants from abroad, who required more lavish amenities for extended periods in addition to safe and protectable warehouse space to store their goods. Yet even the *khan* could not accommodate the masses of pilgrims who stopped in Mocha en route to Mecca, usually for only a few days before continuing on to Jidda. These pilgrims, men and women, sometimes slept in the city's mosques or even constructed provisional housing for their short sojourns at Mocha.[105] But the privilege of renting or owning a house, and residing in it, was granted only to major foreign merchants or important travellers, thus clearly differentiating them from the simple crewmen who staffed their boats and the more modest traders and travellers who stopped at the port.

European trade agreements help to explain why Muhammad Husayn was so resistant to visiting the customs house in 1730, to the extent that he preferred to leave his goods unguarded and out in the open in front of his house as a form of protest. These agreements clearly articulate that the Europeans were allowed to bypass the customs house and unload their goods directly into their warehouses within their residences and residential complexes, where port officials would go to inspect them in private.[106] Once again, this privilege was not limited to the Europeans but also applied to the major Asian and local merchants in town. Muhammad Husayn's vehement reaction to stopping at the customs house illuminates the charged stigma attached to public spaces associated with trade and travel, including the *khan*.

Ample evidence from other trading cities suggests that the public institutions that are often associated with the functions of the overseas trade in the Islamic world were in fact places that many important traders wished to avoid or pass through quickly. In regard to the medieval merchants of the Cairo Geniza, Goldberg describes how those who sailed through customs unchecked were saved the burden of having to reveal the contents (some undeclared) of their tightly packed bundles and bales, privileges and preferences that were closely linked to their reputation and high standing as traders.[107] A smooth and unencumbered journey through the customs house reflected a successful merchant's ability to wield local connections and thus could amplify his standing among his peers. Olivia Remie Constable has demonstrated that the *khan* and *funduq* (temporary lodging establishments for merchants and travellers) found frequently in Mediterranean cities were often viewed with suspicion and reprehension because they "provided lodging to foreigners and travelers who had no friends or family in a given city . . . and were, by their very nature, gathering-points for those people who were to some degree *other*, different or alien to the local context. The very strangeness of foreign travelers could generate distrust, perhaps even fear."[108] In the context of the western Indian Ocean, these negative associations too seem to have been at work, thus confirming the public lodging facility as an unsuitable accommodation for the major overseas merchant and the customs house as a place to be avoided. In the case of Mocha, the *khan* and the customs house, which were open to all, were perceived as the direct social inverse of the much more exclusive house.

Rather than simply a place to sleep, the merchant's house in Mocha played a central role within a local system of commercial privilege and hierarchy where certain preferential trading rights were actually carried out. Even Phipps, who served as the EIC chief in Mocha briefly and was assertive in his efforts to cut operational costs there, acknowledged that the large English house in Mocha was essential for local trade. He stated, "It may be necessary that such a publick way of living be maintained to preserve Respect from these Country People, which I find practiced by other European Nations."[109] Although he singles out the Europeans, his statement recognizes that the house was not a mere accessory to trade or just a site for its everyday operations. Rather it was a necessary attribute in upholding a major merchant's reputation and sustaining the inclusion of the English among others of their stature, namely Mocha's major overseas merchants. Thus the house served as a fitting final point in these ceremonial rites of entry.

It is also worth mentioning that many of the finest houses in Mocha were located along the shoreline and conspicuously adorned with elaborately carved wooden projecting windows. Often hoisted directly above the entrance, these grilled windows provided much-needed shade to Mocha's hot streets and allowed for cooling breezes to enter the stuffy space of the brick-walled house. Although one example (Figure 1.8), evidenced in a later photograph, can be linked directly to Gujarati precedents with its bird-shaped brackets characteristic of western Indian wood carving, most of these windows were more generally evocative of various distant locations, to the north in the Mediterranean and to the east in the wider Indian Ocean arena. Thus the common feature of the projecting window aided in producing a familiar spatial and visual aesthetic across a vast maritime geography.[110] It is usually said that these windows in Mocha, in addition to other cities of the Red Sea, were carved from Asian teak, one of the commodities that served as ballast on ships coming from the east.[111] Imported wood was thus an apt medium for the prominent decoration found on the exteriors of these houses, the exclusive domain of Mocha's major overseas merchants.

Less-Esteemed Entries

It is useful to examine the arrival of the German traveller and geographer Niebuhr in Mocha in 1763 in order to understand other possible receptions in this coastal city. Niebuhr, of course, was not a merchant; he was employed by King Frederick V of Denmark on an exploratory mission to the Arabian Peninsula. Particularly sympathetic to Yemen and those he met there, and proficient in colloquial Arabic, he is an important interlocutor for the region in the eighteenth century, as demonstrated in his publications. He was the sole survivor of his mission, which originally included a philologist, a naturalist, an artist, and a surgeon, and upon his return he was charged with presenting many of his colleagues' findings to the public.

After entering Yemen through the northern port of al-Luhayya, Niebuhr and his group donned "Turkish dress" for most of their visit in order to avoid undue attention, further underscoring how dress was manipulated and strategized for cross-cultural presentation. Like the VOC rifleman Beling in 1709, Niebuhr attempted to present himself as an "eastern Christian," a liminal figure who delicately straddled East and West, during parts of his journey.[112] In figure 1.5 we can see three of the Danish expedition members wearing full-length robes and standing at the lower center of

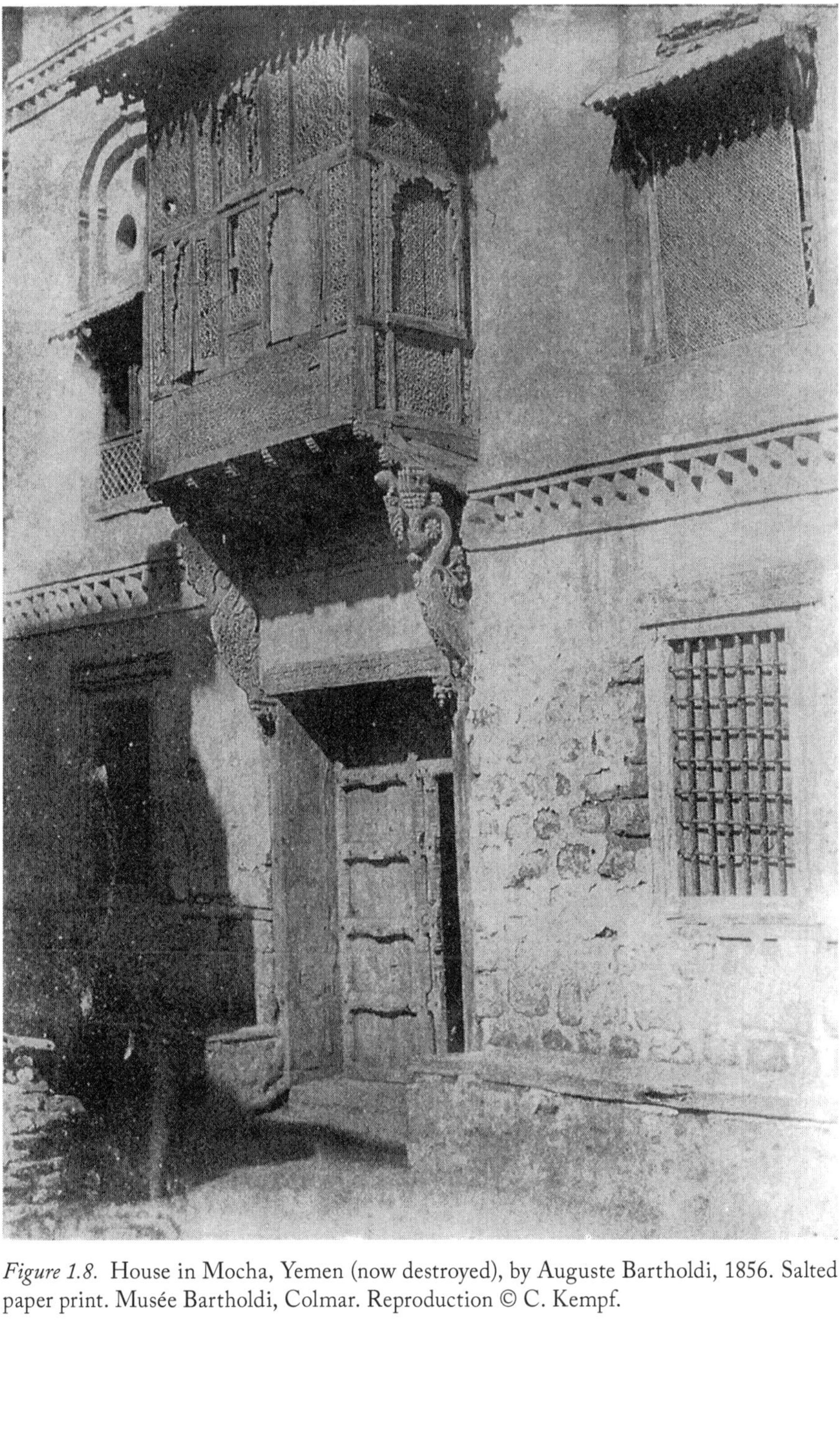

Figure 1.8. House in Mocha, Yemen (now destroyed), by Auguste Bartholdi, 1856. Salted paper print. Musée Bartholdi, Colmar. Reproduction © C. Kempf.

the composition, marked by the number 15. Although their garments are slightly longer than the other full gowns in this particular scene, the group blends in quite seamlessly and would not have stood out had the artist not marked them specifically.

Niebuhr and Peter Forsskål, the naturalist, arrived in Mocha before the rest of their team, on April 23, 1763. Unlike maritime merchants, they entered the city through Bab al-Shadhili, the inland gate on the city's eastern side. Unsurprisingly because of their dress and language capabilities, they were identified as Turks and were directed immediately to the *khan* instead of a private house or the governor's palace. While at al-Luhayya, the team had made the acquaintance of a man named Isma'il who spoke Dutch well. When they met Isma'il again in Mocha soon after their arrival, he advised the two to shed their Turkish dress, shave their beards, and reveal themselves as Europeans. He also helped them find a house to rent. Although they later came to doubt Isma'il's trustworthiness, this local acquaintance confirmed the importance of maintaining their status as foreigners in this cosmopolitan port and setting themselves apart from the less-distinguished groups that took up residence in the *khan*. But at this stage their baggage had already been taken to the customs house, where the governor was presiding over its inspection. Because of the unique nature of their mission, they carried objects that would seem strange to local observers, such as marine specimens and snakes preserved in barrels of wine, which smelled pungent when pried open by local officials. While this aggressive examination was taking place in the presence of Niebuhr and Forsskål, the contents of their rented house were also being inspected thoroughly. Apparently their books and other belongings were thrown out of the windows, and the owner of the house barred their reentry. After these events, which heightened local suspicions about their motives and identity, they had a hard time finding anyone in Mocha who would rent a house to them. Finally an English merchant named Francis Scott allowed them to stay with him. Only after several attempts to visit the governor were they able to get their goods released from the customs house and eventually gain his favor.

Admittedly the Danish mission was quite unique and inspired a special level of curiosity because of the nature of their research. But even so, it presents one possibility of how a foreign traveller who arrived without the signs of recognition and acceptance could be treated. Rather than being welcomed with flags and shots from the forts and an escort to the governor's house, they came in modestly, quietly, and without notice through the landward entrance. Moreover they went directly to the *khan* rather than taking up residence with another merchant or broker, and thus they were accorded the status of petty peddlers or ordinary travellers, which may have contributed to their ill treatment at the customs house. One can see why Muhammad Husayn would have wanted to avoid the possibility of such abuse in 1730.

Niebuhr's entry makes it clear that those of different classes and affiliations were treated to very different modes of reception upon arrival at Mocha, one of the primary gateways to Yemen. Any new traveller that came into the city was sized up immediately based on dress, point of ingress, and, if a maritime voyager, the vessel he or she travelled on. After this initial evaluation, foreigners were sent either to the *khan,* a local broker, or the governor's house. In this process of vetting, material objects, such as clothing and belongings, and the place where they lodged became crucial markers, in fact clues that were used to pin down the identity and intentions of strangers. For Niebuhr, the key stops along the usual itinerary of maritime commercial initiation were entirely inverted and thus resulted in a very different reception from that of a major merchant who came in through Mocha's jetty with all the signs of the local government's approval.

One was never sure who was going to arrive in Mocha's harbor. Even after a ship had been identified based on its flag, those on shore rushed to confirm the presumed identity by sending boats out to the new vessel. Because ceremonies of entry at the maritime threshold were offered only to major overseas merchants, the first moments of appraisal were delicate ones, in which those on shore attempted to size up those at sea quickly and thoroughly. The ceremonial rites of entry I have detailed were not generic examples of pageantry or empty exercises of pomp and display. Nor did they exemplify the petty conceits of Asian merchants and Oriental despots or displays of absolute and uncontested power, as their observers often suggested. Rather they represent important moments of vetting and evaluation, which were essential to the local reception and perception of merchants that arrived at the port. The very first stage of commerce was initiated not by a financial transaction but by these social and cognitive processes, in which newly arrived merchants were appraised and immediately categorized.[113]

This point can be made more emphatically when we examine the ceremonies of exit that were staged for the very same *nakhudha*s and major merchants who were welcomed with the signs of local approval.[114] In a reversal of the entry ceremonies, the departing ship's authorities would first visit the governor, who would bestow upon the captain a *khil'a* (robe of honor), while treating him to the characteristic ceremony of coffee, tobacco, rosewater, and incense that he had participated in upon arrival. Then the departing group was led to the jetty, usually by the *amir al-bahr* and other city officials, again under flags, banners, and the beating of drums. They concluded by boarding their ships. These ceremonies of exit were much smaller than those of entry, and the crucial exchange of the *khil'a* took place outside of the public eye. Moreover there is no indication that exit ceremonies were ever disputed or even closely evaluated, which underlines how important ceremonies of entry were in setting the tone for the trade season. By the time the exit ceremony was conducted, trade negotiations had been closed, deals had been struck, and schedules for payment had been settled.

As an illuminating backdrop, Groebner explores the medieval and early modern origins of the modern passport by looking at the development of processes of identification, which became consolidated institutionally across adjacent regions in Europe by the middle of the fifteenth century. He identifies various practices of vetting one's identity that invariably hinged upon a whole host of material objects, including passes, badges, and letters of introduction.[115] But rather than rendering identity more knowable and attainable, these initiatives inspired new ways to falsify documents and categorically dissimulate one's standing and character. Groebner's insistence on identification as a process, and a fundamentally fallible one at that, that hinged upon the display and reading of material objects is key to the central argument of this chapter. In a commercially oriented society, the vagaries of identification were particularly vexed because misattributions could be extremely costly to the coastal merchant or trade official.

A whole host of objects—mobile, animate, comestible, sensory, and built—were positioned on the leading edge of the cross-cultural commercial encounter at Mocha, where various economic, social, and cultural networks intersected and overlapped. These things may be grouped together, in that all were clearly legible to a wide sector of merchants from the extended maritime world and most happened to be commodities. Thus they were "global" in their ability to function competently as signs within a shared logic of cross-cultural desire and demand at this bustling port. Yet because these goods could move quite fluidly through commodity, gift, consumption, and display systems, their meanings were not obtained solely by their commodity status. Rather most of these goods, particularly flags, clothing, horses, and houses, were used, deployed, and contested within a stratified commercial culture in which privileges for various groups of merchants were sharply differentiated. Rights to them could be given, but just as easily taken away. As such, they were not inert or passive symbols of a natural or fixed status, nor were they simple reflections of local approval. They were unstable signs that were wielded actively in complicated local social matrices. Their meaning derived not from the lulls in their mutable roles but from their dynamic instability. The following chapter follows some of these objects, particularly textiles, into the related realm of merchant tribute.

Two

European Merchant Tribute in Yemen

In an essay of 2001 provocatively named, "Amongst Feigned Friends and Declared Enemies," the heavyweight of Dutch overseas history, Leonard Blussé, suggests that the time has come for VOC historians to shift their focus away from the company's military conquests in the Indian Ocean in order to look more closely at the "soft-handed approach" that Dutch merchants were compelled to maintain when faced with the long-standing and well-established systems of trade that they encountered in Asia.[1] Some, such as Cynthia Viallé, Bhawan Ruangsilp, Adam Clulow, and Martha Chaiklin, have heeded this call by focusing on VOC diplomacy in Thailand, Japan, and other sites.[2] With a keen interest in the ways Dutch merchants managed their tenuous positions at foreign courts, these scholars answered Blussé's invocation while simultaneously contributing to the concurrent movement toward a "new diplomatic history," which has taken shape quite robustly across fields in early modern studies, but under a divergent set of interests and goals.[3]

At the intersection of this new diplomatic history and the VOC-focused history proposed by Blussé, Europeans appear not as dogmatic intruders but as dedicated observers who yielded to local systems of trade and hierarchy, often engaging in necessary accommodations in order to execute their economic agendas successfully. As Jurrien van Goor acknowledges, the VOC position was often an "ambivalent one, in which admiration was mixed with aversion to strange customs and practices."[4] Yet Blussé highlights how readily these merchants assimilated to expectations they construed as demeaning or strange, such as engaging in the kowtow, long seen in the West as a gesture of utter subservience, at the feet of the Qing ruler, or "the Siamese Court's practice of lying sideways and moving, crab-like, across the floor."[5] In Yemen as well, Dutch but also English and French merchants never achieved a preeminent status and were thus required to adapt to the local system of exchange, with all of its unfamiliar trappings.

If diplomacy is to be taken seriously and the activities of ambassadors and intermediaries are worthy of close scrutiny, then the gifts they carried with them must also be given due attention. Certainly gifts were a perennial topic of concern for European merchants as early as 1498, when Vasco da Gama arrived in Calicut only to find that his gift of hats, cloaks, cloth, coral, basins, sugar, and pots of honey and butter was hardly satisfactory as an offering from a prominent foreign visitor.[6] European anxieties about the proper selection of gifts for Indian Ocean rulers and officials would continue as a perennial motif, reflected consistently in the records of the VOC and EIC in later periods as well. As such, it is no surprise that early eighteenth-century documents from Yemen are replete with concerns about gifts as an overriding responsibility for the major overseas merchant.

The Material Content of Commercial Gifts

Inspired by Georges Bataille's notion of the "general economy," this chapter and the one that follows it operate under the assumption that gift exchange as a "non-productive expenditure" was an essential part of Yemen's world of overseas commerce, a point that has been made by previous scholars for other sites in the Middle East and around the Indian Ocean. As Chaiklin has succinctly stated for Japan, gifts were "a necessary cost of business" and an "effective practice of all the East India Companies."[7] Although some gift givers, namely the Dutch and the English, may have considered this type of giving deleterious to their economic enterprises in Mocha and Bayt al-Faqih, they also came to understand that gifts implicitly undergirded the survival of those very enterprises, operating in parallel to more explicit modes of commercial exchange. As Bataille states, "Social rank is linked to the possession of a fortune, but only on the condition that the fortune be partially sacrificed in unproductive social expenditures"; he goes on to mention festivals, spectacles, and games as activities in which the outcome inevitably leads to an overall loss.[8] Participation in the gift economy as a requisite but seemingly unproductive expenditure also allowed entry and sustained membership to an exclusive segment of Yemen's overseas merchant class. Like the ceremonies described in chapter 1, these rites were social privileges to which only some were invited to engage.

I look closely at the commercial gifts the merchants of the VOC and EIC offered to recipients in Yemen, examining them in parallel to the practices and substance of trade transactions. This examination rests on the premise that we must go beyond quick pronouncements about the European perception of gifts by delving into their material content. While acknowledging that gifts constituted a serious preoccupation of local rulers in the Indian Ocean, most historians, with the exception of Viallé and Chaiklin, have not taken the time or energy to explore the actual contents of the thousands of ordinary commercial gifts that were given around the Indian Ocean in the seventeenth and eighteenth centuries. They have generally focused on the fact that gifts were given or not, and the ramifications these items had, rather than what kinds of goods they included. When items are listed, they are rarely treated beyond their value as exotica or reduced to a pure monetary equation.

Indeed scholars of merchant tribute are severely hampered by the fact that most of the commercial gift items from the Indian Ocean sphere have not been preserved for us, thus they can only be considered "tangible goods of a somewhat generic character."[9] In these cases, the art historical initiative to look closely at gifts as individual objects with attention to their formal, material, and visual aspects is impossible. Even so, it is suggested that meaning may be drawn from classes of objects, even those that cannot be studied directly, by sketching their salient patterns of assemblage and bestowal, through close readings of the textual passages that describe them, and by lining them up with comparative objects, however limited they may be.[10] The patterns discerned in Yemen will certainly present similarities to gift practices evidenced in other sites around the Indian Ocean. Yet my hope is to situate these gifts within local and specific rather than generalized circumstances of bestowal and reception while asking what these goods may have signified within the Yemeni context of exchange. The fundamental goal is to determine "the way in which an object is socially consequential."[11]

By the eighteenth century, neither the VOC nor the EIC was interested in dispatching a formal diplomatic mission to Yemen.[12] So merchants were the key conduits for exchange and communication. Through their bestowals we can hone in on commercial gift practices, particularly to provincial officials, without ambiguity. By focusing intently on the detailed dynamics of commercial gift practices rather than personal or diplomatic practices, I turn the focus away from the noteworthy gifts that were exchanged between rulers and sometimes included objects of untold value or rarity, such as exotic animals, precious gems, and unique paintings, legendary items that have merited a certain amount of interest by scholars of historic gift exchange and in the popular imagination. But, in agreement with Clulow, I also reject the possibility that any commercial bestowal may be considered "an appendix to the business of trade, an essentially meaningless object that . . . merchants were happy to offer up in order to secure profit."[13]

Dutch Customary Gifts

Since their arrival in Mocha in the year 1616, Dutch merchants recognized that gifts were crucial in the local world of trade.[14] By the early decades of the eighteenth century, VOC merchants were describing their annual customary gifts as ordinary and cyclical in nature, indicating that they came to conceive of them as a rote responsibility.[15] These gifts were given in addition to the requisite customs and duties that were paid on their goods, as well as the gate tolls, fees, and other charges incurred in the process of trade.[16] Whereas those other requisite costs could fluctuate and thus inspired frustration on the part of foreign merchants, they were usually spelled out quite clearly. By contrast, rules around gift giving were not included as prescriptions in trade agreements, despite the fact that they were unconditionally required of major European merchants. For that reason, one must gather information about gift practices from a number of registers that document bestowals already tendered, thus constituting a record of past practices rather than directives for the future. Even so, we know much more about Dutch and English gift practices than those of Asian and local merchants in eighteenth-century Yemen. It is clear that the practices and the substance of their exchanges, which are conveyed only through more fragmentary information and will be treated in chapter 3, differed starkly from those of their European counterparts.

The scope of Dutch yearly distribution always included the governors of Mocha and Bayt al-Faqih, in addition to workers and other officials and merchants in these two cities. For instance, on June 27, 1717, gifts were doled out to Mocha's short-term governor Sayyid Hassan bin Salih; his second in charge, Faqih Ahmad bin al-Hajj; the top inspector of weights at the customs house, "Abdul Sabna" (perhaps 'Abd al-Samad); and the *qadi* (judge, presumably of Mocha), named "Henning."[17] In addition, they provided a gift to the Mocha merchant Qasim al-Turbati (who was still considered a good friend of the company); the *amir al-bahr;* a certain Muhammad Samir, who was likely a merchant; and the company broker, Virsinsi Trikam. They also offered something to Zayd Jamal, the governor of Bayt al-Faqih.

Following a general pattern that the VOC sustained in Mocha and Bayt al-Faqih from at least 1706 until 1724, these gifts were derived from or produced in many sites within the extended Dutch maritime trading world.[18] As an example, in 1717 the governor of Mocha received various spices: eight pounds of cloves, ten of cinnamon, and ten of nutmeg. Textiles were also given, including thirty-four ells of Dutch *laken* (lightweight wool fabric) in scarlet, golden yellow, and "parrot" green and a few malmals and cossaes (both types of Indian muslin), in addition to a single musket.[19] Various oils that were spiced with cinnamon, clove, nutmeg, and mace were presented in quarter-ounce bottles. When taken on its own terms, the volume of this gift would have been impressive, with its bulk of spices and array of spiced oils, and the bright and lively colors of the European cloth would surely have caught the eye of the recipient, in addition to the pieces of muslin, which was highly desirable locally.

However, the variety and the heft of the governor's gift are much less remarkable when one continues reading the very same list of 1717. Even a casual perusal shows that his gift was by no means unusual in its contents, even if its quantities were larger than those of lesser officials. In fact, every person on the list of recipients from 1717 was given some variation of the same set of goods, albeit in different amounts. For instance, Mocha's *amir al-bahr* received only fifteen pounds of the three types of spices and twenty ells of *laken,* without any of the other textiles, firearms, or spiced oils. The only individuals in that gift cycle who received something that was not included on the governor's list were the imam and his son, whose gifts I treat below as special cases, and Zayd Jamal, the governor of Bayt al-Faqih, who was given two pots of candied (*geconfijte*) cloves, in addition to over thirty ells of *laken.*

At the bottom of the list, the VOC merchants noted that two Bengali cossaes were given to the *chaush* of Mocha. Additionally, two casks of Batavian arrack were doled out in bottles to various anonymous port workers, such as the porters, peons, and weighers at the customs house, throughout the time of negotiations.[20] The merchants conclude by accounting for one bafta (a calico from western India), which had been purchased from Mocha's bazaar to make bags for the gifts.[21] Presumably this bafta was red, relatively coarse, and had been transformed into vessels to deliver the spices, as noted from other years.

This list from 1717, as well as the ones from 1719, 1722, and 1723, show that Dutch customary gifts were chosen from a surprisingly limited number of goods each year, with only slight variations in the contents that were delivered to each recipient during any given cycle.[22] In later years, a few different types of textiles were supplied, such as rolls of Chinese silk or damask, pieces of Persian velvet, and Indian shawls, and other varieties of firearms, such as carbines and pistols. Other spiced products, including pots of candied ginger and nutmeg, appear in later cycles, in addition to other types of *oliteiten* (fragrant oils).[23] Yet in any given year, the gifts came from the limited and remarkably consistent catalogue of certain textiles, weapons, spices or spiced goods, and aromatics. Moreover the gifts were regularized annually, even if there was a certain fluctuation between various years. In this way, the quantity of gifts could be easily calibrated during each cycle to suggest hierarchies of rank and position, as Viallé has shown was generally the gift practice of the VOC.[24] The governors of Mocha and Bayt al-Faqih were designated not by the most lavish and unique gifts but by the largest quantities tendered and the notable inclusion of one or two items not given to others. Figures of decreasing status, such as the inspector of the weights in Mocha's customs house, received diminished quantities of the same types of goods, although some, such as firearms, were excluded for those of lesser rank. In this way, VOC gifts not only honored their recipients but also acknowledged their relative standing within an accepted local hierarchy through clear modulations of distribution and scale.

On one hand, these lists are strikingly similar to gift packages that were distributed in other parts of the Dutch trading empire, such as a gift given to the Sultan of Johor, in Malaysia, in 1687, which also included sacks of the same spices, Indian textiles, and some firearms.[25] However, it should be noted that the much-discussed rarities or special orders from Europe, such as a large brass chandelier made in Amsterdam for the Tokugawa shogun Iemitsu in 1634, never appear on Yemeni lists.[26] Almost everything that the VOC distributed as gifts in Yemen, with the exception of Dutch *laken* and possibly the firearms, came from the intra-Asia trade.

Dutch gifts in Mocha were also relatively modest in terms of their value. The 1717 register did not reveal the prices of the gifts, but later registers did. For instance, in 1722 the governor of Mocha received various textiles: Dutch *laken,* Indian cossaes and malmals, three rolls of Chinese silk, one piece of Persian velvet, and a shawl. Spices and aromatics were delivered in three forms: sacks of cloves and nutmeg; candied cloves, ginger, and nutmeg; and *oliteiten*. In total, this gift was worth 183.9 Spanish reals.[27] In 1719–1720 one Bayt al-Faqih *bahar* (a unit of measure weighing 735 pounds) of coffee could be purchased for 130 to 150 Spanish reals, so these gifts constituted only a small fraction of the overall annual Dutch coffee intake, which, in some years, exceeded a million pounds.[28] In 1723 the value of the gift increased to 240.7 Spanish reals. This increase can be accounted for by the fact that the later gift included one musket, described as fine, and a pair of pistols, which were not included the year before.[29] Otherwise, identical quantities of textiles and preserved spices were given in both years.

It is difficult to discuss the material qualities of these various items, even the textiles, based on the short and simple entries that appear in the gift registers. In fact, historians have struggled to differentiate the various types that are listed in company trade documents, usually with just a name, price, and sometimes a brief indication of its quality. Even so, clear patterns of value and distribution emerge from the familiar groupings that appear on each list. Dutch *laken* came in scarlet red, golden yellow, "parrot" green, and black. These textiles were worth around 2.1 Spanish reals per ell, although the prices varied slightly by color. In contrast to the *laken,* muslin from Bengal was delicate and pliable and thus prized throughout the Arab world for turban wrappers.[30] But it is not clear how the two main types that were delivered as gifts, cossaes and malmals, differed from one another and how fine these examples were, as their prices fluctuated between 5 and 14 Spanish reals apiece, a gap that was clearly correlated with their quality and decoration.[31] Chinese silk was provided in rolls of unspecified length, usually in red and green. Velvet, usually Persian but sometimes Dutch, was offered by the piece (also unspecified in size) and appeared in red, blue, and green. Indian shawls were usually offered singly. In 1723 the single most expensive textile the Dutch gave Mocha's governor was a shawl that cost 28.9 Spanish reals, whereas a piece of Persian velvet was valued at 13 Spanish reals and each roll of Chinese silk at around 17.5 Spanish reals. It is clear that the textiles encompassed a variety of textures, weights, and colors, while also ranging in price, including lavish luxury types along with more modest examples.

Packaged in red calico sacks, the spices would have added a certain heft to the gifts. These large sacks would have contrasted with the small vials of oil that were usually drawn of the same varieties of spices, but in concentrated liquid form. Perfume makers in Yemen mixed such oils along with other aromatic essences, many of which were also imported, to derive unique fragrance combinations or to make incense.[32] Because large quantities of each spice were needed to produce even a small vial of the associated oil, they were extremely valuable. For instance, in 1719 the Dutch listed two ounces of cinnamon oil at 13.3 Spanish reals, whereas fifteen pounds of bulk Ceylonese cinnamon, described as fine, were valued at only 1.9 Spanish reals.[33] Much-desired candied spices were doled out in pots; these sugary substances, which may have been added to cups of *qishr* or used for medicinal purposes, were also markedly more expensive than their dry counterparts, tendered in sacks.[34]

Among the weapons, muskets and carbines were delivered individually, while pistols were always offered in pairs. The Dutch were known for their advanced gun technology and had spearheaded the firearm industry in Batavia, where these pieces may have been made.[35] It is also possible that the muskets, carbines, and pistols were ornamented with Asian motifs or designs, as were other examples intended for recipients in the region.[36]

Records of stock sold at Mocha demonstrate that Dutch gifts rarely overlapped with their items for sale in Yemen, providing evidence that merchant tribute was not simply a scaled-down sampling of goods offered in trade negotiations.[37] For example, in August 1722 the VOC sold thousands of calicos, such as dungarees, Surati cannikens, and guinea cloth (all relatively rough, low-cost cotton piece goods from India).[38] They also sold salempores, sailcloth, and gurras (also types of coarse cloth), referred to as rough or bleached. That year the Dutch sold muslin in Mocha, but not the cossaes and malmals of gift fodder, rather camcanies and luckhowries (both low-cost muslin types made in Patna), which were valued at least a quarter lower than the cloth frequently given as gifts. Aside from textiles, bulk metals, such as tin, copper, lead, and iron, constituted a large part of their sale. Spices such as black pepper, cloves, and cinnamon were also sold, in addition to powder and candy sugar, benzoin resin, and sappanwood.

The Dutch generally dealt in large quantities of textiles, yet those that they sold at the port were markedly different from those that they gave to local officials as gifts. Costly pieces of Persian velvet and rolls of Chinese silk were requested from Batavia only as gifts rather than for Mocha's open market.[39] Yet spices, such as cloves from Ambon Island, nutmeg and mace from the Banda Islands, and cinnamon from Ceylon, appear prominently in both VOC gift and trade registers as bulk goods, but were also offered in candied form and concentrated as oils. It is worth noting that the Dutch guarded, even to the point of violence, their monopoly on and access to these particular spices, which historian Els M. Jacobs describes as the "core activity" and "major products" of the VOC.[40] The conspicuous place of these much-guarded spices in both trade and gift registers mirrors their centrality in the policies and purview of the Dutch overseas trading empire.[41]

Other than these spices, most of Dutch gift fodder was considered unsuitable for the market of Mocha and thus actively held back from the wholesale trade. For instance, in 1735, after a system of cash gifts replaced goods (as I describe later), VOC merchants noted that a piece of scarlet *laken* had been kept in their warehouse for four years and had become damaged by moth holes.[42] They chose to preserve it as a gift if the occasion came up, even if it meant leaving it to deteriorate unsold in their warehouse. Although European woolen textiles were coming to Yemen through both Red Sea and Indian Ocean channels at this time, the Dutch were not the major purveyors of them. Dutch *laken* had catered to a large market in the eastern Mediterranean, particularly in the seventeenth century, and in Iran but was not marketed to Yemen's general consumers in the eighteenth century.[43] VOC merchants also retained other objects in their possession to be tendered as gifts, such as a fine box of *oliteiten*, including cinnamon, mace, clove, and musk oil, each of two and a half ounces, which had been brought over in 1730. In addition, they had kept eight rolls of damask, referred to as *schenkagie damasten* (damask to be used for gifts), from the previous year.

Each July, as they closed their account books, the merchants of Mocha summed up their year of trade and made *eisen* (requests) to Batavia for the coming season, as was the "standard VOC practice" across Asia.[44] Their yearly request (*eis*) specified the type and amount of goods they believed would sell successfully on the next year's market, in addition to the distinct category of goods for gifts and use, "*goederen tot geschenk en gebruijk*."[45] Although *eisen* lists were not always fulfilled as requested, they vividly and tangibly demonstrate a logic in which merchant tribute bestowals were seen in their own cogent category that was distinct from, but also considered alongside, commodities for sale. Both categories of commodity and gift were essential to the maintenance of the Yemen trade.

Although most gifts were supplied based on these requests, a small number of Dutch gifts were procured locally, indicating that in some years their gift obligations outstripped their supply of goods specially imported from Batavia for that purpose. These exceptions were always reported conspicuously on gift registers. On occasion, the Dutch purchased objects from other merchants at port, such as one roll of Chinese silk bought from an English captain and then given as a gift to the second in command of Mocha's government in 1719.[46] Even the precious silk shawls destined as gift fodder could be purchased from Mocha's bazaar, as in 1719, when two were acquired locally and given to Imam al-Mutawakkil Qasim as special gifts.[47] The fact that such goods could be procured so readily from the local bazaar also implies that they were not singular or unique items, even though they were certainly expensive. The Dutch also gave alcoholic drinks to port workers throughout the trade season as gifts in order to ensure that the transport and loading of their goods was carried out smoothly. As I describe in chapter 4, these liquid supplies were requested from Batavia on a yearly basis and thus constituted regular gift fodder. When gift supplies were inadequate to fulfill local obligations, beverages could be pulled from their own precious supplies that were meant to sustain them until their ships returned the next year. They could even buy alcohol from the Dutch ships at port or from other European merchants, as they did from the English in 1722.[48]

As Chaiklin has stated in regard to Japan, "The gifts Westerners brought east ranged from the banal to the fantastic," yet the scholarly focus has rested on the latter.[49] Dutch customary gifts in Yemen were not assemblages of rarities and wonders from Europe that were meant to inspire awe in the receiver, as with the many items that were sought or furnished for the king of Siam and Japanese officials in the seventeenth century.[50] Rather each year's gifts were remarkably rote, repetitive, and expected assemblages of foreign goods from Europe, but more frequently from India, Persia, China, Southeast Asia, and the Spice Islands that only partially overlapped with the conventional roster of Dutch commercial products intended for Yemen's market. Fine-quality textiles, such as costly shawls of silk, were combined with less precious lengths of Dutch *laken* and cheaper varieties of Indian textiles, including Bengali cossaes and malmals. Spices and the products derived from them also ranged in quality and cost. It is difficult to discern how the Dutch arrived at this standardized gift formula, but one can assume that it was deemed relatively successful because they were committed to it for several years. So rather than being an alien practice, Yemen's system of commercial gifts was largely accepted by VOC merchants as a key aspect of local Arabian trade, to the extent that these items were formatted comfortably within the established limits of the company document, occupying fixed places as line items in yearly account books and taking up space next to the many goods for sale in their local warehouse.

English Customary Gifts

Like those of the Dutch, English customary gifts in Yemen were formatted by certain rules and patterns that emerge when one examines their registers from 1718 and 1720 to 1722. Although their distribution lists are almost identical to those of the VOC, including the trade officials of Mocha and Bayt al-Faqih, as well as some individual merchants and port workers, EIC gifts were even more limited in the scope of their content than the Dutch gifts.[51] For the EIC, textiles and cash were the main fodder for bestowal in the first quarter of the eighteenth century.[52] They tendered their gifts at the coffee emporium of Bayt al-Faqih in mid-July and in Mocha in late July or early August, right before the annual departure of oceangoing ships.[53]

As with those of the VOC, English gifts could be easily scaled up or down in terms of content and quantity according to hierarchies of rank and position. The two governors and the second in charge of both cities were given textiles as gifts over these years. At the same time, the anonymous workers at the port of Mocha—the searchers, weighers, and servants—were given small cash sums in local currency.[54] Middle-ranking port officials, such as the *amir al-bahr* and the scribes of the customs house, who were all appointed directly by the imam of Yemen, were given gifts of either textiles or cash, depending on the year. When these officials received cash, it was usually Spanish reals, the international currency of the wholesale trade, and not local coin. The choice to give reals seems to have been based on the larger sums these individuals received, as well, perhaps, as their greater engagement in the world of overseas trade.

The dominance of textiles in their bestowals is not surprising because cloth had constituted the major part of English overseas trade in Asia since the late seventeenth century, after the English had abandoned their interest in direct access to spices. As Willem Floor states in regard to Iran, "For the EIC the cloth trade was a necessity, while for the VOC it . . . remained a marginal activity."[55] The EIC actively conveyed large amounts of Indian-made textiles around the Indian Ocean and back to Europe, while also trying to open up a market for English broadcloth in the East.[56] Their bestowals in Yemen clearly represent their involvement and engagement in these various markets. As an example, in 1720 Mocha's governor, Amir Rizq, was given yardage of English broadcloth in scarlet and blue, as well as dimities, baftas, hummums, and shalbofts (all cotton piece goods from India).[57] The gift also included pieces of taffeta (silk) from China and Bengal. A few pieces of cloth and one carpet were referred to as "embossed," woolen textiles ornamented with designs impressed by rollers.[58] Like the Dutch, the English offered an array of cloth that included homemade varieties of wool along with lightweight Indian muslin and cotton.[59] And like the Dutch textiles, theirs always ranged in quality and value, from less expensive to quite luxurious types. Among these offerings, the most costly was the Chinese taffeta, valued at 12 Spanish reals per piece; the least expensive, the Bengali taffeta, was valued at a fifth of that, 2.4 Spanish reals per piece. The Dutch cut up red baftas or calicos from Gujarat to make sacks for their spices rather than offering them as gifts, a variance in usage that indicates the wide range of quality that any single type of Indian textile could encompass rather than signaling the poor quality of English gifts.[60]

While English gifts to governors and other officials were limited to the realm of textiles, they were relatively dynamic in their choices and combinations, with novel types introduced each year. In 1721 the governor of Mocha was given eight yards of English broadcloth, three silk shawls, four different types of soosies (striped or checkered cotton or cotton-silk blends, some specified as Tatari, Amudi, and "jemakle"), malmals from Bengal, and two different types of allajars (striped cottons or cotton silk blends, specified as "mottercawn" or "dewly").[61] Other than the English broadcloth, none of these types had been included in the previous year's package. It appears the English sought a dynamic recombination of Indian textiles each year, thus keeping the interest of their recipients while sustaining their passive marketing of English woolens.

Although both the Dutch and the English included home-produced cloth in their yearly gifts, their goals were markedly different. Since their early forays into the Indian Ocean, the English had tried to market their broadcloth in the East, and these efforts escalated as a result of the 1693 renewal of the EIC contract that mandated an increase in export of domestic products.[62] However, these endeavors met with mixed results. In India, heavy woolen fabric competed poorly against the large variety of available cloths that fulfilled most local needs and demands. Still, the English tried aggressively to insert their broadcloth into local codes of dress and consumption. However, these fabrics were used more often for decoration and interior design functions, for instance to line tents and palanquins, than for Indian attire.[63] The English were more successful in opening up a market in

Iran for their broadcloth, which they often exchanged for highly desirable local Persian textiles.[64] In the eastern Mediterranean, these items attracted more demand as well, although other competitive varieties were also available there, such as those produced at the Ottoman wool center of Salonika and the "Londrin," a textile fashioned of Spanish wool but manufactured in Languedoc that the French increasingly exported to the Levant beginning in the eighteenth century.[65]

EIC merchants were charged with trying to expand a market for English-made textiles in Yemen as well. In a letter to Mocha in 1722, Phipps, writing from Bombay, encouraged EIC merchants there to sell English broadcloth quickly, even at a lower price, the "aim being chiefly to enlarge the consumption of woolen goods in these Parts."[66] These merchants struggled to understand and meet the subtle needs of Yemen's textile consumers. In many years, Mocha-based merchants wrote with frustration about the cloth that was sent. In 1722 they claimed that black and white broadcloth sold reasonably well in Yemen, whereas the right shade of red was more difficult to identify. Color was not the only problem; the proper weight and delicacy of the cloth were key to its marketability. In 1721 the English claimed that the French textiles that came from the north via Jidda were much lighter and more popular locally.[67] This was surely a reference to the "Londrin," and signals an intriguing migration of those types, some of which were brilliantly colored with cochineal, from the Mediterranean all the way to the southern tip of the Arabian Peninsula.[68] Apparently the cloth also required considerable surface gloss in order to be marketed successfully, as related in 1729, when there was apparently much more demand for English broadcloth at Mocha.[69]

In 1721 Mocha-based merchants attached broadcloth swatches to their commission to show the directors which types of cloth they wanted for the Yemeni market (Plate 5). Small rectangular samples in shades of red and green in addition to blue, black, and white are attached to this document, providing a sense of the quality, weight, and texture of the felted English broadcloth that was destined for the western Indian Ocean market as a commodity and for gifts.[70] These musters or samples were widely used in the cross-cultural trade, but they should not be understood as simple or neutral trade requests. In the case of Mocha, this visually oriented and highly tactile record also signals the difficulty of calibrating in words the sensitive and often shifting local demand for textiles in Yemen. In fact, it was composed with a certain amount of frustration during a time when their unsold bales of cloth were simply sent back to Bombay because they would not sell locally.[71] While it is challenging to gain more clarity about the local consumption of European cloth, we should certainly question Niebuhr, who is usually quite reliable, for his claim that no one in Yemen wore broadcloth circa 1763.[72] The English continued to market European textiles in Yemen with mixed success until the mid-nineteenth century, when the rise of steam travel, the British occupation of Aden, and the opening of the Suez Canal fundamentally transformed the local market for textile consumption, greatly weighing it in favor of European and American products.[73]

Over the years covered by the English gift registers, there is considerable fluctuation in the value of their customary gifts. For instance, in 1718 the Mocha governor was given a package worth 187 Spanish reals, 196 in 1720, and 375.66 in 1721. During the same years, the second to the governor received textiles that were less costly than the governor's, totaling 80 Spanish reals in 1718, 97.85 in 1720, and 207.32 in 1721. The year 1721 may be singled out for its particularly expensive gifts, almost two times the value of the previous year's offering, an increase that may be connected to the arrival of William Phipps, governor-elect of Bombay and temporary EIC chief in Mocha. But it is generally difficult to ascertain how the value of gifts was determined. Some registers account for the amount of the governor's customary gift based on the number of company ships that were served in the port per season. But the associated figures do not reflect a clear relationship. For instance, in 1720 two English ships came to the port, and in 1721 three arrived. The governor's 1721 gift was much larger than the previous year's, but not by an identifiable increment, as with the *amir al-bahr*'s present, which was always tabulated with a standard rate of 30 Spanish reals per ship.

Like the Dutch, the English used and retained very limited formats for their customary gifts in Yemen in the early years of the eighteenth century. Rather than trying to impress the recipient with wholly novel or rare products, their gifts were consistently limited in scope to textiles, both Eastern and Western, in varieties of wool, cotton, and silk, or cash. Although their gifts remained within a circumscribed range of goods, there is no discernible logic in the way their value was determined. Like Dutch gifts, English bestowals can be associated with their trade policies and the scope of their territorial influence, but also more specifically to their larger overseas marketing agendas.

The Turn to Cash

In 1724 'Ali bin Amir Rizq, the governor of Mocha at that time, made a direct request that yearly gifts be tendered in silver.[74] The Dutch agreed to this change, under pressure, and gave the governor 250 Spanish reals, his second 100, and smaller sums of 10 to 35 to the many writers at the port and customs house, the *qadi* of Mocha, and the local *hakim* (judge). Like previous gifts, these were scaled for each recipient according to his administrative rank. The total was 550 Spanish reals, a sum that was increased once, to 650 Spanish reals, in 1729.[75] But aside from that single increase, Dutch cash gifts in Mocha remained consistent in value until 1737 and were given on the same date each year, July 15, the annual closing date for the account books.[76] In Bayt al-Faqih, the Dutch had turned entirely to cash by 1723, when they doled out gifts worth 730 Spanish reals. In 1725 they lowered the overall value, with gifts worth 610 Spanish reals to the governor, his second, the chief weigher, the head of the camel drivers, the slaves of the governor, and the *hakim*. The latter number stayed stable through 1737. The cash system seems to have financially and temporally fixed the gift responsibilities of the Dutch until the trading establishment was lifted formally in 1739.

The English presence in Mocha was less consistent than the Dutch, particularly between 1726 and 1729, when they temporarily lifted their establishment. They were also asked to switch to cash customary bestowals in 1724, which they initially resisted even though the Bombay directors had counseled them to do so. Unlike the Dutch, they claimed that gifts in silver would look more like "a tax or custom" and would thus be subject to periodic increases, without acknowledging that they were already giving some minor recipients cash bestowals at that time.[77] But even with this resistance, they had begun to give the governor of Bayt al-Faqih his gift in silver coin by 1725. By the 1730s, when their gift registers resume in regularity, material gifts were completely dispensed with and everyone in Mocha was given flat sums. The governor received 100 Spanish reals in 1734 and 1735 and 200 in 1736. His second received 50 Spanish reals each year, and the *amir al-bahr* continued to receive 30 Spanish reals per ship. The total gift amount was 309 Spanish reals in 1734 and 1735 and rose to 402 in 1736.

The turn to cash did entail certain increases, as well as one decrease, in the value of yearly gifts, but by fixed increments and on a limited basis for each company. As such, this shift seems to have largely removed the yearly fluctuations in the value of gifts based on changes in commodity prices, which are often discernible in their yearly gift registers. They also provided relatively stable annual benchmarks to budget around and account for. The cash option solidified the relatively rote and cyclical nature of the content of European gifts, which, as I have shown, was present even when goods rather than silver were being tendered in the first quarter of the eighteenth century. Cash presents also allowed for the givers to express clear modulations of rank and hierarchy within the list of distributions. The system of cash gifts remained in place for many years.

In the premodern Islamic world and adjacent areas, gifts often included cash along with other goods. Even when goods were tendered, their value was expressed openly in denominations of specie, evaluations that were usually committed to writing by historians who endeavored to provide a lasting record of gifts conveyed.[78] Moreover both gift givers and recipients in the Islamic world were inclined to make the ready equivalence between a gift and its cash value. This was a world of exchange in which "the price tags were left on," as Linda Komaroff has stated.[79] In contrast to historian John McLane, who contends that the eighteenth-century rise in cash gifts in India represents a shift toward monetization, I do not see the transition to cash gifts, with their transparent liquidity, as an entirely novel introduction in the Yemeni context.[80] To the contrary, these gifts were always seen in liquid terms, whether goods or cash. The shift to cash appears to have crystallized previous practices and formulas by applying increased standardization and introducing more overt valuation rather than transforming their core nature.[81]

Special Gifts

I have characterized the yearly bestowals of the Dutch and English as customary gifts, which were requisite rites of the trade even if they were not always spelled out in trade agreements. But Dutch and English merchants tendered gifts on other occasions as well, usually for specific purposes. These off-cycle gifts were distinct from customary ones, even if they sometimes appear on the same gift registers and are not always differentiated from them by company merchants.[82] Small gifts would also be given casually, for an impromptu meeting with the governor, for instance, and were usually omitted from the account books.

Special gifts could operate as deeply political instruments. The early eighteenth century was particularly tumultuous for the Qasimi imams. Yemeni Zaydism differs from other Shi'i systems in that the imamate does not pass directly from father to son, nor is the imam considered infallible. A Zaydi imam must meet certain criteria of lineage, erudition, and capability, and he also needs to be approved by the notables. For that reason, Zaydi history in Yemen is often marked by struggles between concurrent competing imams, all with certain claims to the title and a number of supporters. By the early eighteenth century, these disputes were frequent and often settled by military efforts. In 1716 a newly declared competitor to Imam al-Mahdi Muhammad emerged in the northern mountain town of Shahara, the original home of the Qasimis, under the title and name Imam al-Mansur billah Husayn (d. 1720, not to be confused with the later imam of Sanaa with the same title and name, who died in 1748). Al-Mahdi sent his nephew, Sidi Qasim, to quash this opponent, but Qasim ended up betraying his uncle and going over to al-Mansur's side. After gaining independent support,

Qasim then shed his allegiance to al-Mansur and declared himself imam with the title al-Mutawakkil 'ala Allah. He proceeded immediately to take the lucrative cities of Mocha and Bayt al-Faqih. From the perspective of the coast, the Dutch describe these dizzying events with great consternation but also a surprising amount of accuracy.[83] Along with the rest of Mocha, they eventually decided to accept al-Mutawakkil's newly declared imamate, thus withdrawing their support from the aged al-Mahdi, with whom they had worked for years, and aligning themselves with his untested yet formidable challenger. On November 19 of that year, the VOC merchant Hendrik Burggraaf visited the new imam al-Mutawakkil in Sanaa, carrying a large gift for him and another for his son. These strategic gifts were sent to signal the VOC's early support for his campaign at a time when three concurrent imams laid claim to Yemen. Burggraaf returned to Mocha in January 1717.[84]

Gifts also accompanied official missives, such as the letter from the governor-general of the Dutch East Indies Christoffel van Zwolle to Imam al-Mutawakkil Qasim in 1719. Al-Mahdi had finally died in 1718, and the purview of the third contender, al-Mansur Husayn of Shahara, had constricted considerably. Thus al-Mutawakkil could claim uncontested control of Yemen's key coastal and highland areas. Van Zwolle's letter acknowledged al-Mutawakkil's now unchallenged rule and confirmed their trade partnership. Of course, the letter and gifts were sent in hopes that the new imam would not diminish the conditions of their established trade agreement. At this time, they also sent smaller gifts to his *wazir*, al-Huraybi, past governor of Mocha, and Amir Rizq, then governor of the port and former *nakhudha* of the imam. The imam's present contained all of the expected contents: copious sacks of spices, Dutch *laken*, Persian velvet, rolls of Chinese silk, Bengali malmals and cossaes, a box of spiced oils, and two shawls from Surat. However, a few unanticipated items were added: five pairs of eyeglasses, twelve Japanese porcelain plates, 120 Japanese porcelain coffee cups and saucers, and 120 Chinese brown coffee cups and saucers.[85] The overall value of this special gift was 389.4 Spanish reals. Although it generally conformed to the standardized formula for annual gifts, this important bestowal, which was sent on behalf of the leading Dutch official in Asia, drew its impact from its overall value and quantity—the spices alone weighed 105 pounds—as well as from the few unique items of interest that were added to the ordinary corpus of customary gifts, like the eyeglasses and the porcelain.[86]

When Burggraaf visited the imam in 1716–1717, he did so in the name of the company but on his own initiative. In other instances, foreigners were called to the court, as in 1712, when the surgeon Barbier of one of the French boats docked at Mocha was summoned to al-Mawahib to provide medical treatment to Imam al-Mahdi Muhammad.[87] Although this visit was quite unexpected and preparations were made quickly, Barbier brought with him some presents. These items were not enumerated individually, but a large mirror, a pair of pistols, and some of the best French cloth were mentioned specifically.[88] Although French gifts are not recorded consistently, this episode shows that, at least on this occasion of the second French journey to Yemen, they followed the Dutch, and to a certain extent English, pattern of giving textiles and weapons as gifts, although the mirror seems to have been a unique inclusion for the occasion of a court sojourn, and probably because it happened to be on hand.

When Phipps stopped by Mocha on his way to Bombay in 1721, the imam, aware of his high status, sent a horse to him as a gift. In return, Phipps sent an impressive assemblage of goods not just to the imam but also his advisers. Unsurprisingly, these gifts, which were delivered on August 3, were almost entirely textiles, in line with English customary gifts for high-ranking officials. A few costly and unique examples that did not appear on the regular yearly rosters were also included. For instance, the imam received a piece of atlas (heavy satin, usually plain but sometimes woven with threads of gold and silver) from Surat that was valued at 60 Spanish reals, the most expensive textile listed on any of the English gift registers. Phipps also sent him five guns, a rare occasion of a nontextile bestowal from the English. In total, the imam's gift was worth 633.4 Spanish reals, which is far more than any of the customary gifts bestowed by the English to the governor of Mocha on a yearly basis. So while these special gifts relied on standard formulas, albeit at larger quantities, apparently they were also opportunities to send a few new or particularly costly items to their recipients.

In October 1737 Mocha's newly appointed governor, Muhyi al-Din al-'Arasi, stopped by the Dutch residence, a rare visit for any overseas merchant.[89] For that reason, they gave him a gift on his departure, undoubtedly chosen with haste, likely from the reserve of gift items held in their warehouse. This bestowal included twenty-nine pounds of cinnamon, two pieces of flowered damask (probably Chinese), two shawls, and two gold allajars. As expected, they also treated him to the traditional welcome, offering him sweets and *qishr*, and they bade him farewell with the sprinkling of rosewater and the burning of incense. Such an occurrence, although rare, highlights the need to have gifts available for unplanned visits and impromptu occasions.

Although the givers of these single-occasion gifts perceived them as one-time commitments, some developed into continuing responsibilities. For instance, each spring the governor of Mocha would travel to the imam's court in the highlands in order to present a large sum of cash from the port's treasury, some of which was converted into gifts. The continuing success of any coastal governor hinged upon the imam's satisfaction with these offerings, as I discuss in chapter 3. After Governor Amir Rizq returned from his trip to the capital in May 1720, the English factor, Edward Say, observed that they needed to give him a gift on this occasion because the governor had spoken to the imam on their behalf, but also because the governor had "already rec'd one from the Dutch."[90] This gift, which included various textiles, had to be purchased from Mocha's bazaar, likely because it was an unexpected expense. This was the first time the English gave a gift for this reason, but within a couple years the governor's return from the imam's court was marked by a regular gift, as indicated by the English register from 1722, which recorded a package comprising textiles from India and valued at 201 Spanish reals. These were given to the governor of Mocha "when he came down from the King as *customary*" (emphasis added).[91]

Disputes over Gifts

Based on a close reading of the VOC and EIC gift registers, my analysis demonstrates that the merchants of both companies understood the general logic of commercial gifts and their material protocols in eighteenth-century Yemen. As such, they duly followed a fixed yearly schedule with appropriately scaled offerings, but sometimes added one-time gifts for specific and even quite self-interested reasons. They planned for these gifts yearly, assuring that they would have adequate items for future gift needs (including impromptu ones), which they then carefully reserved from commercial exchange, sometimes for years at a time. If they lacked the right items for bestowal, they purchased them locally. These gift responsibilities became even more clear-cut after they had turned to the practice of giving flat sums of silver coin. One could go as far as to say that both the Dutch and the English came to sustain a relatively adept engagement with the standard grammar of commercial gifts in Yemen, even as they adhered to their own unique patterns.

The tacit acceptance of the rules and protocols of the local gift economy is clear in the wording of the trade agreement the English renegotiated with Imam al-Mansur in 1729. Unlike the agreement the French had settled in 1709, this one was largely reactive, meant to protect the EIC merchants against possible injustices from the governors of Mocha and Bayt al-Faqih and the delinquency of local merchants. In regard to gifts (an issue that was not even mentioned in 1709), it simply states that they "shall not be oblidged to give any more Presents to The Governour Writers and other Officers at Mocha than has been Customary."[92] With this clause they implicitly accepted the requisite nature of annual gifts and tried to resist any expansion of their rote commitments. It is noteworthy that they did not add any language about the scope, content, or value of these gifts, signaling that they preferred to leave these concerns open-ended and unspecified.

It is also possible to make the assessment that Dutch and English gifts in Yemen were fairly modest, lacking the rarities or specially ordered items that were offered to more prestigious Indian Ocean recipients, such as the Mughal ruler Jahangir, a known connoisseur of art and natural history who was seemingly impossible to please.[93] VOC lists of distribution to the king of Siam at Ayutthaya or the Japanese shogun are also much more impressive than those we see in Yemen, where gifts rarely rose to a fraction of their yearly coffee intake and sometimes included quite inexpensive items. Although, as Viallé has shown, the VOC devoted considerable resources to gift bestowal throughout the Indian Ocean each year, it appears that Yemeni officials were not the beneficiaries of this investment.[94] The same can be said of the English.

But even with this regularized system of commercial gift bestowal, disputes about gifts still arose in Yemen and were often described in the context of other complaints about the corrupt nature of the local trade system. European merchants decried the Mocha governor's undue involvement in the trade, expressed outrage at his shifting policies on taxation and the common practice of asking merchants for "loans" that were to be paid back with credits at the time when duties were due.[95] They also lamented the constant requests for contributions to the local treasury, describing these as "gifts." As such, it is difficult to pull apart this litany of complaints and to see the distinct patterns of gifts tendered, which I have attempted to do.

Moreover a close perusal of these narratives and complaints reveals that the majority of problems emerged around one question—whether the imam should receive a yearly gift from the Europeans—rather than in relation to their customary annual commitments to provincial officials.[96] As described above, Europeans sent gifts to the imam as special bestowals for particular reasons, such as Dutch efforts to signal their early support for Imam al-Mutawakkil in 1716–1717 and the countergifts from Governor Phipps in 1721. But on several occasions, local officials demanded that company merchants provide an annual gift for the imam as well.

The company documents present a certain amount of confusion surrounding the origin of this gift and the basic premises that undergirded it. In regard to the English, it seems that the expectation of the imam's gift may have emerged based on the precedent of Phipps' special offering of 1721, for in 1722, after Phipps had departed Mocha, the English received a request for a gift to the imam. They initially tried to resist this demand, clarifying that it was not customary to grant the imam an annual gift and that the one from the previous year was a notable exception on the occasion of the supervisor's visit to the port.[97] Characteristically, the demanding governor Khazindar replied with threats that he would keep their ships from leaving if a gift was not offered. Eventually the English complied, and the imam's gift became part of their yearly commitment.[98] By 1725 the gifts to the imam and his *wazir* were described as "customary," but this practice came to an end when the year-round factory was lifted in 1726.[99] In this case, a one-time gift of quite extraordinary proportions then became the basis for a yearly commitment to the imam.

In other cases, the imam's gift was tabulated in exchange for the trade concession of duty-free coffee, to which the English, Dutch, and French were entitled six hundred bales yearly. For instance, in May 1733 Mocha's chief *sarraf* (money exchanger), Muhammad Yasin, stopped the English from shipping their coffee to their boat for export, demanding a gift for the imam. He justified this claim with the contention that such a gift "was always understood to be due in such cases." According to his accounts (conveyed by EIC merchants), the English were six years behind on this payment and thus required to pay 5,000 Spanish reals in total.[100] After much discussion, EIC merchants eventually complied by offering 2,500 reals. In their letters, they note with suspicion that this was probably a local scheme to make money, doubting that these port officials ever ended up presenting such offerings to the imam. But they also mention the fact that the company had tendered a yearly gift to the court from 1722 to 1725, citing their customary practices and thus tacitly acknowledging a precedent for this commitment. Even so, in their letter to Bombay, they held stridently to the belief that this gift was completely "exorbitant and unjust" and one of the many "innovations of the government here."[101]

As he had with the English, in 1722 Khazindar also pressed the Dutch for gifts to Imam al-Mutawakkil and the *wazir* (then al-Huraybi). They decided eventually to bestow the requested offerings under the premise that it was sent from Batavia, evidently to separate it from their yearly customary bestowals and to avoid the integration of this gift into their customary commitments.[102] But in 1724 the Dutch were asked to provide another gift for the imam and the *wazir*, this time in exchange for their six hundred duty-free bales.[103] Again, after much insistence, they eventually complied by offering a gift of the usual textiles, spices, and spiced products. However, the governor told them this offering was hardly adequate, so they added more spices and a few costly textiles, raising the total value of this gift to 849.4 Spanish reals, a large sum in comparison to their customary annual commitment. The Dutch were not asked for these gifts again until 1735, at a time when the cash system dominated customary gifts. In this case, rather than tendering cash, as the English had two years earlier, they produced a piece of scarlet *laken* of 60.5 ells, some damask, and the fine box of cinnamon, mace, clove, and musk oils mentioned above, all from their warehouse. The textiles were divided and distributed to the imam, his *wazir*, the governor of Mocha, his second, the head *sarraf*, and the merchant Hasan Hasusa for a total value of 316.9 Spanish reals.

Most of the confusion, complaints, and debates about gifts emerged in regard to those that were demanded for the imam. These demands were most often put forward by the controversial governor of Mocha, Khazindar, who was known for his harsh treatment of residents and his avaricious methods of pressing local merchants for additional funds. Although the Dutch and English wrote about these contested gifts with great indignation, they recognized certain precedents for them and eventually offered them under pressure. During the years they were not asked for these gifts, such as 1731 and 1732, the Dutch noted with relief that they would not offer one unless first prompted, which suggests that such a gift was not entirely unfounded. It is also clear that local officials usually requested these "forced" gifts with a certain rationale, albeit a shifting one, sometimes based on a precedent and at other times as a requisite condition of a trade concession. Although European merchants complained about the imam's gift as a capricious addition to their customary gift commitments, one cannot agree that it was entirely arbitrary or unprecedented.

Writing about Gifts

I have highlighted a fundamental rupture in how we can think about commercial gifts in Yemen. The narrative sources left by both companies are replete with recriminations about the onerous, and seemingly endless, nature of demands for commercial gifts that were put forward by local officials, complaints that were echoed by European merchants across the Indian Ocean. Even in regard to their yearly commitments, the Dutch often grumbled about the port officials who hounded them like "hungry wolves" to obtain these expected offerings.[104] And the English wrote continually about gifts as "oppressions of arbitrary government."[105] Later narrators have tended to repeat these sentiments transparently, lamenting the trials of conducting business among such capricious cohorts and warning against the possibilities of extortion in the dangerous port of Mocha.[106] But the material record of gifts distributed provides quite a different picture of a commercial world hinged upon merchant tribute. And these records show that both Dutch and English merchants were not only aware of the structural logic of this gift-giving system but that they seemed to understand it with a certain amount of subtlety, while also sometimes using it to their own advantage.

In regard to early seventeenth-century India, where gifts were also a constant subject for discussion, literary scholar Ania Loomba describes the English stance toward gifts as a cognitive problem. According to her, the English could see the local gift economy only as corrupt, but, at the same time, they overlooked the fact that gifts were central to cementing commercial and political patronage networks, even in England at that time: "The English assume that the Eastern monarchs live in a gift economy where no one will want, or be able to do, the same arithmetic as the English, and thus will offer returns larger than the value of the gifts they receive, or rather they will return the 'noble gift' with 'ordinary commerce.' . . . Thus they accuse the Indians of violating the rules of the gift economy, of being greedy, and inhospitable, and of offering the wrong gifts in return."[107] Loomba's perspective is important because she warns against taking European subjective judgments about gifts at face value. But she also assumes that the documents left by Sir Thomas Roe in regard to the Mughal emperor Jahangir, in this case, can be read as reflections of overriding cultural insensitivities. I suggest instead that VOC and EIC merchants in Mocha did in fact understand local codes of gift giving precisely because they planned for and abided by them so effectively. But they were under pressure to devalue these very same codes of bestowal in their written documents to home offices in Bombay and Batavia, often making recourse to common tropes about the avaricious appetites of local recipients and the capricious nature of Eastern commerce.[108]

In order to explain this divergence, one must be aware of the position of those writing these letters and documents from Mocha, whether affiliated with the VOC or the EIC. Company trade reports were meant, on one hand, to record transactions made in Yemen and, on the other hand, to substantiate the activities of company merchants to supervisors in faraway ports. These supervisors were always suspicious of resident merchants, who could mishandle funds far away from the eyes of the upper levels of management. Indeed Mocha was famous for abuses in private trade and the malfeasance of company employees.[109] For example, after his 1721 visit to the port, Phipps accused the Mocha factors Edward Say and Thomas Harnett of skimming quantities of coffee beans off the company bales for their own profit, leading to the discharge of Say from company service. Robert Cowan, Phipps' successor in Bombay, arrived as chief in Mocha in 1723; he was later accused of having engaged in private trade before making purchases for the company, although he was eventually cleared of this charge.[110] In this world where accusations of misconduct were rampant, company merchants in Yemen would conveniently highlight, even exaggerate the erratic nature of local trade to substantiate their expenditures to faraway readers who regarded all of their activities with great suspicion and would thus scrutinize their reports meticulously. Their defensive posture in writing is key to understanding the way they portrayed commercial gifts. Merchants of the EIC and VOC became remarkably proficient in the codes of gift giving in Yemen, as they had become elsewhere, but they did so while lamenting the fact that these items were not given "voluntarily" or in constant fear about the possible detriment of these gifts to company activities.[111]

This rupture in writing about gifts does not reflect a cognitive failure on the part of the European merchants of Mocha. Rather it represents one of the core conditions of our documentary sources, which do not concur with the record that is represented materially. Along these lines, I adopt the skepticism suggested by the scholar of English literature Robert Markley, who insists that the "written accounts of shipments loaded and money earned are subject to the vagaries of inscription, transmission, distortion, omission, and downright deceit," in regard to EIC records in particular.[112] As Ruangsilp shows for Ayutthaya, the Dutch proficiency with local protocols and social standards at the Siamese court is often conveyed more clearly by evaluating their actions rather than reading their official reports. According to her, the VOC merchants had "mastered the language of ritual" at the Siamese court, even if they sometimes distanced themselves from it by depicting these same ceremonies with distaste and condescension in their letters to Batavia.[113] Similarly in regard to gifts, we should look closely at the content and material conditions of exchange rather than simply accepting the perennial motifs of greed, extortion, and corruption that are displayed so vividly and repeatedly in our textual sources from Yemen and elsewhere in the Indian Ocean arena.

Gifts in Use

It is clear that these gifts, although easily controvertible to a cash value, were not simple sources of liquidity for the recipient. As such, one must complicate historian Rudi Matthee's assertion for Safavid Iran that gifts may be distilled simply to a "form of taxation," even if their cycles were regularized and cyclical.[114] In fact, after coming into the hands of the imam and provincial trade officials, some of these gifts had the potential to flow into the local realm of conspicuous consumption and display. For instance, robes of green, a color long associated with the Prophet Muhammad, indicated nobility of lineage and were thus exclusive to a select few in Yemen. In the late eighteenth century, Grandpré remarked that the color was reserved for *sayyid*s (descendants of the Prophet), such as the imam.[115] Indeed when

Niebuhr visited Sanaa in 1763, the imam greeted him wearing a light green robe with long wide sleeves.[116] According to Grandpré, those who were named to special posts but may not have been eligible otherwise, such as the administrators of Mocha, were also allowed to wear green robes, but only for the duration of their position.[117] This may explain why Mocha's *amir al-bahr* wore a green robe when he greeted the French in 1709. These striking robes of a restricted hue could have been fashioned from imported cloth, perhaps of Dutch *laken,* Chinese damask, Persian velvet, or English broadcloth (Plate 5). All of these fabrics were available in green and sent to the port yearly, as well as periodically to the imam's court, as gifts. And as Niebuhr explains, in Yemen the size of one's headgear was closely aligned with one's status. Those of higher stature would layer many caps and then wrap them with a long piece of muslin, leaving the two ends hanging down the back.[118] The muslin malmals and cossaes that were delivered by merchants in gift packages could therefore play a major role in the articulation of social difference in a local system of sumptuary hierarchy.

Gift items may have been utilized in ceremonial processions staged by the imam. As recounted in Roque's detailed discussion of Qasimi ceremonial observed in the capital al-Mawahib in 1712, on Fridays Imam al-Mahdi Muhammad and his sons proceeded to the noon prayer with great ceremony, surrounded by soldiers carrying various arms, including carbines. The imam traveled on a fine white horse covered with a canopy made of green damask with a decorative trim in red and gold, topped with a silver globe upon a gold pyramid. One of his officers carried a copy of the Qur'an in a red cloth bag. His standard was square and also fashioned of green damask, with an Arabic inscription and a gold-fringe border.[119] It is tempting to conceive of many of these items, particularly the textiles, coming directly from gift fodder. The green damask was certainly available, although not exclusively, from gift allocations. The red fabric too was copiously provided in many different types in the bestowals documented above. Commercial gifts were one channel by which top-quality (and highly visible) imported cloth appeared in Yemen, whereas the wholesale market was saturated by low-cost, less vibrantly colored varieties.[120] These pieces of fabric could then be fashioned into items that carried a great deal of social weight, such as robes, turbans, standards, and other ceremonial items of display. As James Grehan has stated in regard to eighteenth-century Damascus, color "spoke its own complex language of status and rank."[121] Moreover the Dutch and, to a lesser extent, the English delivered desirable foreign firearms, such as carbines and muskets, to local recipients.

These goods should not be seen only through the prism of their European givers. As Thomas states in regard to Pacific societies, "Goods which

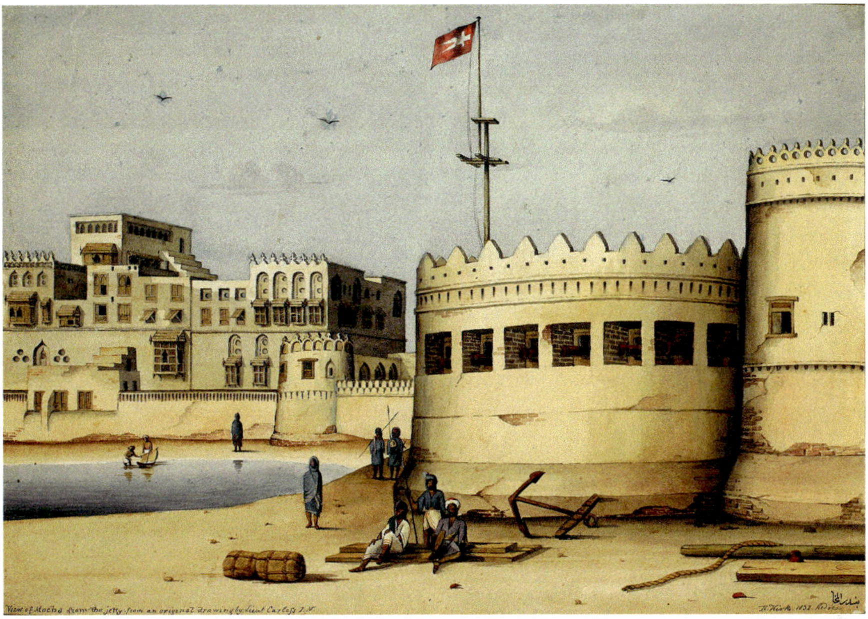

Plate 1. View of Mocha from the jetty, by Rupert Kirk, from an original drawing by Lieutenant Carless IN, 1832. Watercolor on paper, 24.5×35.5 cm. Royal Geographical Society (with IBG), London.

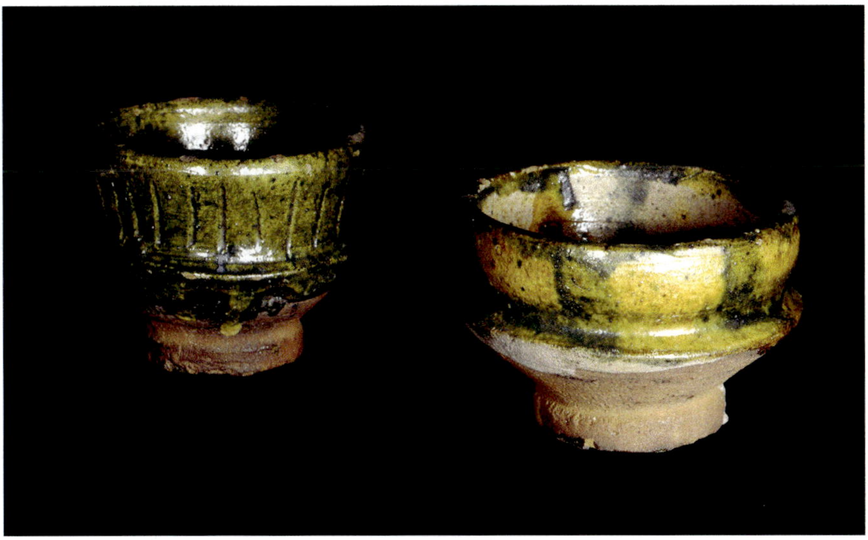

Plate 2. Coffee cups, al-Hudayda, Yemen, 1960s. Partially glazed earthenware, H 5.3 cm.

Plate 3. Rosewater sprinkler, made originally in China, with mounts added later, possibly in Malaysia or Iran, 1730–1750. The bottle was acquired in Iran in the late nineteenth century. Porcelain decorated with overglaze polychrome enamel and silver mounts, H 22.3 cm. © Victoria and Albert Museum, London.

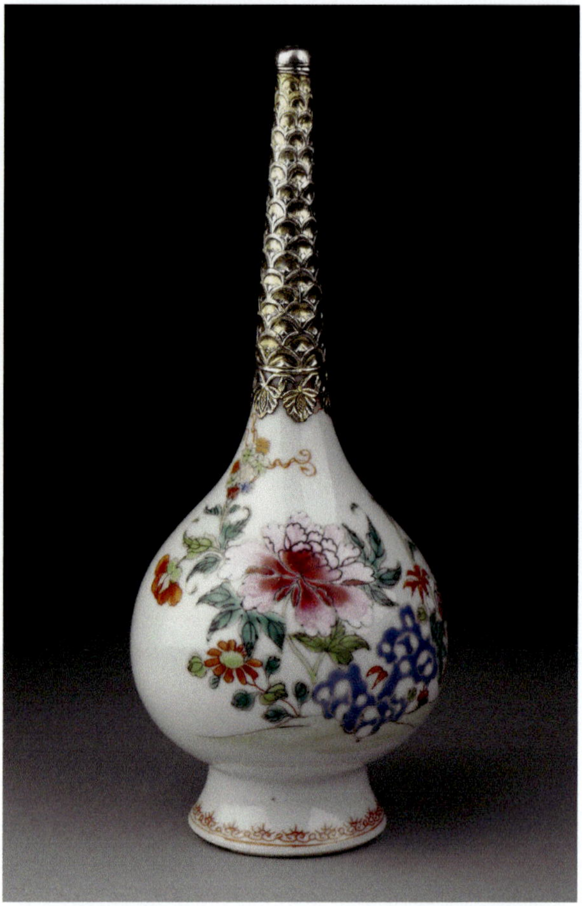

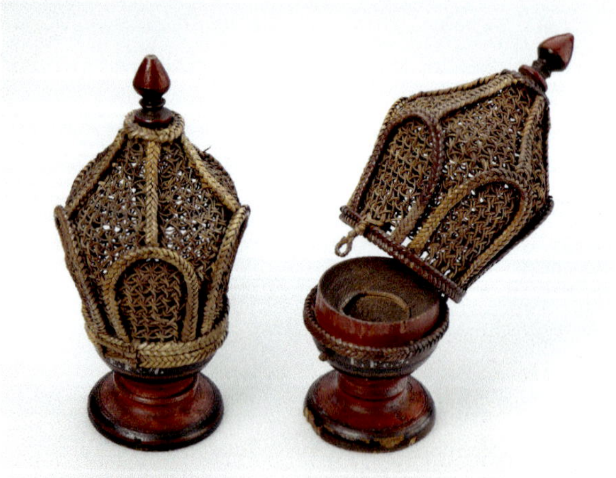

Plate 4. A pair of incense burners, Yemen, ca. 1763. Turned and painted wood and plaited rattan, H (left) 24 cm; H (right) 25 cm. Courtesy of the National Museum of Denmark. Photograph by John Lee.

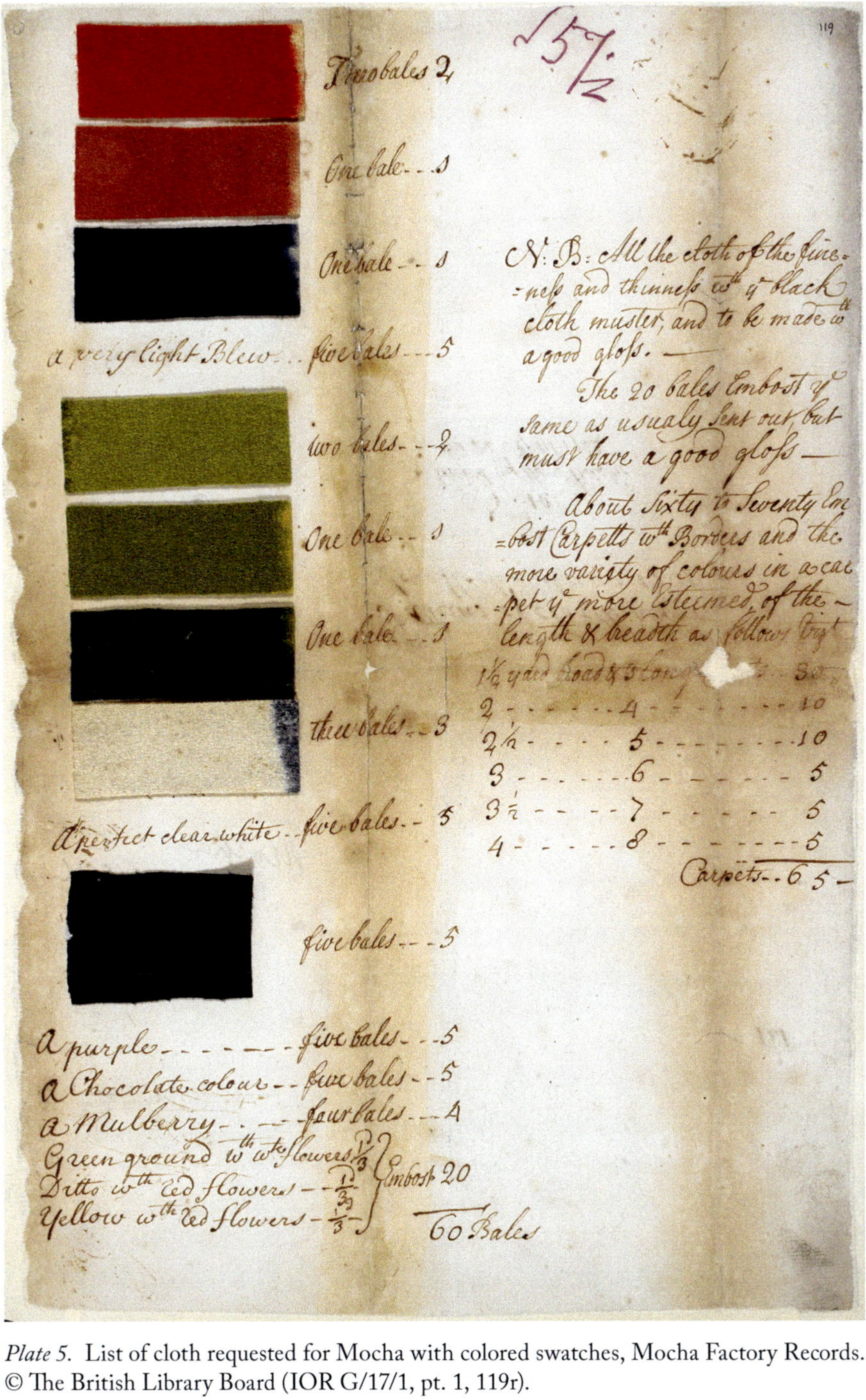

119

Two bales 2
One bale 1
One bale 1
a very light Blew .. five bales 5
two bales 2
One bale 1
One bale 1
three bales 3
A perfect clear white .. five bales 5
five bales 5
a purple ...... five bales 5
a Chocolate colour .. five bales 5
a Mulberry .... four bales 4
Green ground wth wte flowers 1/3 } Embost 20
Ditto wth red flowers 1/3
Yellow wth red flowers 1/3
60 Bales

N: B: All the cloth of the fineness and thinness wth ye black cloth muster, and to be made wth a good gloss.

The 20 bales Embost ye same as usualy sent out, but must have a good gloss—

About Sixty to Seventy Embost Carpetts wth Borders and the more variety of colours in a carpet ye more esteemed, of the length & breadth as follows Vizt

1½ yard broad & 3 long ... 30
2 ... 4 ... 10
2½ ... 5 ... 10
3 ... 6 ... 5
3½ ... 7 ... 5
4 ... 8 ... 5
Carpets .. 65

Plate 5. List of cloth requested for Mocha with colored swatches, Mocha Factory Records. © The British Library Board (IOR G/17/1, pt. 1, 119r).

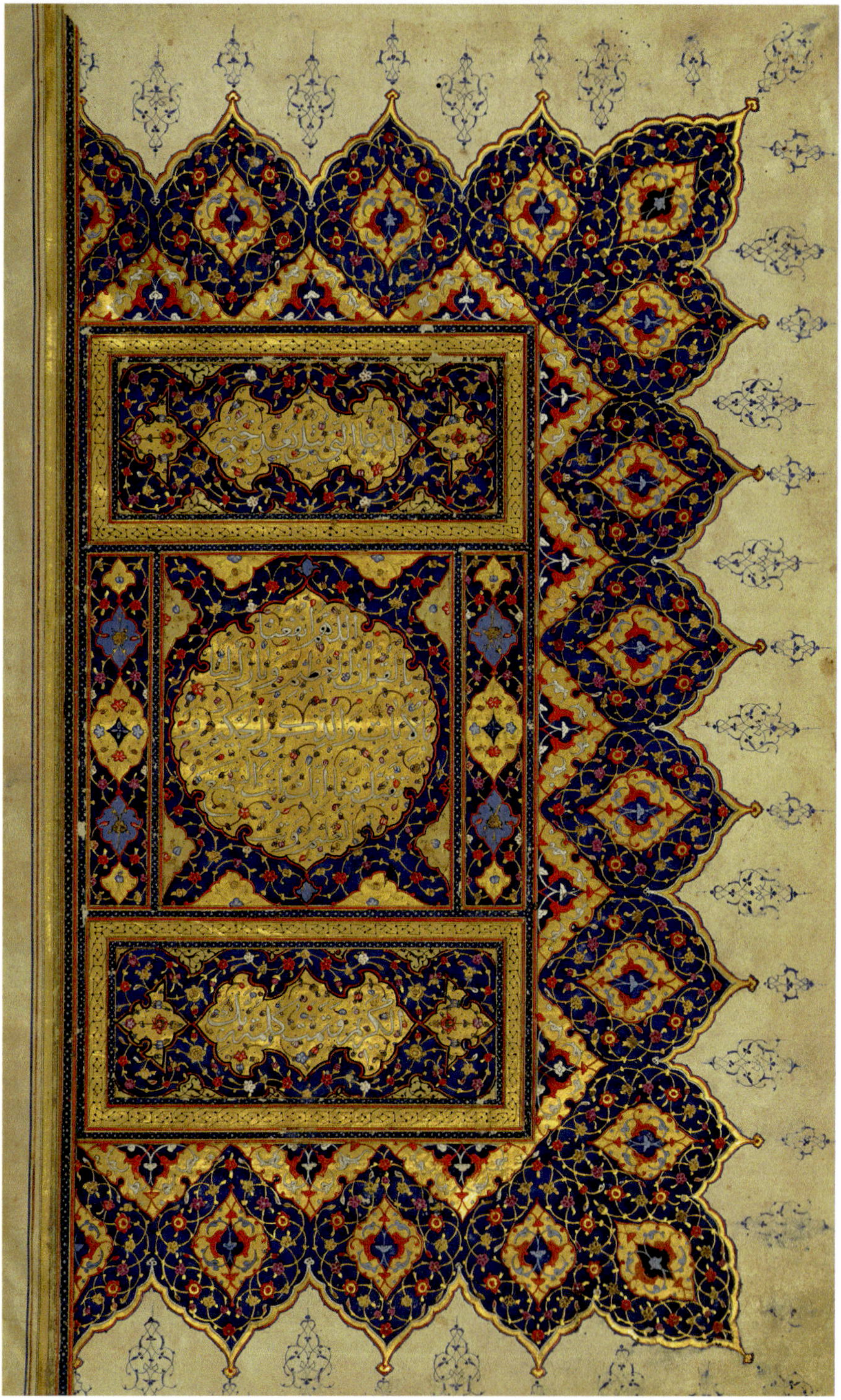

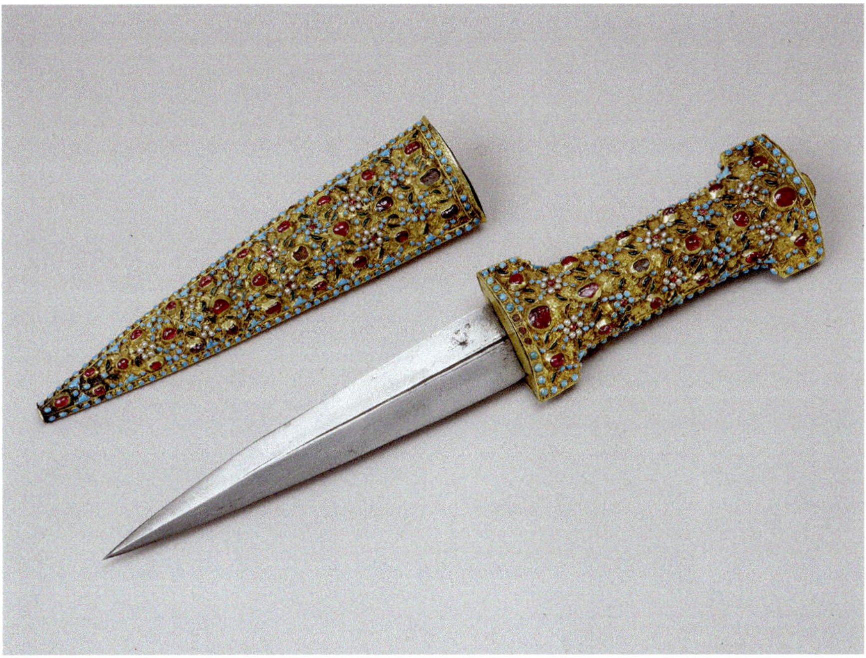

Plate 7. Jeweled dagger and sheath, Safavid, Iran, seventeenth century. Steel, wood, gold, rubies, turquoise, and pearls, H (overall) 12 1/8 in (30.8 cm). © Moscow Kremlin Museums. Photograph by V. N. Seregin, 2006.

Plate 6. Right side of an illuminated finispiece with inscribed prayer, Qur'an, Safavid, Iran, seventeenth century. Ink and pigments on thick cream-colored, gold-flecked paper, H 15 3/16×W 10 1/16 in (38.5×25.5 cm). Courtesy of the Walters Art Museum.

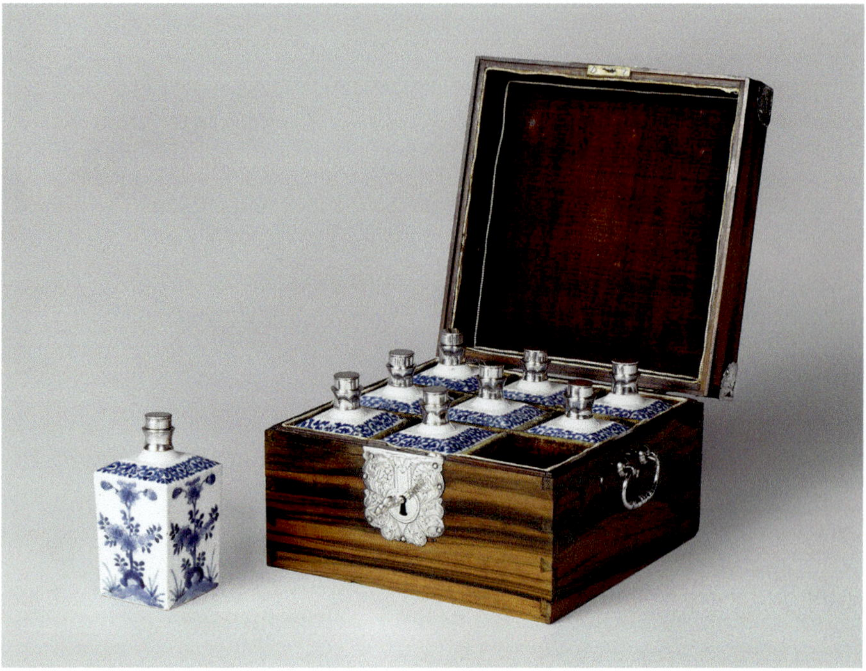

Plate 8. Cellaret, Batavia (Jakarta, Indonesia), with flasks from Arita, Japan, 1680–1700. Calamander with silver mounts and velvet lining, and porcelain, 16.5×26×26 cm. Courtesy of the Rijksmuseum, Amsterdam.

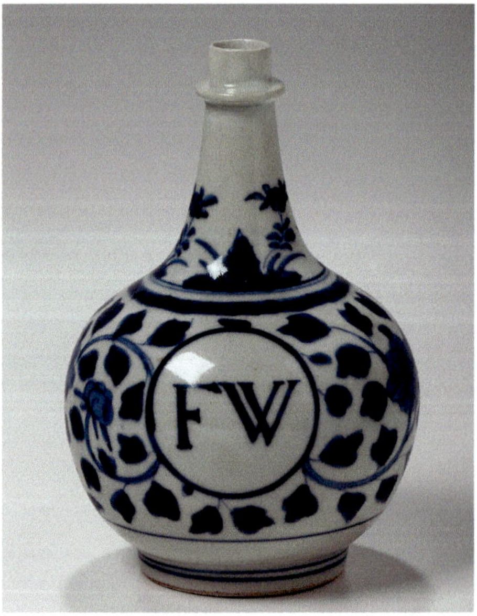

Plate 9. Bottle, Japan, 1670–1700. Porcelain, H 19 cm. Courtesy of the Groninger Museum. Photograph by Marten de Leeuw.

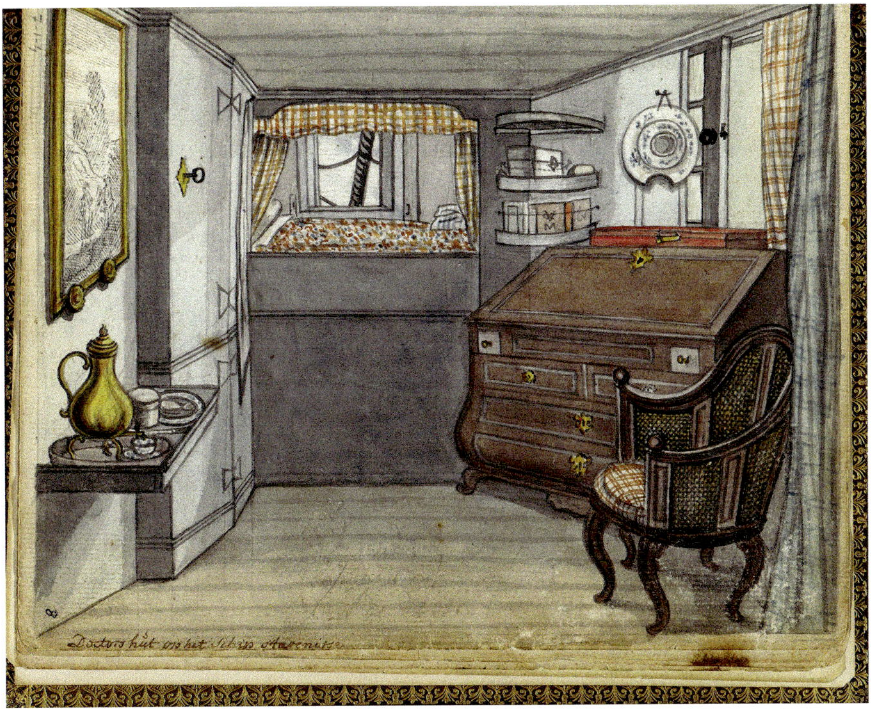

Plate 10. Doctor's cabin on the *Stavenisse*, by Jan Brandes, 1785–1786. Watercolor over pencil, 19.5 × 15.5 cm. Courtesy of the Rijksmuseum, Amsterdam.

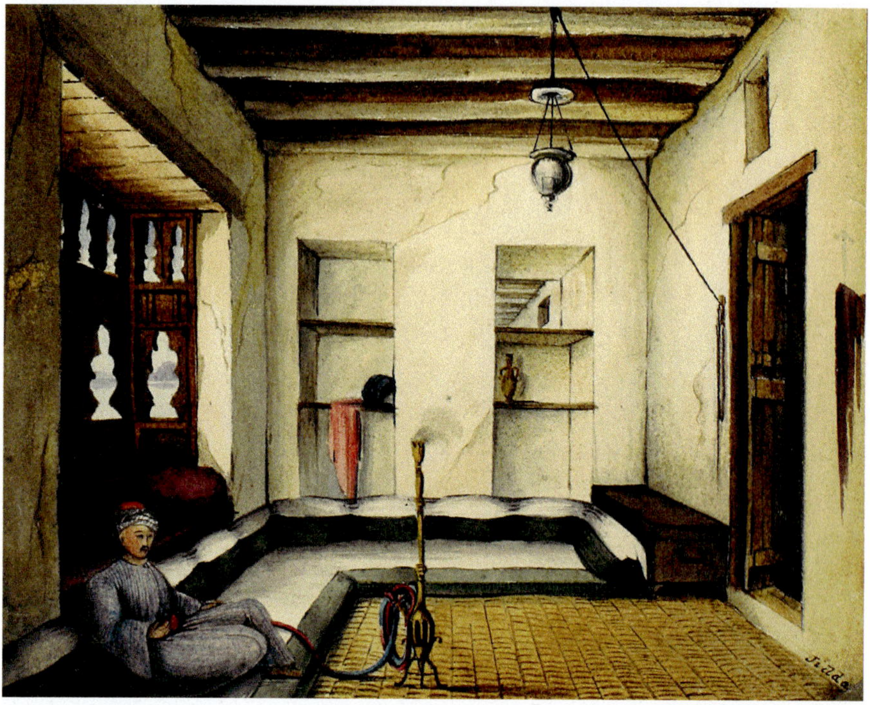

Plate 11. Interior of a house in Jidda, by Rupert Kirk, 1832. Watercolor, 10×12.5 cm. Royal Geographical Society (with IBG), London.

were imported into the Pacific cannot be seen as unproblematic equivalents of whatever we take them to be. To say that black bottles were given does not tell us what was received. This is so partly because the uses to which things were put were not inscribed in them by their metropolitan producers, and partly because gifts and commodities could be variously recontextualized as commodities or gifts, as unique articles for display, as artifacts of history, or as a new category of prestige valuable, the manipulation of which sustained the construction of political inequalities."[122] This point is demonstrated clearly by the precious shawls that were sometimes given as the costliest items in gift packages. As historian Michelle Maskiell has shown, shawls, usually from Kashmir, constituted important parts of *khil'a* bestowals that were tendered by rulers to subjects in India and Iran, but also in the wider Islamic world.[123] These *khil'a* robes were worn by (or at least associated with) the ruler and thus transferred a fundamental aspect of the kingly being to a devoted subject. Yet this widespread understanding of the gifted shawl would have been wholly reversed, if not erased, when it was purchased from the retail bazaar and then given to the imam by a European company merchant.

Merchant tribute in Yemen was composed of annual customary gifts that were locked into a fixed schedule and special gifts offered for particular purposes. Without question, the Dutch and English understood the nature of customary gift practices and planned for them assiduously each year. One could even say they had mastered the core protocol of commercial giving in Yemen, as much as they complained about the practice. Yet there were certain gray areas that were grounds for misunderstanding, such as the question of the imam's gift and the expectation that one-time gifts could become permanent cyclical commitments. But even less regular bestowals followed certain patterns and operated on precedents. As much as they conveyed their dislike for these practices and tried to avoid contributions when possible, European company merchants in Yemen knew how to use them to their advantage, as we saw with the VOC gifts to the new imam al-Mutawakkil in 1716–1717 and 1719.

While attempting to dispel long-standing and widespread opinions regarding the irrelevant or even arbitrary nature of commercial gifts in Yemen, and by extension other Indian Ocean sites, this investigation contributes to the ongoing discussion about the relationship between gifts and commodities, a continuing concern for anthropologists and historians of material culture. In the commercial context of early modern Yemen, gifts and commodities were shipped together but tabulated on separate lists and registers, thus constituting tightly matched parallel economies. As much as I acknowledge a considerable debt to Appadurai, who has helpfully provided a model for seeing how certain goods moved through the cycles of commodity and gift, I also take seriously Thomas' critique of the same framework.[124] By emphasizing fluidity, Appadurai tends to blur the line between commodity and gift to the point where these various rubrics lose integrity. Like Thomas, I make much of rather than overlook how the boundaries between gift and commodity spheres were maintained or transgressed. In the case of European gifts, some objects could move from the wholesale realm to the gift arena fluidly, and others were prohibited from such digressions. Some goods travelled from the wholesale sphere to the retail market and were then offered as gifts. Like the objects described in chapter 1, those objects with the most potential to move fluidly across exchange registers, such as Dutch-procured spices and English broadcloth, were potent markers of wide-reaching economic investments and thus served important purposes for their givers. By contrast, recipients in Yemen placed a high premium on those objects that could be wielded actively in ceremonial displays, including textiles in red and green used for exclusive garments and brightly colored banners.

Foreign goods played an important role both in and out of the open market in the deeply commercial and ocean-oriented society of Qasimi Yemen. We suffer from limited information about these objects, which are not evidenced by extant samples except for a single inscribed commission matched with swatches of broadcloth. Yet we gain insight from thinking about these gifts in assemblages rather than as individual things and conceiving of their value in regard to larger systems of exchange. In fact, we can understand gifts fully only in a larger picture that includes a sketch of the other goods they were shipped with in oceangoing vessels and circulated alongside of in local markets. As Weiner has shown, "in each exchange, participants remain aware of what is not being exchanged and their actions are directed not only to the immediate events but to these events in relationship to the ownership of inalienable possessions and the power they differentiate."[125] In the case of early modern Yemen, certain commercial goods were injected into the gift trajectory and others were withheld from it. Weiner's framework suggests that all forms of exchange operate in parallel and that the meaning of gift encounters can be derived only from a wider view across various types of transactions, including those that take place in the space of the market.

THREE

Merchants from India and Their Gift Practices in Yemen

In contrast to the relatively well-documented gifts of the Dutch and the English, we have little record of what kinds of commercial gifts other merchants distributed in Yemen. However, short references, mostly provided by watchful European observers, offer clues about the gift practices of some of Yemen's other major traders, even if we are unable to determine the contents of these bestowals. In this chapter, I explore a set of indications about the gifts given by merchants who were based in India and who sent their ships to the southern Arabian Peninsula on a yearly basis. It is in this context that we meet, once again, the merchants whose disgruntled *nakhudhas* appeared in Mocha's harbor in chapter 1, namely Mulla Muhammad 'Ali and Sidi Yaqut Khan. While the references to their gift protocols are admittedly scant, they present certain notable patterns that deserve close consideration.

These fleeting references must be located within a wider body of comparative material. In this case, the expected codes of gift giving between Muslim rulers and from provincial officials present the most useful instruction. The historian of the Islamic world will not be surprised with what follows: the bestowal of robes of honor and horses, the giving of unique objects of notable artisanry and value, and the conveyance of gifts in elaborate caravans that were meant to impress all those who witnessed their passing. These standard practices of gift giving in the Islamic world are well documented and have recently garnered considerable scholarly interest, although the case of Yemen and the special role of merchants still remain untreated.[1] The latter lacuna is due, at least in part, to the fact that merchants did not always constitute a discrete category of gift givers. For instance, art historian Anthony Cutler rightly proposes that the line between politics and commerce was often blurry in the medieval Arab lands, an observation that can be extended to later periods as well. Merchants frequently accompanied state campaigns, and diplomats were usually dispatched with commercial interests.[2] Moreover, as we saw in the previous chapter and as I describe below, merchants' gifts were often delivered as annual prestations and hence may be perceived as lacking some of the individualized subtleties of unique diplomatic, pious, or personal exchanges. It may be for that reason that Komaroff did not include commercial gifts among her list of these three major types of bestowals that dominated historically in the Islamic world.[3]

As in the previous chapter, my key concern is to look at early modern commercial gift practices closely, with the understanding that they may not be dismissed as empty generic rituals or meaningless repetitive routines. Rather objects, even conventional ones, such as robes of honor and horses, must be examined in their context of exchange, with a focus on the temporal dimensions of their offering and the types of ties engendered in the act of giving and receiving. These practices provide perspective on the tight relationships that Yemen's imams sustained with entrepreneurs from India, while also shedding additional light on those European gift protocols that were described in the previous chapter.

Usual Yearly Presents for the Imam and the Court's Notables

On March 21, 1729, the Dutch merchants at Mocha reported, "Native servants told us that the *nakhudha*s of the Muslim ships belonging to the renowned merchant Mulla Muhammad 'Ali loaded their usual yearly presents for the Imam and the court's notables on camels today. Under the supervision of two servants and eight peons, they were sent to Sanaa." Several weeks later, on May 9, the register continues the same thread: "Today the servants, who were sent by the *nakhudha*s of the Moorish ships of Muhammad 'Ali with gifts for the imam and the court's notables on March 21, came back with some horses and a robe of honor from the imam and the notables for their masters. The ships' men received them with the usual ceremony outside of the city."[4] While frustratingly short, these paired entries from 1729 are important for several reasons. First, they confirm that the famous Gujarati merchant Mulla Muhammad 'Ali tendered gifts in Yemen, thus undermining the assumption that such expectations were directed only or primarily at European merchants. And although these passages provide no details on the contents of his gifts to the imam and his elite retinue in Sanaa, they suggest a set of conventions for Asian gifts, which are confirmed by other accounts as well.

The Dutch described these gifts of 1729 as "usual yearly presents for the Imam and the court's notables,"[5] thus suggesting that they were regular offerings rather than special or one-time bestowals from this merchant. Although he was not named specifically, the recipient was Imam al-Mansur Husayn, who had consolidated his position in 1728 after settling a difficult struggle with the main contender to the position, Imam al-Nasir Muhammad bin Ishaq. These gifts were the first documented ones that Muhammad 'Ali sent to this imam, although he had delivered gifts to his father and predecessor, al-Mutawakkil, in addition to his advisers, in 1725. He bestowed gifts on al-Mansur and his court officials again in 1730.[6] The notables were not named specifically, but one can assume that the *wazirs* (ministers at court) such as Faqih Muhsin al-Hubayshi, who often intervened in matters regarding Yemen's overseas trade, were included in this group. Although our sources do not convey multiple consecutive years of Muhammad 'Ali's gifts, their description as "usual" and "yearly" and the relatively frequent mention of them in the sources support the view that they were given on an annual basis. During a year when a gift is not mentioned, we cannot assume that it was not tendered; it could have simply gone unrecorded.

It is no surprise that Muhammad 'Ali would seek close ties with the imam of Yemen and his notables for he fully understood the commercial power that such connections could wield. In fact, according to historian Ghulam Nadri, this particular merchant "went too far in harbouring political ambitions" at home in Surat.[7] His efforts to get his son, Fakhr al-Din, placed as the *mutasaddi* (governor) of the Indian port compromised his whole mercantile enterprise, eventually leading to his murder by poisoning in 1733.[8] Muhammad 'Ali may have been one of the most strategic merchants engaged in the Indian Ocean trade, but he was not the only trader from India to send gifts to the highlands, even if his were described the most frequently. For instance, 'Anbar, the other dissatisfied *nakhudha* anchored in Mocha's harbor in chapter 1, who was sent to Mocha by Sidi Yaqut Khan of Danda-Rajpuri in 1730, went to the court with gifts after his arrival that year. The *dagregister*, however, tells us only of his return on July 20. According to the Dutch, when he came back to the port, this *nakhudha* had been "glorified" with a robe and a turban and had been given three horses, two from Imam al-Mansur Husayn and one from his brother (who was unnamed but was probably Amir Ahmad of Ta'izz).[9] One imagines that the other major merchants who sent ships from India to Mocha frequently also engaged in gift exchange with the imam of Yemen. Muslim shipowners dominated this group, such as the Turkish merchant from Surat Ahmad Chalabi, the Sindhi Bohra merchant Sulaymanji, and the Ali Raja of Cannanore.[10] Unfortunately, our sources are practically silent about their gifts.

As discussed in the previous chapter, the English and the Dutch each operated according to their own patterns of gift giving. So it is no surprise that a merchant from India whose family maintained a long history at the port, such as Mulla Muhammad 'Ali, might present yet another set of gift protocols and that this model would stand apart from those discussed in chapter 2. Yet the differences are quite striking. Whereas the Dutch and

English often resisted including the imam in their sphere of annual giving, doing so only for a specific purpose or when they were pressured by local administrators, Muhammad ʻAli did so on a yearly basis. By contrast, we have no records of Muhammad ʻAli's gifts to Mocha's trade officials, such as the governor and the *amir al-bahr*. This, of course, does not mean that they were not delivered. For instance, Indian *nakhudha*s gave gifts to Mocha's governors on behalf of the merchants they represented in the seventeenth century.[11] But in the eighteenth century, such bestowals went undocumented, in contrast to more publicized offerings to the imam. However, it is unlikely that Muhammad ʻAli or his cohorts from Surat ever gave gifts to the trade officials of Bayt al-Faqih, as they were not involved in Yemen's coffee market.

The timing of their gifts also differed greatly. The *nakhudha*s of Muhammad ʻAli and Sidi Yaqut Khan made preparations for the dispatch of their gift packages to the imam soon after arriving on Yemen's shores, thus using their gifts to open each season of trade. For instance, in both 1729 and 1730 Muhammad ʻAli's *nakhudha* disembarked at Mocha in February and then dispatched his delegation to Sanaa in March.[12] By contrast, European bestowals at Bayt al-Faqih and Mocha ushered in the final chapter of each year's trade encounter, thus sealing negotiations that had already been made and settled. The English bestowed gifts in Bayt al-Faqih as they completed their purchase of coffee beans in July, then offered gifts at Mocha as they were loading their ships with those beans in August. Dutch cash gifts were given consistently on July 15, toward the end of the trading season and coinciding with the closing of their yearly account books.[13]

Muhammad ʻAli's tight schedule for dispatching gifts to the imam was probably due to the fact that the trip to the court was a serious time commitment. The journey through the mountains took up to ten days each way, and once at the court, delegations were expected to stay for an extended period of time while being entertained at the imam's expense.[14] In 1729 Muhammad ʻAli's delegation returned to Mocha after six weeks of travelling and residence in Sanaa, where they had surely been received with enthusiasm. For that reason, newly arrived *nakhudha*s usually sent representatives to the highlands with their gifts so they could stay at the port to trade uninterrupted through the duration of the season.

Although in 1729 Muhammad ʻAli's *nakhudha* entrusted two unidentified servants with the task of delivering his presents, on at least two other occasions specific individuals were chosen as his representatives. In 1725 a certain Muhammad, who was called a *wazir*, was selected, and in 1730 someone named Sayyid Husayn served as his *wakil* (agent) to the imam's court.[15]

Both representatives were identified in the VOC *dagregister* by name but without description, which implies that they were known figures in Yemen's commercial world. In 1725 Muhammad also carried a gift equaling 35,000 Spanish reals from 'Ali bin Amir Rizq, the governor of Mocha, which indicates that he was considered to be a responsible proxy by the port's notables.[16] In 1730 the *nakhudha* 'Anbar undertook the journey in person. On the occasions when the Europeans were compelled (or forced) to send gifts to the imam's court, they never brought them in person; they simply entrusted the parcels to the governor of Mocha for conveyance.[17]

Most interesting, the Asian gift responsibilities to the imam were not just cyclical but also apparently reciprocal, resulting in a robe of honor and a horse or horses as return gifts. Robes were tendered to each person individually, sometimes with a turban, but the number of horses varied. This reciprocity contrasts with European customary gift practices, which generally moved in only one direction, to the officials of Mocha and Bayt al-Faqih, and rarely resulted in direct countergifts. The practices of European merchant tribute decidedly confirmed the status of the recipient, usually one of Yemen's trade officials, as well as his responsibility to oversee the trade of the giver efficiently. The merchants of western India were tied into more enduring social and cyclical relationships with Yemen's imam, as I discuss below.

Diplomatic Gifts to the Imam

These brief references to gifts from the merchants of India invite speculation about their contents, which are not revealed by the VOC *dagregister*s that provide evidence of their transmission. But their patterns may be compared to those of diplomatic gifts that were delivered to the imam, which Yemeni chroniclers mention, though they never write of commercial ones. These references aid in broadening the scope of comparative material, thus helping us to better understand the practices described above.

As one key example, according to the chronicler Muhsin al-Hasan, also known as Abu Talib, Imam al-Mahdi Muhammad dispatched an embassy to the Safavid shah Sultan Husayn in 1109/1697–1698, with the Yemeni poet Muhammad bin Haydar Agha as his ambassador.[18] According to Abu Talib, this envoy took to Iran many gifts of swords, horses, objects crafted of carnelian, and Yemeni treasures. Then, in 1113/1701, a Persian ambassador, whom Abu Talib tellingly refers to as *al-ilji* (the infidel), was sent back to al-Mahdi, accompanied by his original envoy and carrying gifts (*tuhaf*) and precious objects (*nafa'is*) that "exceeded comprehension" but were not enumerated.[19] During his four-month stay, the imam rewarded the

Persian envoy with many gifts, in addition to some to be conveyed back to Shah Sultan Husayn.[20]

Other passages in the same chronicle are more precise about a few of the items delivered, mentioning that the Persian ambassador had brought a *mushaf*, a copy of the Qur'an, as a gift for al-Mahdi. Qur'an manuscripts were commonly given as gifts in the Islamic world, and the Safavids were regular purveyors of lavishly illuminated copies as diplomatic bestowals to other Muslim rulers.[21] In this case, the manuscript was likely decorated with gold and colors, particularly on its opening pages. It probably also included a *du'a* (formulaic prayer) laid out over two pages at the end, which was a common feature of Persian Qur'an manuscripts from the time. Comparable examples include a seventeenth-century copy in the Walters Art Museum, an example in the Princeton University library with a mid-eighteenth-century *waqf* (endowment) seal, and one in a private Yemeni collection that, according to its current owners, was given as a diplomatic gift to Imam al-Mutawakkil Isma'il (r. 1644–1676) by an earlier Safavid envoy in 1070/1659–1660 (Plate 6).[22] These gift-quality manuscripts share a standard layout, similar design features, and a corresponding level of lustrous gold and brilliantly colored illumination. A later reference mentions a jeweled dagger that the Persian envoy had given to al-Mahdi. Our chronicler did not single out this gift at the time it was offered but mentioned it a few years later, when al-Mahdi passed it on as a special present to a visiting Ottoman ambassador.[23] A comparative example that the Persian merchant Muhammad Qasim presented to Tsar Mikhail Fedorovich in 1617 is now in the Kremlin collection.[24] Although it was a private offering rather than a state gift, this lavish piece provides a solid basis upon which to imagine the ornamental weapon received by al-Mahdi, which may have been encrusted with gold, rubies, turquoise, and pearls on its sheath and hilt (Plate 7).[25]

The Ottomans also offered diplomatic gifts to the Qasimis in the early eighteenth century. As described in chapter 1, their outreach to them was oriented particularly around commercial policies regarding coffee, a pressing issue at a moment when the global demand for this good had risen sharply.[26] In 1712 an Ottoman ambassador arrived at al-Mahdi's court, apparently to complain about the liberal permission that the imam had granted to Europeans in Bayt al-Faqih, which, they claimed, affected Ottoman sales of the bean. According to the French observers at the court at that time, the Turkish ambassador "appear'd with a great deal of Pomp, and a large Retinue" and presented the imam with many gifts, including a valuable and finely crafted clock.[27] This clock, which was likely from Europe or at least made by a European clockmaker, may have arrived at the Ottoman court originally as a gift. Although Europeans had been sending automata as gifts to the Ottomans since the sixteenth century and watches were sometimes given in Yemen, clocks rarely reached the area; thus this item was received with great interest.[28]

Compared to the legendary cases of exotic or valuable gifts exchanged by Muslim rulers, such as the elephants and lions discussed by Mikhail, these eighteenth-century diplomatic gifts to al-Mahdi may seem quite modest.[29] But it is worth noting that they were different in character from those commercial bestowals that European merchants delivered during the same period, with the limited formula of textiles, spices and spiced products, firearms, and cash. The Qur'an bestowed by the Safavids was sumptuous, valuable, and meaningful in an intra-Muslim context, although the Zaydi Qasimis and the Twelver Safavids did not enjoy a shared Shi'i connection. The dagger's value was concentrated in its jewels, whereas the clock represented modern technology and unique manufacture.

The Safavid dagger, and probably the clock as well, fit into the category of heirloom gifts that art historian Sinem Arcak and others have described as objects with histories of famous ownership that accrued meaning and importance over time as they circulated from one recipient to the next.[30] Thus these objects, even as they were moved, retained a certain amount of inalienability from the initial exchange that began their dispersal, and therefore they acquired an "exclusive and cumulative identity with a particular series of owners through time."[31] The Persian dagger was given first to al-Mahdi, who passed it on to an Ottoman visitor, and the clock the Ottomans brought to al-Mawahib had likely been received initially as a gift. In the Islamic world, the most valuable objects were those that gained compounded social capital through their paths of redistribution among notable recipients and carried with them their histories of exchange as weighty and meaningful aspects of their identity. For this reason, the practice of regifting items in the Islamic world was quite common, although it may seem tactless according to the rules of contemporary etiquette. In this context, the repurposing of a gift indicates that the original recipient had treasured it rather than disdained it. This initial reverence powered the object on a continual path of gifting and regifting that could continue through multiple owners and magnified the object's importance over time through its dissemination. The VOC often repurposed gift items as well, selling them on the open market or giving them as gifts to other recipients.[32] When they did so, however, the origin of the object was never highlighted and did not constitute an important or enduring aspect of the object's identity.

Provincial Tribute to the Imam

Another paradigm for gifts to the imam is represented by the yearly tribute offered by Yemen's provincial officials. Like the commercial gifts sent by Indian merchants and diplomatic missions, these involved lengthy court visits. They also entailed costly remittances as a condition of the lucrative posts that had been granted.[33] Of course, the most advantageous position, but also one of the most fragile, was that of the governor of Mocha, who was by no means a neutral administrator but actively participated in the trade for his own benefit, a feature of Yemen's trading world that Europeans constantly decried. In the early nineteenth century, George Annesley, titled Viscount Valentia, described the possible benefits of this post: "The government of Mocha is the best in the gift of the Imaum. . . . They say, that when a Dola [governor] is appointed, he weighs nothing; that on going out of the gates of Sana he weighs a frasel [a unit of measure of around 12 kg]; that on arriving at his government, he weighs two; and goes on growing heavier and heavier, during his stay; but that he dwindles and dwindles as he returns, till the gates of Sana reduce him to his primitive leanness."[34] With this vivid image, Annesley accurately acknowledged the profits this job could reap but also its many associated responsibilities and pitfalls. The governor was required to send up revenues from the port to the court on a yearly basis, and the imam evaluated these offerings and could recall the governor based on insufficient remittance. As a key example, in January 1724, when Faqih Ahmad Khazindar was serving in his first stint as governor of Mocha, Imam al-Mutawakkil called him up for his yearly visit. Khazindar reportedly prepared 140,000 Spanish reals for the journey, with the intention of giving 80,000 to the imam and using 60,000 for himself while in Sanaa. According to a later report from the English, the imam considered this sum inadequate.[35] The governor was immediately removed from his post, and his son, who had been serving as deputy in Mocha during his absence, was called from the port abruptly. While in Sanaa, this governor was disgraced publicly and then fined an additional 55,000 Spanish reals. The Dutch suggest that the amount of his gift was the determining factor in his removal, but it is also likely that Khazindar's main enemy, the powerful *wazir* al-Hubayshi, had a hand in this upheaval. Even so, this incident signals the tangible importance of these gifts to the permanence of a port official's post.[36]

However, even after this fall from favor, Khazindar was able to regain Imam al-Mutawakkil's approval, for he was named to another high-powered position, the governorship of Sanaa, in August 1725. And then in 1729 Imam al-Mansur Husayn reappointed him as Mocha's governor. During his second coastal tenure, he clearly understood that his gifts for the imam needed to be adequate in type, quality, and quantity. In the following year, the Dutch observed that the governor had ordered the production of "gold and silver horse harnesses as well as costly men and women's clothing" and presumed that these were intended for the "insatiable Sanaa court."[37] Their presumptions were correct, for a few weeks later, the governor sent his son to Sanaa with 18,000 *rijksdaalders* in cash, ten horses with gold- and silver-studded harnesses and saddles, chintzes, textiles, and gold cloth, in addition to male and female slaves.[38] Fortunately for Khazindar, this gift was received well. Two years later, in 1732, the same governor prepared a set of comparable gifts, for the Dutch noted that he had "forced all the Baniyan gold and silversmiths to make gold and silver horse harnesses that will make his present to the Sanaa court more distinguished."[39] And again, in June 1736, he arranged for his trip to Sanaa with "gold and silver work for the horses and for women's jewelry."[40] These disparate and offhanded remarks make it clear that a local governor like Khazindar had to endeavor to adequately calibrate his gifts to the court. They also show that, with manufactured items of silver and gold, the content of official tribute from Yemen's most lucrative province differed starkly from European merchant tribute and the diplomatic bestowals mentioned earlier.

Even lesser port officials were required to send tribute to the imam. In 1729 the Dutch noted that Mocha's second in charge had left for Sanaa with many camels that carried gifts, in addition to slaves, some described as Abyssinian and others as female, to offer to the imam.[41] Qasim al-Turbati, perhaps the most important local merchant of Mocha, visited the imam once a year and brought tribute to him at that time. It is unclear whether these yearly visits were a function of the various administrative posts that he held in the city, such as being the second to Mocha's governor and the imam's *wakil,* or as a requisite distribution because of his stature as a major local merchant. Like that of the governor, his yearly tribute often comprised several tens of thousands of Spanish reals, in addition to some goods. Yet, like a provincial governor, he was also subject to penalties. On October 30, 1725, the Dutch heard that al-Turbati's gifts tendered in Sanaa were considered too insignificant, and so Imam al-Mutawakkil had charged him another 40,000 Spanish reals.[42] But the same merchant also received rewards for some of his court journeys, as in 1731, when he visited the court of Amir Ahmad, Imam al-Mansur's brother, in Ta'izz and returned with a robe of honor and some horses.[43]

The imam was thus the recipient of many different types of gifts from merchants, diplomatic envoys, and provincial officials, who provided a direct channel to coastal revenues. It is clear that the amount of these gifts far surpassed those customary ones that the Europeans tendered in Yemen, which fluctuated in value but were always less than 1,000 Spanish reals per year. Unlike the Dutch and English assemblages of global trade products and the more unique diplomatic gifts from other Muslim rulers, port officials offered high-value manufactured items made of silver and gold, particularly horse fittings, jewelry, and tailored clothing, in addition to some Indian textiles. Copious amounts of silver coins outweighed these various goods as a key liquid component. African slaves, procured from across the Red Sea and likely purchased in Mocha's slave market, were also a significant part of these provincial contributions.

Robes of Honor

I have provided a sketch of the range of gifts that appeared at the Qasimi court from diplomats and provincial officials, yet we can still only speculate about what Indian merchants gave to the imam as gifts. By contrast, we do know what he returned as countergifts, the *khil'a* (sometimes written *khil'at*), or robe of honor, in addition to a horse or horses.[44] Both have long histories of bestowal in the Islamic world.[45] The *khil'a,* in particular, resonates far beyond Yemen and across a wide "region of robing," as Stewart Gordon has termed it. This arena extended around the Mediterranean, into sub-Saharan Africa and to the east across Central Asia.[46] Of course, these robes were not unique to the commercial context, but as Gavin Hambly points out, more often "robes of honour and the *Khil'at* ceremony served the political objectives of rewarding, honouring, and bonding servants of the state, personnel of the imperial bureaucracy, and the representatives of foreign rulers."[47]

According to Gordon, the "bedrock characteristic of the system was that *khil'at* established a client relationship between the giver and receiver" while also "reinforc[ing] the image of the ruler as a font of largesse," cementing a fundamentally asymmetrical relationship.[48] These implications of subservience and inequality, but also loyalty, were universally associated with the *khil'a.* In fact, during the reception of the Safavid delegation to the Qasimis in 1701, the court poet Ahmad bin Ahmad al-Anisi refused a *khil'a* from the Persian ambassador after accepting one from the imam.[49] By doing so, al-Anisi publicly represented his allegiance and deference to the imam, while denying an equally elevated status to this foreign visitor, an obvious snub. In this way, the acceptance or refusal of a robe could send a clear message about individual relationships and one's perceptions of the larger social order.

It is useful to consider the particular place of the *khil'a* in the world of merchant gifting, looking at how and when it was offered and what it may have meant, especially when its bestowal was formatted to the exigencies of the long-distance maritime trade. Generally, the *khil'a* was given within the precinct of a palace with many court officials present, as with the Persian delegation. Because the robe was draped over the shoulders of the recipient, the *khil'a* bestowal constituted a direct corporeal tie, with the movement of an intimate item directly from the body (or hands) of the giver to that of the receiver. Scholars have focused on the public ceremonies staged around the giving of the *khil'a* as a salient part of its meaning. Yet aside from Barry Flood, who states that the *khil'a* was "transvalued through contact," few have highlighted the underlying assumption that, in its ceremonial context, the transfer of the *khil'a* commemorated the face-to-face meeting of two individuals and thus confirmed a social bond forged by direct human interface, which allowed it to convey corporeal associations quite lucidly.[50] Moreover it was most often given as a singular offering to a recipient in a particular setting, unlike horses, which were more frequently given in multiples and often bestowed to recognize past events.

Indeed direct contact at the court visit appears to have been an essential component of these gift bestowals, but the question of social interface was complicated when it came to the maritime traders who were active in Yemen. For the famous merchants of India, their *nakhudhas*, but also their *nakhudhas*' representatives, played a key role as proxies in sustaining their relationships to Yemen's imam. Because the Yemeni capital was far from the coast, the imam never travelled to meet merchants in the ports. Similarly, the major ship-owning merchants of India almost never made the overseas journey in person. As an exception, Muhammad 'Ali visited the region only once in 1727, stopping by Mocha briefly for only ten days on his way to Jidda for the pilgrimage. He was received well at the port, "with all of the signs of one of the city's government," but he did not visit the imam on this trip.[51] For this reason, proxies were invested with the authority of a given merchant, not just in matters regarding the trade but also to maintain the merchant's relationship to the imam, as one would expect with a diplomatic envoy for a faraway and sedentary ruler.

The court visit was an important component in the delivery of provincial gifts as well, but usually for reasons of accountability. Officials from the lowlands, namely Mocha's governors, were generally expected to make their yearly journey to deliver tribute to the court in person, although I have noted some exceptions to this practice. Of course, these visits encompassed more than the mere sending of gifts; they also entailed the firsthand delivery of a report on port activities. Sometimes officials were asked to vouch for their conduct in their administrative roles. There were certainly cases when governors actively shunned this directive, as with Khazindar, who avoided making the visit himself in 1730. With their usual scorn for this governor, the Dutch noted that he was supposed to go in person but sent his son for fear that he would have the government taken from him again and be subject to familiar humiliations in Sanaa. But biases aside, their comments make it clear that the governor himself was expected to appear at the court. If successful in his offering, he would return to the coast wearing a new robe from the imam and bringing back some horses, all of which would be highly visible upon arrival in Mocha. The court visit was an integral part of the process of provincial remittance that validated the goods and money carried therein.

This focus on the court visit rather than solely on the material content of gifts given during it allows us to understand the commercial gift protocols of the Europeans with more clarity. When Mocha's local officials asked for or even forced gifts from the Dutch and English for the imam and his *wazir*s, they may have been trying to align their practices with the codes of exchange their Indian merchant counterparts regularly engaged in. Along these lines, on July 7, 1731, Imam al-Mansur Husayn sent a message to the Dutch through Mocha's *shahbandar* asking that they come to the court with a gift. He also expressed curiosity about the Dutch, whom he had never met.[52] The Dutch responded cursorily to this request, indicating that the visit would be too costly and would require advance permission from Batavia. This exchange characterizes the divergent perspectives on the value of a visit to the imam's court and the opportunity to deliver gifts to him directly. The imam placed importance on these face-to-face visits, as demonstrated by his relationships with other merchants, such as Muhammad 'Ali, albeit through their proxies. But the Dutch and English merchants of Yemen did not see the highland visit as a privilege or prerogative. Rather they saw the inclusion of the imam's gift as an additional burden to their yearly financial commitments and tried to avoid the long journey to the capital, which they considered a costly distraction rather than an aid to their trade endeavors.

On the rare occasions when European merchants made the court visit, they also received the *khil'a*. Characteristically, we have more information about these bestowals than we do for those of local administrators and merchants from India. For instance, in 1706 the VOC surgeon Otto Mueller was called to al-Mawahib to treat the aged Imam al-Mahdi of an unidentified ailment. In gratitude for his medical service and upon the delegation's departure, the imam granted Mueller a *khil'a* and a horse. The imam gave only horses to each of the two lower-ranking soldiers who had accompanied Mueller, in addition to one to be shipped abroad for Pieter de Vos, the previous VOC director in Surat.[53] The *khil'a* acknowledged that Mueller had undertaken the arduous journey from the coast to the capital and cemented an intimate relationship between doctor and patient. A few weeks before the surgeon's return, the imam had sent a *khil'a* and a horse to Joan Josua Ketelaar, the chief VOC merchant in Mocha, who had approved his journey. At this time, Ketelaar referred to the robe as a "sirpau [a variant of *sarupa*] or robe of honor," using a Persian term to describe it.[54] That he made this translation from the Persian quite seamlessly suggests that Ketelaar encountered the *khil'a* in Yemen with a sense of familiarity, drawing on his long experience in India.[55]

The imam was not the only one who had the right to bestow robes in this manner. In Mocha, the governor would award a *khil'a* to the ship's captain and its officers as they left the port each year. These robes played a distinct role in concluding and finalizing a relationship between the governor and the foreign merchant that had been sustained throughout the trade season. European merchants do not always mention the receipt of the *khil'a* during these exit ceremonies, which points again to the sense of familiarity with which they came to record these repetitive events that surrounded their entry to and exit from the port.[56] It is also unclear whether or not the governor gave robes to the Indian *nakhudha*s in these cases because their port departures received little attention from our primary observers, but it is likely that he did.

On July 28, 1706, the VOC merchants prepared to leave the port for the year. They did not yet hold a year-round establishment in Mocha, so the entire factory would be shut down after their departure. No one was left behind, and any unresolved affairs were entrusted to their broker. In preparation for their departure, Ketelaar, along with the *Oostersteijn*'s commander Jan de Wenzijn and the junior merchant Joan van der Needen, went to bid farewell to the governor, al-Huraybi. Other port officials, such as the city's second 'Ali and the imam's *nakhudha* Amir Rizq, were also present for this sendoff, which involved the familiar serving of coffee, sprinkling of rosewater, and burning of *'ud*. As they left, the governor gave each of them a *khil'a*, which was described as a "red woolen Arab cloak."[57] They were then escorted out of the city and to their ship. The fact that they were given robes as they left the port rather than when they entered it means it punctuated the final stage of a relationship sustained throughout the trade season rather than initiating a new tie. In this way, the governor's *khil'a* bestowal at Mocha was quite terminal, crystallizing the inverse meaning of the ceremonies of entry described in chapter 1. By contrast, in the early seventeenth century, when Mocha was still under Ottoman rule, robes were given to new merchants upon arrival at the port.[58]

Other indications provide further support for the *khil'a* as a terminal gift. After the yearlong VOC residence was established, a small cadre of merchants remained behind at the port each winter to maintain company affairs. In 1709 the senior merchant, Ketelaar, left Daniel Haagdoorn and Christiaan van Vrijberghen to oversee the establishment. Ketelaar's farewell to al-Huraybi was particularly poignant because he had developed a close relationship with him and many other locals during his visits to the port. When he went to the governor's house for his farewell, he was given a robe of honor, as were the commander of the departing ship, the *Koning Karel,* two junior merchants, and the warehouse master.[59] Five robes were given in total, but only to those who departed. The merchants who remained at the port, Haagdoorn and van Vrijberghen, were not recognized with any gifts or robes.

The 1706 reference to the "red woolen Arab cloak" is also important because it suggests, ever so briefly, the material attributes of the Yemeni *khil'a.* In 1790 Grandpré added further evidence to this impression, describing it as "an elegant cashmere robe" in red, which he received as a parting gift from Mocha's governor.[60] Apparently the imam distributed the same type of robe from the highlands. In 1712 Major de la Grelaudiere of the French mission to al-Mawahib received two "Habits after the Fashion of the Country, one of fine Scarlet, and the second of another beautiful Cloth of a Rose Colour" in addition to golden vests and a nicely equipped horse.[61] Similar items were given to the doctor Barbier. Fashioned of red, scarlet, crimson, or even pink wool of an unknown origin,[62] these robes probably had long wide sleeves, like the one pictured in figure 1.2. Although no examples of the eighteenth-century Yemeni red woolen *khil'a* remain in contemporary collections, it was clearly distinct from those tendered by the Ottoman governors of Yemen in the seventeenth century, which Brouwer describes as valuable cloaks of silver or gold brocade.[63]

The distributive practices around the *khil'a,* as much as they were shared around Gordon's "region of robing," had variable cultural and temporal attributes in Yemen when given by the imam to a foreign merchant. At Mocha, the practices around the giving of the *khil'a* were by no means stable as the port went from Ottoman to Qasimi rule over a period of 150 years. When located within these circumstances of bestowal, at the imam's court or at the port of Mocha upon departure, the red woolen *khil'a,* sometimes with a turban and a vest, forged ties that could be enduring and cyclical or could conclude a relationship that was decidedly terminal and finite.

Horses as Gifts

The *khil'a* was usually given as a singular offering—one per person. But when the imam offered the robe, it was commonly paired with the gift of a horse or horses, although on a few occasions mules or donkeys were given instead.[64] Horses were customary gifts around the Islamic world, but in Yemen they were also precious local commodities.[65] According to Niebuhr, a horse purchased in Mocha could be sold for double the price in Bengal and four times the amount in England.[66] Yet they exceeded their economic value as luxury commodities, as Hedda Reindl-Kiel has described them, because of the social status accorded to mounted riders, which was crystallized in the sumptuary laws discussed in chapter 1.[67] In this way, horses, as socially significant animals, could condense their commercial value, outstripping their monetary worth. That Indian recipients also adhered to this socially dense understanding of the horse is clear. Jagjeet Lally has shown that "the horse was firmly entrenched within cultural-political practices and material exchanges in South Asia."[68] Thus these beasts served as ideal return offerings to gift assemblages that were often much more complex and diverse.

Their impact could be scaled up when allocated in multiples, although too large a number could be misconstrued as a tributary offering.[69] In 1725 Mulla Muhammad 'Ali's representative, Muhammad, returned to Mocha from Sanaa with two horses for the merchant's *nakhudha,* which the Dutch considered "a wonderful honor."[70] In 1729 no number was given, but then on May 22, 1730, his other representative, Sayyid Husayn, returned from Sanaa with six horses, four from the imam and two from his son, Sidi Ibrahim, which the Dutch describe as "lean stallions."[71] By contrast, the Dutch described others as "fine" and always specified when they received a stallion. They created an even more favorable impression when they were given with expensive equipment, such as lavish fittings in silver and gold, which may have exceeded the value of the horses themselves.[72]

The distribution of horses was restricted not only by their monetary value. As Reindl-Kiel has shown for the Ottoman realm, thoroughbred horses were not traded liberally to Christian lands. Limited numbers could be procured from the Ottomans, but only through carefully orchestrated treaties or as gifts. According to Grandpré, in the late eighteenth century the imam was the owner of all the horses in Yemen, which he could distribute as a clear measure of his favor and could just as easily remove to show his displeasure.[73] Grandpré may have exaggerated the imam's dominion over Yemen's horses, because evidence shows that those other than the imam distributed horses too. Yet even if overstated, his comment represents how central horses were to a local economy of royal approval.

Horses were sometimes given as gifts independent of the robe of honor. As such, they could entail a range of meanings and initiate different types of social ties or intentions than the *khil'a,* which was much more limited in its context of distribution. More specifically, horses were commonly given outside of face-to-face encounters and the court visit and thus were a much less personal bestowal. The imam would often send some to recipients on the coast as unexpected gifts. For instance, on August 18, 1729, the English received two horses from Imam al-Mansur and were asked to convey both to India. One was for Robert Cowan, who had been chief at Mocha in 1724 but at that time was the governor of Bombay.[74] Historian Timothy Davies argues that Cowan used his lucrative position in India, as well as his previous contacts from his Mocha stint, to build his own private trade network and was thus an important player in the world of Indian Ocean commerce.[75] Although the Dutch, who narrated this transfer, did not speculate on the reason for it, the gift was likely meant to recognize the successfully renegotiated trading contract of the EIC, which the merchant Francis Dickinson had just concluded after a period of absence from Yemen. The other horse was intended for ʻAli bin Amir Rizq, a former governor of Mocha, who had left the port suddenly on an English ship for Bombay in 1728. At that time, he, along with the rest of the city, had accepted the rule of the new (but temporary) Imam al-Nasir and thus breached loyalty to al-Mansur, who later regained his coastal foothold. When al-Mansur's allies closed in on the city from the east and it was clear that his treachery would be punishable, ʻAli went into exile, leaving the city by the sea. Al-Mansur's 1729 gift of a horse was tendered to him as a pardon, suggesting that he should return to Yemen the following season and would not be held accountable for his actions at a time of crisis.

Although the imam and others gave horses as gifts to represent their approval of a merchant, on the receiving end horses could be difficult possessions, particularly for the Europeans. The VOC mandated that all gifts received at company outposts were to be sent back to Batavia in order to discourage merchants from engaging in private business or reaping unwarranted incentives in their overseas positions.[76] In 1717, when VOC merchant Hendrick Burggraaf returned from his highland visit to the new imam al-Mutawakkil Qasim, he brought back with him four Arabian stallions outfitted with their equipment that the imam and his sons had given to him. These were then sent to Batavia on the ships that left Mocha late that summer.[77] The merchants duly noted the fees incurred by this shipment, which were to be assumed by the company.[78] While horses were considered the property of the company and had the potential to move between different transactional registers quite freely, the *khil'a* was treated as a personal item that was not demanded back from individuals, a testament to its enduring potential to crystallize social bonds and its nonconvertibility to a mere commodity.

By contrast, the English initially kept their gift horses in their stable in Mocha, even though these animals were expensive to maintain. In May 1720 they listed the recurrent charges associated with them, which included necessary supplies such as straw, horseshoes, feed, and nails, in addition to the wages for the horse keepers and farriers, who were given gifts in some years as well.[79] That year, horse expenses amounted to 733 Spanish reals, a significant percentage of total house expenses, which came to 8,508 Spanish reals. These horse-related charges equaled much more than the total amount spent on gifts that year, which was only 220 Spanish reals, and 150 for salaries.[80] When Phipps arrived in Mocha in 1721, he made great efforts to trim unneeded costs at the factory and identified horses as a significant drain on company resources. He eventually relished the success of his efforts on September 30, 1722, when he thanked the Mocha factors for sending one of their horses to Bombay, where he was then based, citing both their exorbitant cost of maintenance and the fact that there were local restrictions on riding in Yemen, as described in chapter 1.[81] He praised them for making do with three donkeys, which were cheaper to maintain and useful for transporting cargo.

Horses were distributed to provincial officials and merchants—local, Asian-based, and European—in Yemen as marks of the imam's favor. These highly sought-after Arabian horses were also central to the articulation of a set of localized social privileges, as described in chapter 1, thus fixing intangible hierarchies and highlighting varying levels of status in a diverse trading community. But as much as these bestowals occupied a prized place in the Indian Ocean world of exchange, the recipients did not always accept them with the gratitude one might anticipate. The Dutch saw them as costly possessions that could not be retained in their Mocha establishment because of VOC mandates. For the English, they became a financial burden for a factory at which expenses were being closely scrutinized. In this deeply commercial society, horses could not uniformly project the royal power their givers intended. They could be viewed as precious commodities and prized gifts or as cumbersome possessions and liabilities to corporate trade endeavors.

Entourage and Presentation

These accounts suggest that the gift encounter was not entirely oriented around the material aspects or commodity value of the objects given, and many of these accounts convey the impression that gifts were situated within a whole host of entangled social codes and expectations of both givers and receivers. The acknowledged history of ownership of the objects bestowed, the context of the court visit to the imam, and the burdens posed by various gifts to their recipients are other important aspects of gift encounters in the commercial world of eighteenth-century Yemen.

One also needs to consider the circumstances of gift presentation, which art historian Avinoam Shalem has described as the elaborate "performance of the object" that often undergirded the delivery of major royal gifts in the premodern Middle East.[82] According to Shalem, this performance began long before the object entered the hands of its recipient. As Arcak has shown for the famous 1568 Safavid embassy to the newly appointed Ottoman sultan Selim, crowds gathered to witness the elaborate parades staged as the gifts were brought along a long land route to their eventual destination point in Edirne.[83] These parades were intended to speak to two sets of audiences, like the ceremonies of chapter 1. They were meant to impress local onlookers with the size and scale of the visiting entourage, which attested to the important standing and opulent world of the sender, in this case the Ottomans' archrival, the Safavid shah. And these hordes of people were called together in order to astound the passing envoys, thus attesting to the ability of the host, the Ottoman sultan, to mobilize vast numbers of people. According to Shalem, this "latent-competitive atmosphere" of gift exchange and diplomacy was part of a "total scenario of exercising power, instigating astonishment, and memorializing the event as exclusive and unique."[84] In these parades, the gift parcels and packages were wrapped up and arranged on multiple pack animals overseen by countless servants. The overall effect was of a never-ending procession of undoubtedly precious, yet mysterious goods. The masses that looked on could only imagine the brilliant objects encased within these copious bundles, which suggested abundance because of their quantity but also because of their implicit mystery; the vast majority of viewers lacked knowledge of their shrouded contents.

Such performance and staging were surely enacted in Yemen as well, as attested to by the Safavid embassy of 1701. In preparation for this visit, al-Mahdi had ordered the cities along the route to be ornamented and to generously welcome the embassy at each stop along the eight-day journey, which included the major cities of Ta'izz, Yarim, and Dhamar. The imam staged these welcoming parties with both locals and the foreign visitors in mind to indicate the wide extent of his dominion and with a desire to represent the wealth and resources of his imamate. According to our narrator, onlookers in Yemen duly responded with awe at the impressive scale of the Persian retinue. As another example, Mocha governor Ahmad Khazindar's 1724 remittance to the imam comprised ninety camel loads. Although it was deemed insufficient in Sanaa, it would have made a profound impression on all of those who witnessed its passage from the coast to the capital.[85]

In the case of Indian merchant tribute, similarly lavish performances were staged on the return, to receive those back in Mocha after the delivery of gifts at the court. As recounted in 1729, when Muhammad 'Ali's servants returned from Sanaa with the *khil'a* and some horses, the crews from this merchant's ships gathered to meet the returning group outside of Bab al-Shadhili, the major gate to Mocha on the landward side, in what was described as "the usual ceremony outside of the city."[86] The VOC surgeon Mueller was also received in this manner when he returned from al-Mawahib in 1706, after having successfully treated the imam's unnamed ailment. In that case, the governor specifically called the city's notables and the VOC merchants to come out to recognize the success of Mueller's medical mission and followed with a banquet at the palace.[87] These ceremonies provided an opportunity for the returning figure to don the robe received in the highlands and display the horses acquired, thus maximizing the social capital gained from the court visit and doubling the value of the gifts that had been received.

Within the city of Mocha, the preparation and packaging of commercial gifts to the imam must have constituted a type of spectacle as well. Again, we can recall Muhammad 'Ali's 1729 gift that required the labor of two servants and eight peons to be conveyed to the recipient, which suggests its considerable scale and scope, even if it was much smaller than that sent by Khazindar in 1724. These observations delivered by the Dutch also suggest how closely various merchants scrutinized each other's gift preparations. Whether directly or through their "native servants," the Dutch and other merchants carefully observed the loading of these gifts and their passage through the city, undoubtedly to ascertain what their competition was doing. At the same time, the assistants who packed and delivered these goods engaged in certain efforts to keep their contents secret. Had the contents been known (or even rumored), they would have been recorded by the Dutch, who described gifts given by other merchants in detail, usually with associated value amounts, even uncertain ones. As an example, in 1709, on their initial mission to Mocha, the French delivered their first gifts to the governor. These consisted of silver horse furniture, a pair of pistols, broadcloth, and pieces of crystal, worth around 2,500 Spanish reals and carried by their broker Vira, two of their officers, and ten soldiers.[88] These observations are important not just because they describe with a certain amount of detail the scope of this early and costly French gift and the entourage that carried it but also because the Dutch, not the French, recorded it, thus confirming that merchants were watching closely as gifts were being prepared and transported by their rivals, in an effort to enumerate their value. It is also clear that these efforts at gathering information were sometimes fruitless and that the merchants of Gujarat may have been particularly successful at concealing the content of their offerings.

Art historians have paid specific attention to the packaging of imperial gifts, particularly because many of these cases, wrappers, and receptacles were also lavish art objects. In fact, some of these boxes and containers have survived after their original contents have long vanished.[89] The tight packaging and closure of objects helped to keep their contents secret and, as Shalem has suggested, heightened the pleasure associated with gift receipt in the premodern Islamic world.[90] Some medieval gifts were nested within other precious objects, such as a finely carved ivory casket, or wrapped in equally valuable textiles. As each layer was opened, another stunning container was found within. The various layers might be scented with valuable aromatics, thus adding another sensory dimension to the process. These features furthered the excitement and experience of opening any gift and contributed to the ever-present notion of abundance because each object appeared as a bottomless cornucopia, with more surprises nested inside.

Indications from Yemen suggest that even commercial gifts were "wrapped" in special ways. For instance, as noted in the previous chapter, VOC merchants bought red baftas (calicoes from India) in the bazaar to make sacks for the spices that were included in the yearly gifts to Mocha's governor. Although these red sacks were likely quite simple, they indicate that one could not simply deliver spices in the ordinary packaging they arrived in from the east, which would have been made of an extremely coarse material, and also that basic commodities had to undergo a type of visual transformation in order to become suitable as gifts. Red, a color that was used extensively in Yemeni ceremonial and for the Mocha *khil'a,* was mobilized for these deliveries.

Along the same lines, the oils scented with spices that were often tendered in small vials to the governors of Mocha and Bayt al-Faqih might be specially packaged when offered to the imam, such as the box filled with two-ounce glass vials of cinnamon, clove, and nutmeg oil that VOC merchants presented to Imam al-Mutawakkil in 1719 on behalf of Christoffel van Zwolle, governor-general of the Dutch East Indies.[91] This gift may be compared to a wooden cellaret held in the Rijksmuseum today (Plate 8). Lined with red velvet and segmented to hold nine square bottles, it is fitted with porcelain rather than glass vessels. In the late seventeenth and early eighteenth centuries, VOC officials in Batavia ordered such boxes from Japan to be doled out to recipients in Ayutthaya, Banten, Abyssinia, and elsewhere.[92] Their orders were strikingly specific on which type of wood was to be used, if the fittings were to be of silver or brass, and the precise capacity of the bottles and the boxes. The box given to the imam in 1719 was much smaller than the Rijksmuseum cellaret, but even so, it represents the desire to impress. That this gift was deemed successful was confirmed in 1735, when the Dutch provided another boxed set of oils to Imam al-Mansur Husayn. This box, which was singled out as "fine," was larger, with four vials, each of two and a half ounces, of cinnamon, mace, clove, and musk oil.[93] That such an offering was not intended for general distribution is clear. The box had arrived in the factory in 1730 and was held there for five years, until the right opportunity for a gift to the imam arose. Their extended retention of this item suggests that they would not deign to give it to a lesser recipient in the intervening period.

Additionally, like the gifts Shalem describes, the segmented cellaret offered a complex experience of opening. After the wooden box was unlatched and the lid lifted, the recipient would find a sumptuous interior with individual containers of contrasting colors and textures nested inside. Each had to be removed independently and uncapped before it revealed the oil within. This type of wrapping thus enhanced the visual, tactile, and olfactory experience. Some of these VOC gift boxes were made of aromatic woods, such as sandalwood, with oil drawn from the same substance within, a choice that doubled the sensory impact.[94] Although the boxed sets of oils given in Yemen were not of the high caliber of the Rijksmuseum specimen, or even equivalent in size, we can be certain that the Dutch were conscious of and quite capable of adhering to the subtle codes associated with the presentation and offering of gifts in Yemen and other places where similar items were bestowed. These boxes also further demonstrate the elaborate planning and forethought that went into the act of VOC merchant tribute in Yemen and around the Indian Ocean. High-impact gifts necessitated the production of specialized containers for storage, shipping, and presentation, calling upon the skills of artisans and officials in Batavia and Dejima for a roster of recipients that stretched from the Red Sea to South East Asia.

When compared to the copious line-by-line registers we have for the Dutch and the English, the evidence for the commercial gifting practices of merchants from India in Yemen is indeed scant. For that reason, much of this chapter used comparative information from the noncommercial context as well as from the European experience to explicate these elusive acts of gift giving and what they may have meant. Ultimately, Asian gifts were different in character, timing, conveyance, and meaning than those of their European counterparts. These differences compel us to look at each group's gift practices closely and specifically rather than resorting to sweeping generalities.

Whereas the commercial gifts described in chapter 2 were situated alongside trade practices, the commercial gifts of Muslim merchants from India, such as Mulla Muhammad 'Ali and Sidi Yaqut Khan, were within the diplomatic and regional norms of gift bestowal that were widespread in the Islamic world, involving the presentation of the ubiquitous *khil'a* and the transfer of horses as signs of honor, preference, and acceptance. Representatives conveying these gifts cemented personal relationships between a faraway merchant in India and Yemen's imam, even if by proxy. Thus travel and receiving audience were tightly coded into these intra-Muslim, yet still cross-cultural, commercial gift encounters, shifting the emphasis from goods to social interactions, ceremonies, and the conventions of visitation.

These gifts were conveyed in impressive caravans that travelled through Yemeni cities and would have provided a striking scene to those who witnessed their passage, thus underscoring the status of both the gift giver and recipient. Some of these gifts may have been wrapped or delivered in special containers that enhanced their presentation, while also inspiring curiosity and awe of the unknown contents within. As expressed in brief passages from the Dutch *dagregister,* the gift practices of the merchants from India in Yemen may have shared certain features with diplomatic practices. Because of this, it is tempting to conceive of these major overseas merchants as operating their commercial enterprises with relative independence and thus staking out relationships with sovereigns whose territories they traded in on their own terms. As such, their yearly visits to Yemen's imam functioned like embassies and their proxies like ambassadors.

Similar to the ceremonies described in chapter 1, some of the gift practices may appear generic and conventional. Yet I argue that these familiar bestowals had special inflections in the maritime trading world of Yemen. The imam and the governor of Mocha bestowed robes and horses on various merchants, but even when given together these two classes of objects were variable in terms of the ties they expressed and the relations they forged, sustained, or concluded. Horses were precious commodities and honorable gifts, but also cumbersome and costly to maintain, as European records show. The meaning of these gifts was circumscribed by the specific context of exchange in a world dominated by the cycles of the maritime trade and all of its contingencies.

Four

Everyday Objects and Tools of the Trade

In 1992 archaeologists began to bring the remnants and cargo of the *San Diego* up from the murky depths of the South China Sea.[1] Almost four hundred years earlier, this Spanish trading galleon was sunk outside of Manila during a battle with a Dutch ship, for which it had been quickly prepared. Although some of its cargo had been removed in this transformation, it still held around twelve hundred pristine pieces of Chinese porcelain when it went down. These were crated and packed for sale, perhaps in Mexico, where lustrous blue-and-whites sold well. In addition to the goods intended for the market, the excavators found the remains of many other items that were meant to sustain the crew and passengers during their long sea voyage: hundreds of large stoneware vessels that stored food and drink, candlesticks and lamps for lighting the dark cabins and holds below decks, various types of metal, glass, and ceramic tableware, and even remnants of a chess set that point to the need for recreation while travelling.

These types of items are usually characterized as those related to "life at sea" or "life on board" and feed modern fascination about the arduous experience of maritime travel before the age of steam. But they also hint at the extensive structural apparatus that undergirded the enterprise of premodern maritime trade. Eight hundred recovered stoneware storage jars, some with remains of their culinary contents, do not just speak to the need to feed four hundred people for a journey that could last seven months. They also point to the presence of an effective industry of provisioning on land to outfit the voyage to the Americas and other locations. And those storage containers, which were diverse in shape, size, form, and place of origin, require study, just like the more treasured porcelain pieces that were packed for sale and have inspired the interest of art historians, economic historians, and collectors.

The more mundane finds of the *San Diego* shipwreck and other sunken archaeological sites compel us to think about the objects that were carried on boats to sustain the wide-reaching endeavors of maritime merchants.[2] By doing so, we can displace the more common focus on cargo items intended for sale in far-off ports and direct our attention toward the supporting material culture of trade, travel, and foreign settlement. Merchants carried with them an assortment of imported items that they required for their daily life and commercial endeavors in Yemen but could not procure there. Characteristically, we know the most about the needs of Dutch and English traders, thanks to inventories of goods held at their establishments and requests for items to be sent there each year from Europe or other Indian Ocean ports that hosted large foreign communities. Like those excavated from the waters around the wrecked *San Diego,* these highly mobile products speak to the complexity of the maritime enterprise and its dependence on an array of material goods that were destined for endpoints other than the wholesale marketplace.

Inventories

Inventories that enumerate the holdings in the English factory at Mocha provide a starting point for understanding how this trading establishment was outfitted. During the period from 1716 until 1726,[3] the factory was inhabited around the year. But in 1726 the English pulled up their residence and did not reestablish it until 1729. After that time, they stopped overwintering at the port. Although their building, which was located along the shore near Bab al-ʿAmudi, remained in their possession continuously throughout this period, they would entrust it and their remaining goods to a broker or private merchant during the slow season (Figure 1.6). Many, but not all, of their effects would be retained in their factory until their return the following year.

In January 1722 they enumerated the contents of their establishment under the title "dead stock," a list that documents company possessions by room.[4] Eight pages in length, it comprises various types of goods needed to sustain the everyday activities of company employees. Not surprisingly, many items are related to their culinary habits, which were quite different from local ones and thus required a whole host of specific objects for meals and their preparation. Tableware was extensive, including dishes, plates, and bowls, some of porcelain, one large tankard, one mug, one cup with a cover, salvers, saltcellars, and various knives, forks, spoons, tablecloths, and napkins. Implements used for preparing food, such as pots and pans, are listed, in addition to mortars, pestles, and nutmeg graters. In terms of their stored food, they mention forty pieces of English beef, presumably cured, seven bottles of oil, two bottles of capers, canisters of candy sugar, and many bags of rice, described as coarse and fine. A few jars for storing water and ghee appear on the inventory. Alcoholic beverages were copious and diverse in type, including Batavia arrack, white and red wine from the Cape and Spain (specified as Mountain, Sack, and Galicia wine), palm wine (probably from India), beer, and brandy.

Lighting was clearly an issue, as represented by the many candlesticks, some of brass, a snuffer, countless boxes of wax candles, lamps, and lanterns. Tools included hatchets, chisels, saws, planes, pincers, a mallet, a hammer, and a shovel. Minor pieces of hardware were also enumerated, such as nails, hinges, bolts, locks of many types, and rope. Firearms are mentioned, including muskets, bayonets, blunderbusses, musketoons, and pistols, along with bullets and gunpowder. Six fusees and six pairs of pistols were specified for gifts, clearly differentiated from the other weapons for use of the company. There were also many objects related to the weighing and enumeration of goods, such as scale boards and weights in an array of denominations. One frasel of ruddle (red ocher) would have been used to mark bales of goods. Three flags were catalogued with these various tools and supplies.

The list indicates that this factory was extensively outfitted with upright furniture and some decorative items. The halls were equipped with four mirrors, a caned couch from Surat, twenty chairs, a basin and ewer of white copper, seven tables of various sizes covered with pieces of green cloth, glass lanterns and sconces, a weatherglass, a carpet, and a paper press. The other rooms contained an additional mirror, two more couches, twenty-three additional chairs, some described as new or old, two desks covered with green cloth, one cot, and various quilts, pillows, sheets, and pillowcases. The doctor's room held chairs and a cane couch in addition to a chest of medicine. Miscellaneous items, which were not sorted by type or room, included a parcel of stationery ware and a box of glasses. The inventory lists one horse (which was sent to Bombay later that year),[5] three donkeys, and a mule, in addition to saddles and bridles for them. They also kept two rosewater droppers with five flasks of rosewater to fill them.

This long and detailed roster of items of consequence held in the English factory in the year 1722 is similar to the one taken the following year, although the one recorded in 1740, when the establishment was inhabited only seasonally, was much shorter.[6] Dutch inventories were much more provisional than their English counterparts, despite the fact that the VOC had maintained its year-round establishment on a more consistent basis from 1709 until 1739.[7] But even in their brevity, VOC inventories list the same types of items. In an inventory taken in 1734, we see various vessels for food preparation, including many types of cauldrons, pots, and pans, with and without lids. Tableware and comestible items were not included, although surely present. Sconces, candlesticks, and lanterns were noted, as were diverse tools, such as handsaws, hammers, pliers, drills, and a grinding wheel, as well as some wooden beams. As with the English, a whole range of scales, balances, and weights was included. The furnishings of this establishment were much scanter than the English factory, with only three dining tables, one long writing desk, and six chairs.

The impression is that the English and the Dutch possessed a great number of items to accommodate many of their needs in Mocha. Some were essential to the basic functions of trade, such as scales and weights, others to look after their safety at this foreign port, including firearms of various types. Tools, hardware, and sailcloth were required to maintain and repair ships, which would take place while the vessels were docked at the port, but also to service the chests used to transport goods and to make minor repairs on their house and its furnishings. Many items made a stay in this land more comfortable and familiar, such as pieces of raised furniture and those related to conventional Western dining and drinking habits.

As historian Giorgio Riello has suggested, early modern inventories such as these provide a wealth of knowledge about the world of consumption, but they must be understood as "subjective representations," which omit some items while including others. They also present a misleading "notion of a stable society."[8] As such, one must keep in mind the purpose of the inventory when using it as a source. In the case of the East India companies, inventories were not just neutral documents of property enumerated. Rather they were created with the distinct purpose of verifying that all goods that were sent to Yemen had been duly received and were being used properly for the good of the company. As an illustration, the two lengthy EIC inventories from 1722 and 1723 directly postdated the visit of the supervisor Phipps to the port. While in Mocha, Phipps scrutinized the workings of the establishment and suggested various means for trimming unnecessary costs. His visit also prompted the implementation of more complete measures of documentation in Mocha, as indicated by the extremely ordered and tediously detailed stewards' registers from 1722 that mention each instance when limes, eggs, and chickens, for example, were purchased for the factory. An explanatory note that appears on the 1723 inventory provides further indication that EIC employees felt pressured to substantiate the presence or absence of company property during this period: "NB the appearing deficiency of the Stores here with the former Inventory is accounted for by the removal of part into other Godowns and allowing for Factory Expenses."[9] By 1740 this directive for comprehensive documentation appears to have been dismissed, or even forgotten, as demonstrated in the concise, one-page inventory that the EIC employees recorded that year.

Moreover, as presented in the format of the inventory, various goods at both the English and the Dutch establishments are neutralized in their meanings and functions. Arranged in a single and undifferentiated list, a donkey is rendered as roughly equivalent to a candlestick, for instance. More important, certain items that had social significance in the context of local ceremonial activities or systems of gift exchange, such as flags and horses, were seamlessly aligned with items that were absent from those displays and transactions, such as pots and hinges. Rosewater and the special droppers to dispense it signal the adoption of certain local habits, while the imported chairs and tables suggest the resilience of European customs abroad. Yet all of these items are aligned in the inventory without comment or differentiation. The task of this chapter is to tease out some of the social uses and meanings of these goods, with particular interest in those imports that were visibly present in company establishments or commonly requested as necessary supplies annually.

The impulse to look closely at these inventories is undergirded by a growing body of scholarship that explores the material culture of other Indian Ocean ports, such as Batavia and Cape Town. The work of historians Ross, Groenewald, Nigel Worden, and Antonia Malan, who also treat inventories and relevant material records but deal primarily with the Cape, has been pivotal in situating this discussion. However, the case of Yemen adds a needed dimension to this ongoing consideration of early modern Indian Ocean material culture because it was a relatively contingent and remote site for both the Dutch and the English. Unlike the long-established Indian Ocean bases of the VOC or EIC, which catered to the needs of diverse and relatively large European settler communities, Mocha was a much more transitory place of residence. As such, it provides a useful example of how European traders had to negotiate a foreign lifestyle far from the comforts of home, thus representing another key dimension of merchant mobility along the edge of the Indian Ocean in the eighteenth century.

Eisen (Requests)

The VOC *eisen* lists, mentioned in chapter 2 for their information about gifts, are also useful in this task, for they provide a sense of what the Dutch found to be of necessity on a yearly basis and indicate clearly what was brought to Mocha from elsewhere, an important characteristic that is not always apparent on inventory lists.[10] Of course, the request lists include only supplies that were exhaustible and had to be replenished on a yearly basis, in addition to more permanent items that may have required occasional renewal from constant use.

One request list from August 1735 was particularly lengthy and detailed. It enumerated the goods that remained in the Dutch warehouse from the past year's trade season, paired with those they were requesting from Batavia for the following year's market, mostly consisting of coarse piece goods from India, spices, and bulk metals.[11] They also listed a category of gifts, including the expected pots of candied cloves, nutmeg, and ginger and a piece of Dutch velvet. At this time, when the system of cash gifts dominated in Mocha, they did not require many goods for the following year's presents, although clearly they wanted to have some appropriate items on hand in case a sudden opportunity for a bestowal arose. Their request for two *kelders* (boxes fitted with compartments for individual bottles, usually of fifteen each) of Dutch spirits and eight of *jenever* were to be doled out to the port workers to facilitate the landing and loading of their goods as they did each year.[12]

The rest of the request list is divided into four categories: provisions, goods for use, stationery supplies, and medicine, all of which supported the everyday life and trading activities of VOC merchants. In addition to the two hundred pounds of wax candles that they requested, most of their provisions were related to their culinary needs, a category that was wholly omitted from their inventories. They asked for two half *leggers* (casks of around 614 liters) of coconut oil, a half *aam* (a barrel of 155 liters) of olive oil, and two *aamen* of Dutch vinegar. Alcohol appears prominently on this list, including two *leggers* of Batavia arrack (distilled alcohol made of rice and sugarcane), 230 bottles of French wine, and two casks of beer. As for the goods for use, they requested twenty-three pieces of flag cloth from the Coromandel Coast and many pieces of porcelain—forty dishes, one hundred plates, and twenty-five bowls—for their own tableware. Carpentry supplies were also requested, including 150 pounds of nails, fifty wood planks, and a new set of tools to replace those that had become worn-out. The list of stationery supplies is long enough to necessitate its own category. It is also quite specific, including eight reams (each of around twenty-two quires, or 550 pages) of paper,[13] in large, medium, and small formats, six book cartridges, three hundred quills, six penknives, a quarter pound of silk binding cord, four pounds of good sealing wax, four rulers, and twelve lead pencils and ruddle pens, along with their sleeves and additional lead and ruddle to fill them. The list ends with medicine, which was filed in a different brief that was not retained.

A VOC *eis* from 1712 is similar in content, albeit with fewer details, thus confirming the cyclical nature of these yearly requests.[14] There were, however, a few notable differences in content and quantity. In addition to those goods requested in 1735, they asked for a case of rosewater, some firearms, five hundred quills rather than three hundred, four pieces of guinea cloth to cover tables, twelve chairs, some lamp oil, and sixty pounds of ink. They also specified the need for Japanese gilded coffee cups of porcelain, but without exact numbers. Rather than listing individual provisions, as they had in 1735, they left it to those in Batavia to decide what to send.

In contrast to their detailed inventories from 1722 and 1723, the few English request lists that were retained from Yemen were hardly as standardized or lengthy as their Dutch counterparts. For example, in 1720 they sent a short "List of necessarys wanting for the use of the factory" to London. Like the VOC *eis* of 1735, it included medicine according to the doctor's enclosure, which is no longer attached. Alcohol was specified in twelve chests of wine and twelve of table beer. Various pieces of horse equipment were requested, including six saddles, bridles, housing, and holsters, during a time when horses were still kept in the factory.[15] In 1722 they requested six chests of red wine and six of white, ten puncheons of beer (one puncheon was between 70 and 120 gallons) of the same sort they had sent the year before, but also three tons of small beer, which was lower in alcohol content than the regular variety, two leaguers of Cape white wine and two of red, one chest of stationery ware, three large glass lanterns and three small ones, and five hundred wooden deal-boards.[16]

These request lists reveal certain particularities related to each company's system of provisioning. Batavia served as the VOC's home base in Asia, and all goods destined for other Indian Ocean outposts passed through that port, even if they were originally from Europe or the Cape. By contrast, EIC ships came to Mocha from London and Bombay, so both sites provided certain provisions for the trading establishment. But even with these differences, both sets of documents show similar categories of demand. The Dutch and the English imported tableware and certain condiments but purchased most of their perishable food locally. Alcohol was imported in large quantities and many varieties every year. Medicine required constant renewal, as well as the specialized knowledge of a surgeon or physician who would draft a list separate from other provisions. Stationery supplies, which did not appear prominently or in detail on the inventories, were requested continuously and in large quantities, suggesting that much writing was to be done in Mocha. Wooden planks were required to seal chests and cases of goods. While many of these items appear mundane, the following sections reveal that merchants used them in very specific ways, so they may not be relegated to an undifferentiated world of utilitarian functionality. Indeed these objects were wielded, consumed, and displayed in a manner that was localized to the commercial context of eighteenth-century Yemen and requires elucidation.

Food and Drink

Both the inventories and the yearly request lists were largely oriented around the preparation and consumption of food and drink, which entailed considerable quantities at these establishments that would each house around twenty people, including merchants, scribes, soldiers, and at least one surgeon.[17] Even so, as historian Joji Nozawa has stated in regard to the Dutch presence in Japan, "the VOC was above all a mercantile enterprise, and therefore the internal consumption of food has been treated as only of secondary importance. The consumption of alcoholic drinks has been equally considered peripheral, even though the provision of drink was essential for all meals."[18] The same can be said for the VOC and EIC in Yemen, which brings to light the need to look at the culinary aspects of these mobile merchant groups closely.

The lists examined above indicate that Dutch and English merchants in Mocha imported many durable objects to prepare, serve, and consume their food in their Arabian establishments. Whereas the caudle cup that the EIC merchants owned must have come from England, the ubiquitous copper cooking vessels of both the Dutch and the English could have been procured locally, perhaps imported originally from the Gulf. In fact, when the VOC closed their establishment in 1739, they chose to sell these well-used copper vessels locally for their weight in metal, suggesting that these items could be easily repurposed in Mocha.[19] The English caudle cup, probably with a handle on each side, was eventually traded in Yemen for a pair of candlesticks and snuffers, which suggests that there was demand for such an item locally, although it is unclear who purchased it.[20]

Comestible products, which were mentioned only selectively in these documents, were obtained from various sources. Perishable foods, such as chicken, fish, mutton, butter, eggs, milk, vegetables, and fruit, salt, vinegar, currants, and certain spices, in addition to fresh water and firewood, were purchased in Mocha's bazaar.[21] These are documented consistently as monthly expenses in the EIC steward's accounts from this time, but were quickly expendable and thus never included on inventory lists of either company. By contrast, the English carried other edibles, such as capers and cured beef, all the way from Europe. However, spices, sugar (packed in reed canisters), and rice were surely obtained from India or Southeast Asia, which provisioned these items for the local market as well. Similarly, many ingredients were imported. The Dutch requested vinegar, which was also used as a disinfectant, all the way from Europe.[22] Their olive oil came from Majorca via Batavia, whereas their considerable casks of coconut oil likely came from Batavia or Colombo.[23] The available records do not mention what menu items dom-

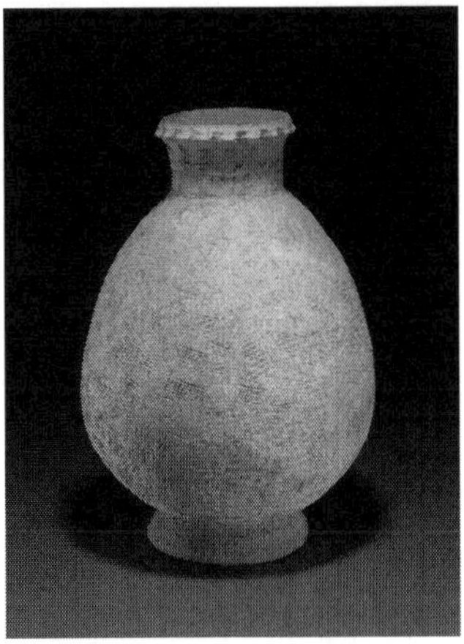

Figure 4.1. Water vessel, made in al-Mimdara, southern Yemen, twentieth century. Clay, H 51 cm.

inated at the company establishments in Yemen, but the cooks, who were local, surely relied upon available fresh ingredients to prepare food in the manner they were accustomed to for their patrons, many of whom had been exposed to cuisines different from their own. These dishes would have been served in tableware fitting European consumption rather than on large communal plates without cutlery in the local manner.

Fresh water was a precious commodity in Mocha because the city wells delivered only brackish supplies. Potable water had to be hauled from far out of the urban precinct or even shuttled to the port from the other side of the Red Sea. After purchase it was distributed into large water jars, probably of earthenware and purchased from the local market, like the modern example from the Aden area featured in figure 4.1.[24] This simple unglazed vessel would allow for some water to evaporate through its surface, thus cooling the liquid within.[25] But the most important beverages to the Dutch and English were alcoholic. Arrack, beer, spirits, *jenever,* brandy, and multiple types of wine appear prominently on inventory lists, request lists, and gift registers. Wine came from France, Spain, and the Cape and brandy from France. Beer was brewed in Amsterdam, Rotterdam, and Delft using methods that allowed it to last the length of the ocean journey and also withstand further distribution in the East.[26] Spirits, including *jenever,* came from Europe or Batavia, whereas arrack was distilled in Batavia and palm wine in India.[27] Alcohol provisioning in Yemen thus relied upon wide-reaching networks for the delivery of these various products from many different origins.

That a group of European men living in a remote port on the Arabian Peninsula would cherish strong drinks is not surprising. Residents of the

Mocha factory complained about the boredom that would set in, particularly during the slow months of the winter. There were few local entertainments or diversions at this port, aside from the "taverns" in the extramural Jewish quarter located to the south of the city, which was all but closed off after nightfall. These establishments were unique in offering alcohol. Yet, according to Niebuhr, Europeans generally did not find the wine served there, which was made in Sanaa, palatable.[28] Most of their alcohol was imported from overseas, and Mocha served as the gateway for this controversial commodity.

It is clear that imported alcohol served more than this small European community, however. As I mentioned, the Dutch merchants distributed alcohol to low-ranking port workers, namely the weighers at the tollhouse, porters, and peons, as part of their yearly gift system. In 1717 and 1719 they doled out bottles of arrack amounting to two *legger*s to these workers.[29] In the 1730s they switched type, dividing up anywhere between two and twelve *kelder*s (thirty to three hundred bottles) of *jenever* and between two and four *kelder*s of other spirits each year.[30] The Dutch distributed these bottles to individual workers on top of the payments made for services rendered in order to assure that their goods would be handled, transported, and loaded with extra care and added security as they prepared to depart the port.

Alcohol was tendered to higher-ranking officials in Mocha and Bayt al-Faqih as well. In 1706 Mocha's governor al-Huraybi suggested to the VOC merchant Ketelaar that he bring some spirits to the governor of Bayt al-Faqih as a gift, in addition to some spices (by the sack and pots of candied ones) and various textiles.[31] Amir Rizq, governor of Mocha from 1718 to 1721, was famous for his love of hard drinking. Before being appointed to the governorship, he had served as the port's *amir al-bahr*, a post he relinquished to become the *nakhudha* of Imam al-Mahdi Muhammad. In this role, he commanded the imam's ships across the Arabian Sea to Surat each autumn, which may have been where he cultivated a taste for alcohol.

In 1719 the Dutch merchant Abraham Pantzer wrote about Amir Rizq's habits extensively. He claimed that the governor "drank day and night with a gang of thugs" and that he needed a half bottle of *jenever* in the morning and another in the evening each day in addition to wine.[32] The Dutch proposed that the best way to maintain his friendship was by providing him with bottles, which the English also did. The Dutch went so far as to convey his particular tastes to Batavia, specifying that he preferred red and white wine, as well as brandy, but could make do with arrack if nothing else was available. These extreme comments seem exaggerated, but they point to the central role alcohol played as a medium of exchange in an informal economy of favors in this commercial port, a system that European shipments fundamentally sustained. For instance, on January 12, 1720, as they awaited the arrival of their ships, the Dutch merchants recorded, "The governor here [Amir Rizq] is very sick because of a lack of alcohol. He longs for the company's ship from overseas because he heard that it has wine and *jenever*, which will be like medicine for him."[33] As Nozawa has noted for Japan, where the Dutch were also instrumental in inspiring a local taste for foreign drinks, imported alcohol could be both a provision and a gift in Asian ports.[34] A similar economy of distribution seems to have been at work on the coastal edges of the Islamic world as well, although their frequent liquid distributions to Amir Rizq constituted a use of provisions that was not recorded on the gift registers.

While describing Amir Rizq's drinking habits, Pantzer stated that alcohol was sold quite openly in Mocha, as opposed to other Arabian Peninsula cities where its public sale and overt consumption would have been unwelcome.[35] Niebuhr confirmed that some people he met in Yemen were fond of hard drinks, specifically "in the cities along the Arabian fringe, because there are often many Jews and Christians."[36] But at the same time, he notes the risks of these habits when describing a merchant in al-Luhayya, a port to the north of Mocha, who possessed the tools to produce spirits but did so covertly for fear that others would find out. In Mocha, where many and more diverse foreigners resided, the social codes were clearly looser, although an English visitor in 1737 stated that locals could be fined 500 dollars if caught drinking.[37]

Even so, Europeans were the major purveyors of alcohol not just for trade officials and workers but also for other port dwellers who were accustomed to alcohol consumption. Niebuhr claims that some English merchants brought arrack to be sold in Mocha as a commodity.[38] One wonders if these EIC merchants actually filched supplies from the company stores and sold them privately for their individual profit. In fact, in 1722, after calculating their "extraordinary" consumption based on extant supplies and newly shipped provisions, Phipps in Bombay accused EIC employees in Mocha of "tippling."[39] Although Phipps' perceptions are in line with his generally conservative stance on factory expenditures, in this case these merchants may have sold some of the copious company stock meant for internal consumption rather than drinking it all in house.

These liquid supplies were exhausted each year either through consumption or distribution. Yet they must have left some lasting material remains in Mocha even after all of the imported casks and bottles had been drained. Referring to an iconic ceramic soy sauce bottle from Holland, historian Anne Gerritsen suggests that it is fruitful to reunite empty vessels with their former contents when looking at global material culture.[40] Similarly, in

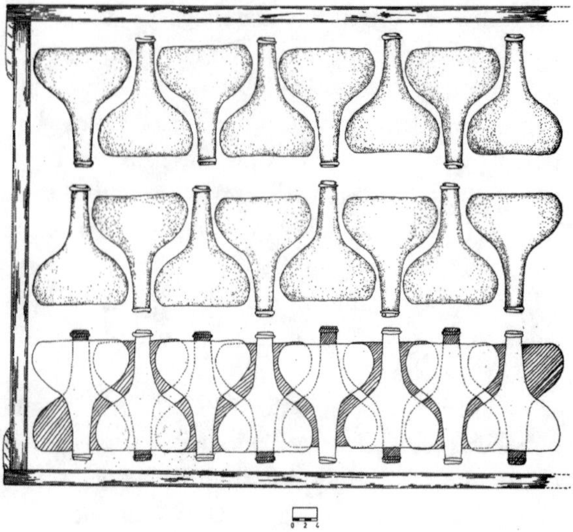

Figure 4.2. Diagram of the packing of wine bottles based on finds from the *Amsterdam* shipwreck. Courtesy of Stichting VOC-schip *Amsterdam*, drawing H. Maxwell Stuart.

his compelling study of Madeira wine, from vine to the early modern American table, David Hancock implores us to think about the intricacies of storing, packing, transporting, and consuming wine across and around the Atlantic sphere.[41] In this case as well, it is worth considering how these various beverages would have been packaged, disseminated, and consumed.

According to Niebuhr, Jewish vintners in Yemen usually stored their locally made wine in stoneware jugs, but then transported it around the region in large copper vessels.[42] By contrast, the Dutch used wooden barrels or glass bottles to house and ship wine, spirits, and beer. As an example, green glass bottles filled with French wine were packed in straw and placed in wooden crates to avoid breakage during transit. As reconstructed from the *Amsterdam* shipwreck of 1749, the largest crates could carry 252 wine bottles (around 221 liters total), laid horizontally and stacked efficiently to maximize the space (Figure 4.2).[43] When, in 1735, VOC merchants requested 230 bottles of French wine for Mocha (with a special request that individual bottles be sent rather than large casks), they were probably referring to a box of that size. Spirits would have arrived in durable *kelder*s, wooden boxes that were segmented to prevent damage, although our narrators give us almost no clues about the details of these packing conditions.[44] Even so, it is clear that thousands of bottles and hundreds of boxes and barrels were shipped to Yemen in the period under consideration.

Once these beverages reached Mocha, most were decanted into other vessels for table presentation, especially if they had arrived in barrels or casks.

We have few details about these decanters and pieces of tableware, but the Asian ceramics industry produced specialized containers to serve different types of alcohol. Japanese-made porcelain bottles with bulbous bodies and thin necks carry the initials FW, which scholars have suggested stands for *franse wijn* or French wine (Plate 9).[45] Although we cannot say that such vessels ever made it to the port of Mocha, the Japanese bottle marked FW hints at the wide geographic scope of the industry that provisioned bulk drinks for the Dutch overseas trading empire and its many beneficiaries. Strangely, the EIC and VOC inventories from Mocha are devoid of large quantities of specialized glasses to drink wine or beer, leading us to wonder if the oft-mentioned porcelain coffee cups were used for other beverages as well.[46] It is certain that the three drinking vessels mentioned in the EIC inventory of 1722 (a tankard, a mug, and a cup) would have been insufficient to support the beverage consumption of the whole establishment. One presumes that remnants of these practices of packaging, distribution, and consumption would come to light more clearly if the port of Mocha, particularly the sites of the Dutch and English trading establishments, were excavated.

Conventional logic may dictate that alcohol would be shunned as a reprehensible foreign habit in eighteenth-century Yemen. Yet, as Matthee has shown, alcohol was a considerably more ambiguous substance than prevailing Islamic prohibitions suggest.[47] Particularly in the early modern period, several private and covert spheres of alcohol consumption could be found throughout the Islamic world, such as the halls of the Safavid palace and the less savory venue of the Ottoman tavern. Matthee also highlights ports as places where such consumption took root naturally because of the presence of many itinerant non-Muslims and foreigners, who were both suppliers and consumers of alcoholic drinks. In Mocha some local residents, particularly those who were associated with overseas trade functions or had travelled to other ports, were apparently quite accustomed to strong beverages. And the European companies, with their large stores of imported wine, beer, arrack, and spirits, were common purveyors of these products for locals who had developed a taste for them.

In Mocha, Dutch and English merchants doled out rosewater in decorative droppers and served coffee in gilded porcelain cups to entertain local merchants inside their homes in the manner that dominated locally. They periodically requested the replenishment of rosewater from India or new coffee cups from Japan via Batavia, which suggests that they saw these imported items as necessary for their social engagement at the port. But some locals heartily consumed various types of alcohol and gladly received bottles of wine and spirits as official or informal gifts. These habits of consumption suggest that in the undeniable contact zone of Mocha, these practices were not sharply circumscribed along cultural or religious lines, as one might expect. While Europeans abroad consumed alcohol on a daily basis, the practice did not simply represent "Dutchness at the table," as Lodewijk Wagenaar has declared.[48] The companies sent most of these beverages as provisions, but after arrival these goods could be sold as commodities or distributed as informal gifts, even if such practices were not in accordance with the companies' strict rules regarding accounting and the use of supplies. Thus alcohol operated on several registers of exchange and circulated in various unexpected spheres of consumption among Mocha's diverse overseas merchant class.

Medical Services and Supplies

Sickness was quite familiar to the foreign merchant, and fatalities were all too common at the port of Mocha. As reported by the Dutch in their *dagregister*, on November 2, 1719, the junior merchant Pieter Zegens was so sick that he was sent to the English doctor, who claimed he had an "ordinary Mocha fever," which could be cured with a dose of "cina cina" powder. This treatment seemed to alleviate his condition slightly by evening, but the next day he was incomprehensible, and in the following days his fever worsened. On November 13 he died.[49] Zegens was one of many merchants to be buried in the European cemetery located to the north of Mocha during the eighteenth century, although such a dedicated burial ground was quite unique to the port; other Yemeni cities offered no possibilities for a Christian burial.[50]

The companies tried to prevent the attrition of their staff abroad by posting doctors or surgeons on each boat sent overseas and usually one as a resident in each overseas trading outpost. As historian Iris Bruijn has shown in her detailed study of the ships' surgeons of the VOC, most of these men were not university-trained physicians but rather surgeons or barber-surgeons, who gained their expertise from a combination of study and empirical training, some of which took place on board ships and in foreign ports. Unlike physicians, these surgeons focused on external procedures, such as bloodletting and setting bones, although the gap between these two fields of medical practice and knowledge was closing precisely during this time.[51] The larger European settlements, such as the Dutch one in Batavia, had an established hospital with a considerable staff, which Bruijn has credited for playing a leading role in shaping early modern medical administration in Europe as well as Asia. Yet in Mocha, the medical team was generally limited to a single provider per nation. During the years when the Dutch or

English establishment lacked a resident doctor, the surgeon from their ship at port would disembark to care for patients on shore, thus bridging the realms of water and land.[52]

These surgeons were expected to provide care primarily for their own company employees.[53] But in Yemen, their actual purview extended outside of the company limits, as demonstrated by the case of Zegens, who visited the EIC medic because the VOC surgeon had fallen ill.[54] Of course, Europeans posted at Mocha could visit local healers if their surgeon was unavailable, although they rarely did so, unlike the Portuguese and English who had freely adopted local methods of medical care upon arriving in India and avidly studied long-established Asian treatments for tropical diseases, assimilating many of them for their own use.[55] By contrast, in Yemen native medical techniques received little acclaim. Niebuhr explains that medical work was hardly a respectable profession on the southern Arabian Peninsula. Various practitioners, including chemists, veterinarians, and herbalists, worked as healers, but many had a hard time earning a living.[56]

According to Bruijn, both early modern and modern historians have unjustly tainted the image of the VOC surgeon, often disparaging his expertise and capabilities.[57] Yet in Yemen, locals avidly sought Western surgeons and physicians, including those associated with the VOC, for medical treatment without questions or concerns about their qualifications.[58] During Niebuhr's stay in Mocha, which started off under an air of suspicion, he and his cohorts gained the governor's favor only after their doctor had treated his foot injury.[59] And, as mentioned, two European ships' surgeons, Otto Mueller of the VOC *Oostersteijn* in 1706 and the French doctor Barbier of *Le Diligent* in 1712, travelled to al-Mawahib to treat Imam al-Mahdi, who was particularly prone to illness.[60] The delivery of medical care to such important local patients was a delicate exchange. In 1706 the VOC merchants deliberated over the decision to send Mueller to the court. Only after the governor had visited them three times with the same request did they finally comply. They wrote, "We could no longer excuse ourselves from the imam's request, fearing that if we did not agree now we would come into his disfavor and there would be some harm against us. It was weighed and in the end we agreed."[61]

In 1712 they were faced with the same quandary when the imam again requested the help of the VOC surgeon, then Jan Abraham Zimmerman. This time they declined. In a letter to Batavia, they acknowledged the possible benefits that such a visit could yield, but worried about their own patients in Mocha who required Zimmerman's treatment. They also feared the liabilities associated with caring for this aged patient, whom they described as recklessly taking hundreds of types of medicines given by "various doctors from various nations."[62] Ultimately, the Dutch worried that the imam, who was in his eighties at the time, would die in the care of a European doctor, which could cause problems for all of the European merchants residing in Yemen. Their ruminations provide a clear sense that involvement with the imam's medical care could be useful to merchants but was also a risky endeavor given his fragile state and history of medical care.[63]

After they declined, Mocha's governor directed the same request to the French, who agreed, seeing the opportunity to deliver medical treatment to Yemen's imam in a more positive light, as a way "to make known the *French* Nation to the King of *Yaman*, and to become better acquainted, than any yet had been, with the Country under his Subjection, in Order to draw from thence all the Advantage possible for their Commerce."[64] Apparently these objectives were met successfully. When Barbier, the surgeon of *Le Diligent,* returned to the port with the news of the imam's full recovery, Mocha's governor came to the aid of the French merchants who were completing their coffee transactions for the year. He helped them to dispatch their coffee quickly and without hindrance and also intervened to remove a new tax on coffee that had just been levied at Bayt al-Faqih.[65] The French attributed this assistance directly to the success of their medical mission in the capital. Ten years later, in 1722, the French sent another doctor to the imam, then al-Mutawakkil Qasim. After doing so they were granted six hundred bales of duty-free coffee annually, according to the English at Mocha.[66] However, we should be wary of confirming an exclusive correlation between this privilege and the doctor's visit because both the English and the Dutch received the same concession without offering medical treatment in exchange. Even so, these French and English observations demonstrate the perception that medical favors led to certain tangible trade privileges in Yemen at this time. It is also important to underline that the Qasimi imam's reverence for outside medical knowledge was not limited to European expertise. According to the Dutch, during the 1701 Safavid visit to al-Mahdi's court, a Persian doctor had successfully treated the imam, who was suffering from a case of hemorrhoids.[67]

The inventories and request lists from Mocha also underline the fact that foreign medical care was deeply dependent on a number of essential material items. In the 1780s the artist Jan Brandes depicted a unique view into the barber-surgeon's quarters on board the Dutch East Indiaman the *Stavenisse* (Plate 10). This image provides some clues about the material aspects of this mobile trade, representing a spacious private cabin that held some of the medic's tools, such as the surgeon's manual and the ship's medical log on the small bookshelf in the corner.[68] A barber's plate, with a concave recess on one side, hangs from the wall. Although it is closed, we can

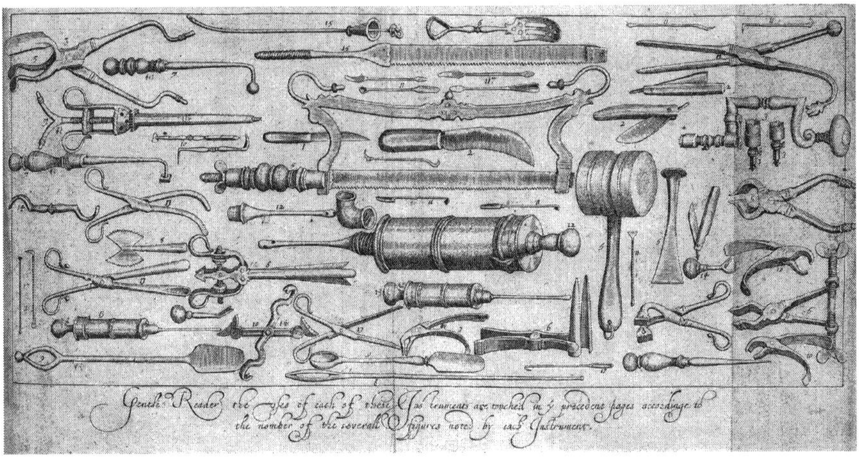

Figure 4.3. Surgical instruments, published in John Woodall, *The Surgeon's Mate* (London: R. Young, 1639). Courtesy of the Wellcome Library, London.

surmise that the flat sealed case resting above the desk held his surgical instruments, probably including the types of tools pictured in John Woodall's seventeenth-century book *The Surgeon's Mate* (Figure 4.3). Woodall, the first surgeon-general to the EIC, standardized a portable kit with the essential supplies for sea travel and foreign residence, such as scissors for cutting bandages, saws for amputation, spatulas for dosing medicine, a scale, knives, clamps, syringes, and hoses.

Medicine and other pharmaceuticals, however, were not depicted in Brandes' image, for they were likely hidden away in one of the storage cabinets in another part of the ship.[69] Unlike surgeon's instruments, these valuable supplies were exhaustible and usually quite closely guarded. They also had to be replenished for each overseas trading establishment on a yearly basis. The company covered the costs and the responsibility of maintaining these stores, which were enumerated in the request lists drafted by surgeons from Mocha. In the case of the VOC, these items were sent from the medical repository at Batavia, the centralized dispensary for the Dutch overseas empire, although some may have been supplied originally from the home apothecary.[70] Of course, certain items, such as clove oil, rosewater, cinnamon water, tamarind, and Chinese licorice, were readily available in Batavia and other Asian ports.[71] Indeed as A. M. G. Rutten has shown, many key pharmaceutical products and ingredients overlapped with the spices and dyestuffs that were the main fodder of the Indian Ocean and Atlantic trades.[72] Only a few needed items were locally available in Yemen, such as aloe. In February 1706 the VOC surgeon Mueller was given permission to seek out herbs and medicine in Mocha's bazaar, but this was an isolated event.[73] Although none of the attached documents that list the medical supplies requested by the VOC in Mocha survives, one freestanding request list from the EIC surgeon remains. It is dated August 5, 1722, and was recorded by John Mackenzie. It lists turpentine and juniper oil, sambucus flowers, absinthe, *saccharum saturni*, and vitriol, among other items. The urgency of these needs is noted at the bottom of his request list, in Mackenzie's interjection: "The above are absolutely Necessary here."[74]

Some of these stores of medicine could be doled out as informal gifts in Yemen, where foreign medical care, knowledge, and products were sought out avidly. For instance, we know that the Dutch can be counted as contributors to Imam al-Mahdi's reportedly large stockpile of drugs, as they had delivered medicine to him at least once in 1709.[75] And of course, in the medical visits to the imam that I have described, the Dutch and French surgeons took supplies, along with their expertise. In this way, foreign medicine could be bestowed as another effective yet unofficial gift, in this case to gain the imam's favor, along with or independent of medical treatment. In 1737, the EIC medic William Fergusson complained that Mocha's *amir al-bahr* had not compensated him for his services and the costly medicines that were expended, which suggests that certain local officials believed that these services could be accepted without remuneration.[76] As with the wine and spirits given to Mocha's governor Amir Rizq, these substances were generally funneled from the company supplies to this purpose.

And like the wine and spirits I described, the ointments, salves, oils, tinctures, and pastes that were shipped to Mocha came over in various containers.[77] Some items were wrapped simply in paper, but various pots and jars of different sizes and materials, often of plain white porcelain and made in Japan, were used as vessels, although they were never mentioned or described specifically.[78] The transitory scope of these wares is vividly demonstrated by the remains of the 1697 *Oosterland* shipwreck off the Cape coast. This westbound VOC ship, which had stopped in the Gulf before rounding the Cape, carried at least eight *albarello*s (drug pots) in undecorated porcelain. These jars did not come with covers but were closed with pieces of paper or parchment tied under the lip of the rim. There were also square medicine flasks and bottles, also of undecorated porcelain, that would have been closed with small stoppers. Some of these vessels were encrusted with the residue of their past medicinal contents, thus confirming their use.[79] Undoubtedly, these types of receptacles would have been used on land as well as at sea.

The specimens from the *Oosterland* suggest that many types of containers in various sizes were needed on board ships and at VOC trading outposts every year, although our registers mention only their more precious contents. These relatively plain and undecorated Japanese wares stand in sharp contrast to the gilded porcelain coffee cups from Japan and China, which were sometimes given as gifts in Yemen or used for drinking coffee.[80] Together they demonstrate the multifaceted role the Asian ceramics industry played for the VOC. Not only did it furnish considerable commodities for sale in Europe and within Asia, but it also supported the gift economy and the functional infrastructure of the Dutch overseas medical system.

So European medical care in Yemen, with all of its imported instruments and medicines that required yearly renewal, did not serve just European patients. Medical services and products were greatly sought after by prominent locals as well, particularly Yemen's imams. Dutch, English, and French merchants and a Persian doctor used medical care and imported pharmaceuticals as informal gifts to gain favor from the imam, as well as Mocha's officials, which could also support their commercial endeavors.

Scales and Weights

Food, drink, and medicine were items of daily consumption and necessity for residents in a foreign port. The scales, scale boards, and weights made of different materials and of varying sizes were needed to conduct the core commercial activity of the company. For that reason, they were always present in the European factories and usually described in detail. From 1722 to 1740 the EIC establishment relied primarily on a brass tray scale set with various iron and lead weights of different sizes, while the VOC used a few different scales; one was designated for products up to four hundred pounds, and another tallied a maximum of one thousand pounds. Individual metal stool weights, with looped handles at the top, were numerous, ranging from an eighth of a pound to fifty pounds. They also had a scale with copper plates to weigh money, which may have been similar in its components to the set featured in figure 4.4. Bundled together in a box for easy transport and storage, this assemblage contains the yoke and pivot of the scale, along with balance pans and weights for various denominations. A steel weight that equaled the mass of 128 Spanish reals was also available to measure large quantities of silver.

These scales and weights were used on a daily basis for incoming and outgoing goods, as we can see from the *dagregisters* and account books. The money weights, particularly for the Spanish real of eight, were essential during a time when coins were never of a standard weight, thus requiring that their value be confirmed for each transaction. While these scales appear consistently on factory inventories of the EIC and VOC, they never show up on the available yearly request lists. This suggests that these durable

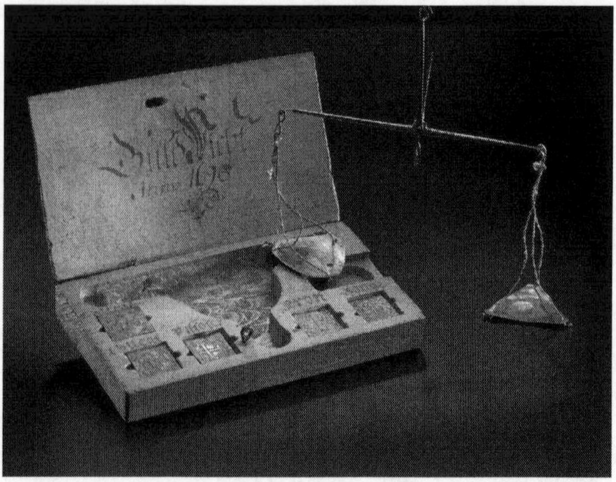

Figure 4.4. Boxed set of gold weights and scale, Dutch Republic/Northern Rhineland, 1696. Wood, brass, iron wire, marbleized paper, 11.2 × 6.4 × 1.9 cm. Courtesy of the American Numismatic Society.

products rarely needed replacement and were likely brought to the factory upon its initial establishment.[81] Although it was not stated specifically, these scales and their accessories were probably imported from Europe, as with the example featured in figure 4.4 and those that were excavated from the remains of the mid-eighteenth-century *Amsterdam* shipwreck and had been destined for Asian use.

Not surprisingly, each group desired control over its own scales and measures.[82] But in order to conduct trade locally, all merchants had to be proficient in the system of weights in use in Yemen's main markets, which was quite complicated judging from the many accounts and reports that attempt to gloss and convert them.[83] The most common local measure for coffee was the *bahar*, which was calculated differently in the two main cities where the Europeans did business. In Mocha, the bahar weighed 405 pounds and in Bayt al-Faqih 735, a divergence that led to a certain amount of confusion in accounting. Outside of these concerns, which were oriented mainly around conversion, European merchants disparaged the local scales as wholly inadequate. They were concerned primarily with the two scales in the customs house at Mocha and at the coffee market of Bayt al-Faqih. French observers described the latter as "great Scales, and for Weights huge Stones wrap'd up in Cloth."[84] These devices generated readings that were used to determine annual duties and fees in Yemen. As such, their accuracy was of primary concern, causing the supervisor Phipps to write with frustration to directors in Bombay about the one in Mocha: "Y^{r} Hon^{rs} may please to observe by the account of Weights, Measures &c.^{a} sent you of this Place how very incorrect these People are therein, that 'tis impossible to frame a just Calculate of them, the Weights of this Place for Merchandize made use of in the Custom house, and no other permitted are nothing else than Stones sewed up in Gunny, which every day weighs not alike. . . . The Uncertainty of their Weights gives for great Abuses."[85] These comments are not surprising from the exacting Phipps, yet the sentiment that the local system of weights was primitive, fickle, and imprecise must be looked at closely, particularly in the context of English concerns at this time. As Witold Kula has argued, historical systems of weights and measures, even standardized ones, were never simple scientific tools and schemes; "what is additionally necessary is an understanding of their varied, but hidden, social content."[86]

Phipps' intense scrutiny of the local system of weights and measures stemmed from events involving the EIC chief Edward Say. In 1720 an officer named Mark Anthony Crommelin was sent to Mocha in order to remove Chief John Hill from his post and to have him answer to charges of malfeasance from Bombay. Soon after doing so, Crommelin died unexpectedly, thus leaving the post of chief to Say, who was already present at the port. The next year Phipps stopped by Mocha on his way to Bombay in order to continue Crommelin's unfinished inquiry. He was particularly concerned with the fact that Say had not sent Hill to Bombay, as was required. He also alleged that Say had helped an Ostend captain with his coffee purchases to the detriment of his own company's overall yield during the previous year.[87] Throughout the trade season, Phipps interrogated company employees, including Say. He also inquired about the local system of weights and investigated the scales carefully, leading him to believe that the seemingly primitive and ineffective system of stones tied up in sacks may have resulted in company losses, as characterized in his quote.

Eventually, Phipps found that he could not blame the unpredictable local scales for the inconsistencies in the weight of coffee bales that were sent on English ships. Rather Say had been overseeing a system of embezzlement that began at Bayt al-Faqih. There small amounts of coffee beans were removed from each of the company bales after they were officially weighed. These amounts were then sold at the chief's profit, a scheme that was aided by the EIC writer Thomas Harnett.[88] However, the remaining beans in the coffee bales were arbitrarily redistributed so that each one would tally at a different weight and the overall amount they had skimmed off would be harder to detect. Once Phipps found out about this, he carted Say off to Bombay to answer to these charges. As geographer Miles Ogborn describes for the first English mission to the east, "The most elaborate regulations . . . were designed to protect the Company from its own crews," which suggests that fear of internal misconduct was equal to the suspicion of local wrongdoing in Indian Ocean ports.[89]

Even after this incident was resolved, questions about the coffee volume purchased at Bayt al-Faqih and the ability to assure that the scales' readouts were correct and consistent continued to be a concern for both the EIC and the VOC. Phipps' obsession with the inaccuracy of local scales inspired later EIC employees to generate a number of reports about them.[90] But reasons other than faulty scales needed to be taken into account as well. Newly harvested coffee had to be dried before it was packed for shipment, but even after packing, the weight of any bale of coffee was bound to decrease slightly as the beans continued to dry naturally. Moreover each bale of coffee that was purchased changed hands many times. Both the Dutch and the English alleged that the camel drivers from Bayt al-Faqih would take small amounts from the bales for their own profit as they brought the loads overland to Mocha or al-Hudayda, an accusation that was also directed at the boatmen of the ports, who shipped the bales on small lighter boats that connected the jetty to the ships in the harbor.[91]

So one must view the imported metal scale hardware, scale plates, and weights as items of grave importance within this atmosphere of suspicion in the EIC trading establishment, but also to a lesser extent among the Dutch. And their material significance may be correlated to a commercial world in which officials scrutinized the weight of each consignment of coffee that arrived at its destination and endeavored to figure out why it did not equal its official stated volume. But these imported weights and scales were not simple correctives to the seemingly inefficient sacks of stones used in Mocha and Bayt al-Faqih that Phipps ridiculed. The discourse around local weights was clearly more complex and situated within a competitive atmosphere of trade, where multiple agents were trying to make a profit off these large bales destined eventually for the markets of London and Amsterdam. Ultimately, the standardized imported scales and weights could not solve problems that were endemic to the functioning of the company and its local investments, such as the possible malfeasance of those it employed, European and local.

Writing Utensils

The VOC *eisen* indicate that copious and specific writing supplies were needed to keep records for its company outpost in Mocha, as was the case in Dutch establishments throughout their extensive maritime empire. For instance, Dutch merchants asked for between three hundred and five hundred quills for Mocha each year, suggesting that a large amount of written output was expected from this establishment annually.[92] Although they are less detailed, the EIC records also account for the steady usage of their stationery supplies in their expense accounts.[93] Almost all of these items were brought from abroad and mostly from Europe.[94] For instance, quills were not available for sale in Yemen, where reed pens were used primarily. Other products, such as ink, could be purchased in Mocha but were still imported frequently and in large quantities. Although also available locally, paper for company use was sent from Europe via Indian Ocean channels.[95]

In addition to these yearly requests for stationery supplies, the voluminous extant records that company employees left are "a testament to the power of writing in its operation."[96] These records constitute the historical backbone of the present study but must also be considered as the material products of this scribally oriented commercial culture. Recent scholars of trade have devoted considerable attention to merchants' letters, looking not only at what they reveal about commerce but, as with the work of Goldberg, the "culture of writing." Goldberg, Aslanian, and Trivellato look closely at modes of address, inquiries into a correspondent's health and well-being, and how letters were folded and addressed.[97] My discussion also owes much to Sood, who has inspired early modern historians to think about the many collaborative steps that writing a single letter entailed, with a concern for the material dimensions of this process.[98]

As the most complete example, the VOC's Mocha outpost kept a number of different types of records. The *dagregister* was a continuous log that was added to on a daily basis, with price updates, observations about the weather, accounts of political upheavals in Yemen, and everyday events that took place in the city. Each decision that was made in the establishment was documented with a *resolutie* (proceeding), which identified the date, circumstances, and conclusion taken. A *resolutie* marked the settlement of a trade agreement with details on weights, prices, and expected dates for delivery and payment, but this format was also used to treat internal company matters, such as how the possessions of a sailor who died at port would be distributed or sold. Account books recorded transactions made and the overall losses and profits to the company. Lengthy letters were sent to Batavia at the end of each trade season, as well as to outposts in associated ports, such as Surat, Colombo, and Bandar 'Abbas. The material that was received in Batavia was then copied for the *kamers* (VOC chambers) back at home. Some of these copies are held in the National Archives in The Hague. Even with the loss of many of these records, the sheer volume of what remains hints at the wide scope of the scribal project of Dutch trade in Yemen.

The prevalence of these writing tools in company establishments and the remains of so many documents that were produced using them (or copied from originals that were) demonstrate that writing and commerce were intimately linked activities for the Dutch, a point that Ogborn has made eloquently for the EIC. He showed that the "Company's world was one made on paper as well as on land and sea" because overseas trade was enabled by the transfer of written documents, such as official letters and treaties, and by recording transactions and negotiations that took place in the abstract space of the marketplace.[99] In Mocha, where many items were bought or sold on credit and much of the city's financial activity took place with bills of exchange that were cashed in faraway ports, the textual character of trade was particularly palpable.

VOC merchants in Yemen continually demonstrated the power and resilience of this culture of commercial documentation. For instance, on December 24, 1730, the Dutch merchants in Bayt al-Faqih, fearing a raid, sent their books to Mocha, which indicates that they saw these registers as inherently valuable, even as they risked their own safety by staying in that city.[100] In 1738 Willem van den Bergh, the last Dutch chief in Mocha, decided to shut down the factory provisionally, with the recommendation that the Dutch return the next year with force to retrieve unpaid local debts, clearly inspired by the French attack on the port of the previous year.[101] While he prepared to make this bold but unapproved move, even renting two ships from Indian merchants, including the Ali Raja, to transport the staff and cargo out of Yemen, he documented all of his plans in detailed letters that were sent to Batavia, Cochin, and Bandar 'Abbas. He even kept the *dagregister* for the factory up until the day he departed, then locked it up in the deserted house. Although he was unsure of how Dutch affairs in Mocha would progress, in van den Bergh's worldview the daily logbook was a necessary holding of the factory, even if its doors were shuttered and his supervisors never read the book.[102] After he arrived in Surat, he engaged in "curious conduct," according to historian Ashin Das Gupta, ignoring VOC orders to return to Batavia to account for his decisions. After a short (and unauthorized) trip back to Mocha, he returned to Surat and eventually took refuge with various Dutch competitors, the English, French, and Portuguese and was thus deemed a fugitive.[103] Even amid these erratic actions, van den Bergh's conduct reflects the deeply engrained logic of scribal work, which this company servant had a hard time abandoning even as he readily diverged from other codes of expected behavior mandated by the VOC.

Characteristically, these official VOC records and correspondence from Mocha followed strict rules in format and thus appear as generic documents that were meant to normalize company activities across the vast and unruly spectrum in which the Dutch operated.[104] *Dagregister* entries were recorded by the date, but even if the day was uneventful, a note had to be made: "Nothing happened today." Letters were written to the directors in Batavia replete with honorific terms of address and the writer referring to himself consistently as "the undersigned." Marginal notes periodically summarized the content of these missives, and earlier letters were often excerpted, indicating the problems of adjudicating commercial matters across both space and time. All of the documents and letters were formatted for the stationery products that were provided for them from Batavia, thus adding to their uniform character.

The survival of so many of these European documents from Yemen should not suggest their local dominance, for this was not a case of Westerners introducing commercial writing practices to an unlettered region.[105] Mainly relying on letters, Aslanian and Sood have shown that various Indian Ocean trading groups employed robust scribal practices that are worthy of close study.[106] Along these lines, the port of Mocha hosted diverse and long-standing commercial writing customs that predated but also coexisted with these European customs. For instance, a series of scribes (*katib*s) kept the official records of the port in Arabic. They took stock of the goods that each merchant brought to shore and registered them in their books, documenting how much they were worth and where they came from. All of this data was essential to the proper collection of taxes and duties upon the merchant's departure. In one case, the imam called for the scribes to come to the court and rectify Mocha's accounts in his presence, which indicates that these port ledgers could be subject to official scrutiny.[107] It also suggests that the role of the port *katib* entailed great accountability and thus went beyond the simple task of transcription.[108]

Other foreign merchants at the port kept their own commercial records for private use and also engaged in commercial correspondence with their compatriots. For instance, the Baniyans maintained records of their own trade activity, as well as that of the wholesalers for whom they worked. They were active in corresponding with other Baniyans around the Arabian Sea and in Yemen to convey essential commercial information and political updates that would affect the status of the trade. These letters were quite useful, especially to the Dutch, who often heard about events in the faraway Yemeni highlands through "Baniyan letters." Because they were written in Gujarati, these missives could include confidential or sensitive information that would not be divulged even if opened by an unintended recipient. And for this reason, these letters had to be mediated and translated through a Baniyan recipient. The various *nakhudha*s from Asia must have had their own record-keeping systems in languages such as Persian, Gujarati, Marathi, or Malayalam, but unfortunately we know almost nothing about them.

All of these commercial documents were essentially internal, meant for the eyes of a cohort, partner, or supervisor who could read the language of the writer. But foreign merchants also sent many letters to the imam of Yemen or his *wazir*s in the highlands. In these cases of early modern cross-cultural communication, the process, which Sood has pieced together from fragmentary indications rather than any thorough or stated directives for it, involved many intermediaries.[109] In the case of VOC letters penned from Mocha to the imam, the original was written first in Dutch and then translated, perhaps by the company's Baniyan broker, who would have possessed appropriate language skills. The English, however, often relied upon the services of a local translator named 'Abd Allah Ramadan.[110] Each company had at least one European employee whose language proficiency surpassed the others, such as the VOC's Joan Josua Ketelaar, who excelled in Urdu and Persian, and the French merchant D. Courbesatre, who spoke Arabic well. These internal linguists would also consult on the correct translation of company missives.[111] After being translated (either by dictation or on paper), an Arab scribe would then compose the letter, as Sood has suggested, adapting it to local conventions of address and style.[112] A number of freelance scribes in Mocha could fulfill such a role, which was distinct from the official charge of the customs house scribes. Yet this job could be particularly sensitive, as with the independent scribe 'Abd Allah Hajjaj, whom Mocha's governor Khazindar banished from the port in 1731.[113] The Dutch believed his crime was writing too many incriminating letters about the governor's misconduct to the imam on behalf of the Europeans. We can also presume that these independent scribes and translators were enlisted to write documents and letters for non-European foreign merchants, particularly those major merchants from India who would have needed assistance in drafting letters that conformed to the protocols of written Arabic composition.

Unlike the imported alcohol and medicine sent over for company use, imported stationery supplies did not travel far from the realm of the European factories. Although, as described by Viallé, pencils were sometimes given as gifts to curious recipients in Asia, this was not the case in Yemen.[114] There VOC letters, penned using imported tools of writing, usually ended up in company hands, at another Dutch trading establishment or with company merchants residing temporarily in Bayt al-Faqih. It also appears that the imam of Yemen never read (or even received) an original Dutch letter, based on the human processes of translation and the material chain of production I have described, which involved many different individuals, each working with his own body of writing products. Undoubtedly, Mocha scribes would have written final translated letters for the EIC and VOC in Arabic with reed pens and locally made ink on paper procured within the region (although possibly of Italian or Ottoman origin), albeit marked with the company's distinctive stamp.[115]

The Europeans received letters in Arabic from Yemen's imam and other court officials, for which they immediately commissioned a translation. However, VOC merchants copied only the Dutch versions into their registers and generally sent the translations to Batavia without the Arabic originals.[116] In 1706 the Dutch received a letter for Governor-General Joan van Hoorn in Batavia from Mocha's governor right before the departure of their ships. Due to the sailing schedule they had no choice but to send the original Arabic letter, but they did so with apologies, knowing there were few reliable Arabic translators in that port.[117] Their apologetic stance conveys the expectation that these documents were to be transformed into a legible format before dispatch. The perceived uselessness of original Arabic missives to VOC merchants was confirmed in 1739, when the Dutch formally closed down their Mocha establishment. At that time, they burned many original Arabic letters along with other documents they declared to be *onleesbaar* (unreadable).[118] It appears that letters, as material objects, were surprisingly isolated in their circulation even if their contents were conveyed fluidly across linguistic and cultural boundaries.

A rich, multilingual, and diverse tradition of commercial writing and record keeping was in place at Mocha, and the European merchants of the port joined this tradition rather than challenging or replacing it. Trade records were kept in Arabic, Gujarati, Persian, Malayalam, English, French, Dutch, and Portuguese, in addition to other languages. Of these the European practices are the best-preserved and most fully understood today, but they were certainly not the only or dominant ones. Moreover their world of writing and its material outputs were relatively limited in terms of their circulation. Like scales and weights, stationery supplies were necessary for carrying out company trade in Yemen, but they never cultivated local demand or inspired desire across cultural borders. It is this relative isolation that we must keep in mind when we use these documents as essential sources for writing Indian Ocean trade history.

Furniture

EIC and VOC inventories suggest that the European factories, particularly the English one, were outfitted with many pieces of upright wooden furniture. In 1722 the English had three couches, two of which had caned seats; eight tables of various sizes and functions; forty-four chairs, some of which were from Surat and had caned seats; and one cot. This amount of furniture is considerable and much more substantial than that at the scant Dutch factory, which in 1734 had only four tables, one of which was used for writing, and six chairs. However, it is possible that more pieces of furniture were kept but not recorded at the VOC house.[119] Certain merchants travelled with furniture, and their items may have been present but not listed on the inventories because they were not considered company property.

While the presence of raised furniture at a European house, even in eighteenth-century Yemen, may not be surprising, it requires discussion because almost all of these pieces were brought from somewhere else, from India or Southeast Asia, and a few perhaps from China, Japan, or Europe.[120] Furniture historians Pedro Moura Caravalho, Amin Jaffer, and Jan Veenendaal have celebrated the early modern Indian and associated Southeast Asian tradition of cabinetmaking, with its reliance on European forms and Asian motifs, along with the use of tropical hardwoods. Their research shows that Europeans did not introduce raised chairs, thrones, tables, and bedsteads to South and Southeast Asia, but their extended presence there certainly bolstered the furniture industry by increasing the demand for products to accommodate the needs of new settlers, beginning with the Portuguese in the sixteenth century.[121] With the widened European presence, furniture workshops flourished in places that were already renowned for their woodworking traditions, such as Gujarat and the Coromandel Coast. Craftsmen from Coromandel and Sri Lanka were brought to Batavia, where they transferred many of these skills.

These products are characteristically difficult to identify because of their thoroughly syncretic character and the untraceable mobility of associated materials and craftspeople. For instance, a late seventeenth- or early eighteenth-century ebony armchair, now in the J. Paul Getty Museum, may have been made in India, Sri Lanka, or Indonesia, although this type was long miscast as a classic exemplar of Tudor artisanry.[122] With its upright back and turned rails it replicates a form that was widespread in Europe at that time, but its iconography combines cherubs with parrots and other forms from India, thus confirming its Asian manufacture (Figure 4.5). Along with the others in its multipiece set, it was acquired for Longleat Castle in Wiltshire, England, in the early eighteenth century and thus attests to the mobility of these pieces in the era under consideration.

EIC records confirm that many of their pieces of furniture came from India, particularly chairs and couches of cane from Surat, a major furniture production and distribution site as well as a key trade center that was closely tied to Mocha. The Dutch, by contrast, asked for chairs from Batavia, which had a special quarter devoted to woodworkers and craftsmen. But these inventories and request lists clearly do not tell the whole story about furniture in company establishments in Mocha. For instance, we have no extant requests for furniture to be sent to the well-outfitted English factory, which leads us to wonder how so many pieces ended up there. Many were likely carried to Yemen with individual merchants as personal items, and some

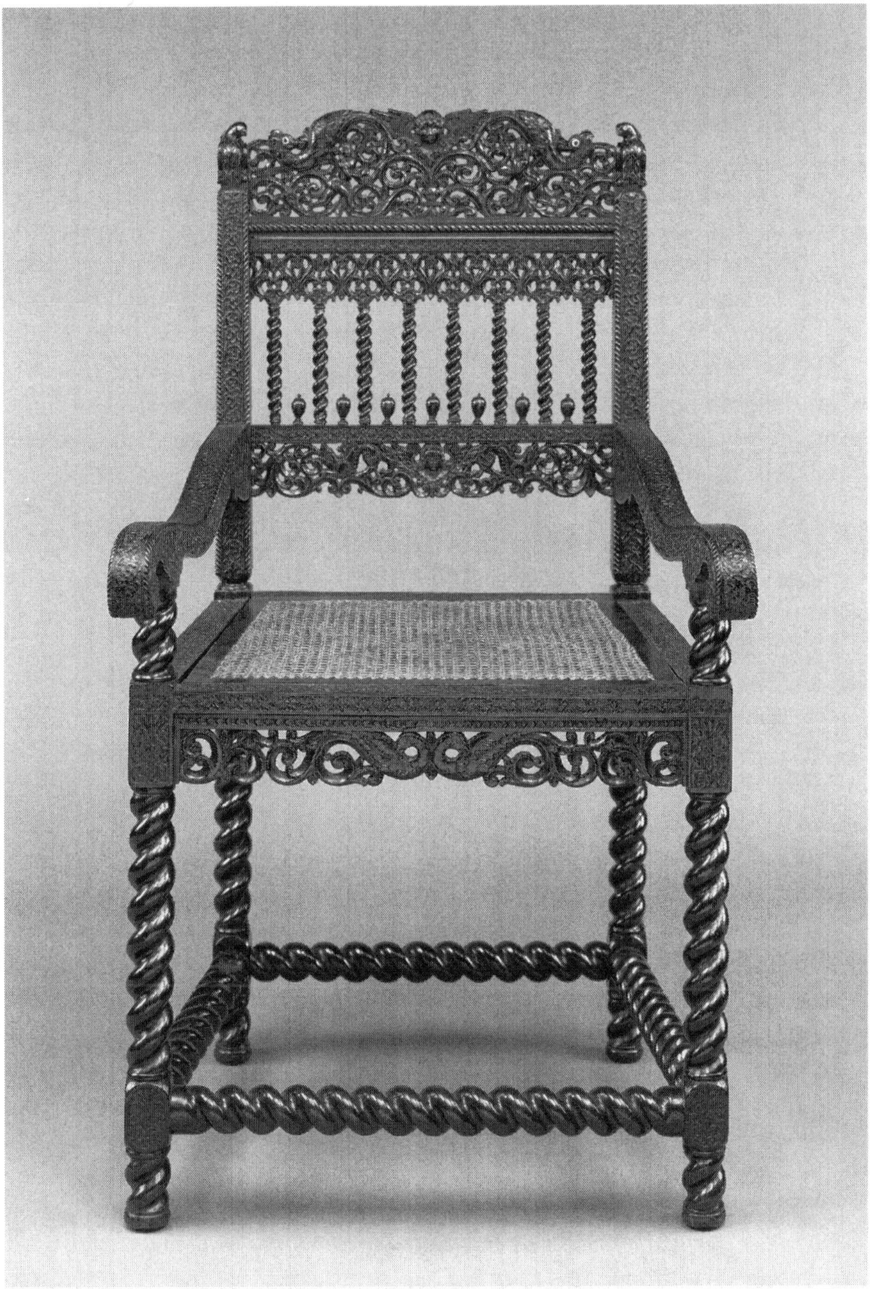

Figure 4.5. Armchair, probably Coromandel Coast, India, 1680–1720. Ebony, ebonized hardwood, ivory, ebonized walnut inner-seat frame with cane, 106.7 × 61 × 49.4 cm. J. Paul Getty Museum, Los Angeles. Digital image courtesy of the Getty's Open Content Program.

probably came off the boats that docked at the port yearly. For instance, on August 21, 1731, the VOC merchants noted in the *dagregister* that the English merchant Francis Dickinson had just left the port for Bombay. His boat, *The Bombay Galley,* departed along with a number of English private ships and a *ghurab* that was rented to carry the merchant's furniture.[123] The Dutch do not tell us exactly what was transported, but the fact that Dickinson rented an entire boat to carry his household belongings suggests that the amount was considerable. Moreover his sojourn in Bombay was relatively short—he returned to Mocha the following season, presumably carrying his furniture with him—which suggests his great reliance on these objects (even for a short time) while also demonstrating the perception that these items were implicitly mobile, despite their size and weight.

Indeed it appears that wooden furniture was brought from land onto boats and then back on land again quite fluidly. When the VOC merchants left Mocha at the end of their trading season in 1706, before they opened their year-round establishment, they sent all of their house furniture and baggage to their ship the *Oostersteijn*.[124] These pieces of furniture were surely used on board as the merchants travelled to their next destination. Turning back to Brandes' image of the surgeon's quarters on the *Stavenisse* in 1785 (Plate 10), which is singular in picturing the interior of an eighteenth-century VOC ship, we see a large wooden desk with a lockable roll-down top that may have come from Europe.[125] However, the wooden chair with a caned seat was likely made in India or Batavia. This image suggests that there was a parallel between the space of the ship and that of the overseas factory. The two were tied together by the pieces of furniture that were brought fluidly from port to port and used on board ships in the meantime. The ship was not just a method of transportation; its space, Richard Guy writes, functioned "to separate its crew from the lands and peoples they traded with."[126] In this way, the accouterments that were used in ships' cabins and then brought on land served as material anchors around which one could outfit company life abroad.

Although these major items of wooden furniture were imported from elsewhere, EIC and VOC merchants did procure certain smaller pieces locally. However, Mocha's bazaar sold only low tables and string-woven charpoy beds, like the "China cott" the merchants of the EIC ordered in January 1722.[127] They also commissioned four beds, which were likely large mattresses similar to the cushions that outfitted Mocha's sitting rooms. Although such beds and mattresses appear on expense lists for the EIC factory, they do not appear on inventories, an omission that suggests they were not seen as significant pieces of property. It also underlines the possibility that locally acquired items were excluded from official inventories, thus pointing to the variable yet undeclared rules behind these systems of record keeping.

Bulky pieces of imported furniture were not suited to the scale of Mocha's architecture. A nineteenth-century watercolor of a reception room in a house in the closely connected Red Sea port of Jidda portrays the layout of these spaces, in which the windowpanes and shelves were placed low to the ground to accommodate floor seating and the room's intimate size facilitated direct social interactions (Plate 11). Moreover rooms in Yemeni houses were functionally flexible and generally lacked fixed pieces of furniture that would pin down their use. Residents could use each sizeable room to sleep in at night, to eat in during meal times, and as a living room in between, with portable items such as cushions, textiles, and trays marking these temporally contingent functional shifts. In 1790 Grandpré complained precisely about this aspect of Mocha houses, declaring them "much less convenient than ours." He specifically noted that "they have no looking-glasses, nor any costly articles of furniture," an absence he clearly viewed as unfortunate. Yet he recognized the incompatibility of such items for these spaces, for he added that the floor "has very little solidity, and is never level, so that a table with four legs will never stand firm."[128] A fatal accident in 1719 demonstrated the unsuitability of these bulky pieces of imported furniture for use in Yemeni domestic spaces. One evening the third floor of the Dutch factory in Mocha collapsed and brought a heavy dining table crashing down below when several people were eating at it, resulting in one death.[129]

But even with the comforts afforded by these familiar items in their establishments, it is very likely that the Dutch and the English kept at least one room furnished in the manner that dominated locally, such as that pictured in plate 11. They always offered coffee, rosewater, and incense to visiting guests during the common local reception.[130] It is difficult to imagine these conventional observances taking place around a large wooden table while seated in upright chairs, as all of the material items involved were oriented to the floor. It is also apparent that raised furniture was limited in use to the European factories and did not inspire local demand. By the end of the eighteenth century, the governor of Mocha had acquired an armchair made of wood for his residence. It was brought out only for European guests, which suggests that by this time such an accessory was seen as useful for foreign reception, although Grandpré condemned the item as old and worm-infested.[131] Yet the fact that this chair was singled out for European visitors also indicates that these types of objects did not have a wider audience in this diverse port city.

Of course, these pieces of furniture also accommodated many of the activities that were facilitated by the material items that appear prominently on Mocha's inventory and request lists. Tables and chairs served the culinary habits of the Dutch and English in Yemen, where eating was generally done on the floor around a communal tray or a low table. Similarly, the desks and other raised surfaces supported the act of writing, which the local scribe performed while seated on a cushion, perhaps with a single knee raised and a writing board upon it.[132] Unlike other European imports, such as coveted bottles of alcohol or vials of Western medicine, these foreign items were not acquired by locals and had very little permanence in Mocha outside of the European scope.

When people are on the move, their concept of utility is hardly stable. The foreign traveller must calculate what he or she needs to carry abroad, what can be procured locally, and what can be done without. In the context of early modern Yemen, seemingly mundane items, such as casks of beer, stores of medicine, scales and weights, reams of paper, quills, and pieces of furniture, fulfilled a set of practical purposes for travelling European merchants. These items were carried over long distances from home or sites within the Indian Ocean. Hence we can confirm that those who requested or carried them from region to region perceived them to be essential objects. But the meanings of these various objects that were brought or sent to the Arabian Peninsula become increasingly complex when located within a cross-cultural matrix, which places pressure on single-dimensional notions of the functional or the utilitarian.

Although categorized as basic provisions, certain items such as alcohol and medical supplies were not just consumed in the factory but were also distributed to gain favor in informal ways. These types of bestowals constituted an unofficial local gift economy that operated in parallel to the more formal gift systems, further underlining the intertwined nature of commodities and gifts. Many items traveled quite promiscuously from one category to the other, albeit in different temporal contexts, and some without express permission of the company.

The world of the overseas trading establishment was deeply connected to the oceangoing merchant vessel. Certain items, such as chairs and tables, were brought back and forth between land and ship on a regular basis, regardless of the fact that some were not designed for easy mobility. Likewise, stores of alcohol were packed in *legger*s and *kelder*s, containers that were designed to prevent breakage at sea and were formatted to the size and capacity of the ship's cargo hold. These pieces of raised furniture and bulk containers were then brought on land for company use in the residence. Ships' surgeons served their crew on board but also serviced landed patients, including the imam of Yemen, travelling with their medical kits and supplies.

Written inventories point to a material world that words can only partially reconstruct. This inquiry suggests that we bring together that which can be made known through archaeological fieldwork with textual scholarship in a more integrated fashion.[133] Although our records faithfully list wine, spirits, beer, and medicine, the archaeologist who goes to the former site of the VOC or EIC establishment in Mocha would find only the shards of the containers that held these substances, some bearing the residue of their former contents. The glass and ceramic containers to be unearthed by the archaeologist's trowel were, by contrast, consistently omitted in the inventory and request lists. Therefore the material and textual evidence constitute complementary realms that must be brought together to explicate the world of cross-cultural shipping, consumption, and distribution. Because the historic quarters of Mocha still await systematic excavation, this unfulfilled project can be initiated only by the proposals presented here.

Vessels of storage, transportation, and consumption help us imagine a commercial world in which Asian porcelain, for instance, played many roles for those who traded on the wholesale market or had dealings with foreign merchants. Cups of porcelain were used in elite Yemeni homes for drinking *qishr*, and silver-clad porcelain bottles dispensed imported rosewater. Glass, earthenware, stoneware, and porcelain vessels were used to store or dole out additional substances, including water, alcoholic beverages, and imported medicine. No historian can dispute the significance of Asian ceramics in the long-distance early modern trade of the Indian Ocean. But the task remains to discover the various ways and forms in which Asian ceramics were meaningful across spheres and particularly within the world of intra-Asian consumption rather than the acknowledged sphere of European desire.

Most of the products treated here were relatively exotic to Yemen, brought from Europe, but also the Cape, Gujarat, or Batavia. Yet their foreign identity did not determine their specific meaning in the local context of maritime Yemen. Some items never left the confined sphere of Dutch or English use, such as imported scales, stationery products, and raised furniture. Other items were adopted and sought after by certain local residents, such as French wine and spirits, despite the prevailing atmosphere of disapproval. Foreign medicine may be understood as representing the triumph of outside over local expertise. The varied use or denial of these products prompts us to consider the multidimensional nature of the import as well as the Western good. Some entered the local sphere of demand fluidly, while others resisted this ready absorption. As Thomas has argued, "indigenous people are no less powerful and no less able to appropriate than the white who imagine themselves as intruders," and "indigenous perceptions of, and reactions to, foreign people and goods must be taken seriously."[134] These products did not point to the inevitable future captivation of Western modes of consumption. To the contrary, they represent a moment when this impact was uneven, imbalanced, and unresolved.

Conclusion

It goes without saying that the early modern maritime merchants of the Indian Ocean were implicitly oriented toward material concerns, for the long-distance trade was a complex engine that served to move goods of all sorts. It is also clear that their material engagements were not limited to the commodities destined for the market, even if these goods occupied a dominant place among their concerns. A wide array of other objects was used in the social rites and repetitive ceremonies that took place at Mocha's jetty and in the houses of its major merchants. Moreover countless items were delivered as gifts across Yemen, some of which were held back expressly from the world of commerce or everyday use. The seemingly nontransactional social engagements that Yemen's major overseas merchants participated in allow us to understand the world of maritime trade in an expansive light, not just as a series of financial deals but through the personal encounters and exchanges that took place outside the market as well. These engagements were formatted to the schedule of the maritime trade and closely linked to its cycles and routines.

Objects at the Center of the Cross-Cultural Encounter

I have relied heavily upon the Dutch, English, and French merchants of Mocha as both observers of and participants in the Yemen trade and its social protocols in the early eighteenth century. Their copious records, while undoubtedly oriented by their own distinct interests and preoccupations, serve as an important means to understand the cross-cultural encounter in the western Indian Ocean, particularly when we look beyond the copious quantitative and seemingly empirical data they have yielded and examine them as intensely social documents. At the same time and at each juncture, we must interrogate these sources with the understanding that they are not transparent records awaiting historical examination. As Ogborn has aptly stated, "Writing was not simply a commentary upon what happened, it was very much part of the action."[1]

So it is fitting to end with an account from an Arabic source, provided by the eighteenth-century Yemeni historian Lutf Allah bin Ahmad Jahhaf al-San'ani, who narrated the 1737 French bombing of Mocha, an event I have referenced frequently in this study, from a local perspective. According to him, the French siege took place under the following circumstances:

> The *firanj* [Franks] took possession of the fort 'Abd al-Ghafur in Mocha and fired their guns on it.[2] They took it and remained there until they received a peace treaty. And it was said that the reason for their hostility and attack was that the governor of Mocha Faqih Ahmad Khazindar oppressed them and did not look after their concerns and did not allow them the freedom to commit reprehensible acts. They said that he prohibited them from riding inside of the port, having relations with prostitutes, and drinking wine. So they arrived late at Mocha that year after complaining to their "sultan" about the actions of the governor of Mocha toward them.[3]

On a certain level, sections of this passage echo what we know about the attack from much lengthier French and Dutch accounts.[4] Whereas at least one Arab biographer touted the generosity of Khazindar (who was also his patron), the French merchants of Mocha protested his wayward policies and greed.[5] This governor's notorious mistreatment of merchants also merited countless entries in the Dutch *dagregister* and the EIC documents from the port. However, the French would hardly agree with the other reasons Jahhaf offered for their attack: prohibitions against riding within the city precinct, visiting prostitutes, and the consumption of wine. It may not be surprising that this eighteenth-century Yemeni historian described the French siege of the city by repeating familiar tropes about the inability of Europeans to conform to the social codes that governed the activities of non-Muslim communities in Yemen, highlighting their perceived immoral sexual behavior and their penchant for imbibing illicit substances.[6] However, after reading the sources cited in the previous chapters, these references appear more meaningful and pointed. Horses were distributed and displayed prominently within a local system of uneven social privilege, as described in chapters 1 and 3. They could also be grounds for contestation, through which difference was performed and mediated among Mocha's diverse trading community. As conveyed in chapter 4, Europeans were the primary purveyors of wine and alcohol in Yemen, although these beverages certainly exited the realm of the companies and did not simply exemplify European difference, as Jahhaf would have us believe. Even so, this brief reference by one of Yemen's key historians of the period should be taken seriously, for it suggests, ever so subtly, that cultural and religious differences in the ports and emporia of Yemen were often understood in material terms and that the anxieties and discomforts generated by the cross-cultural encounter were expressed most readily in a language of things.

The same recognition is discernible when we read the trade agreement forged by the French and Imam al-Mansur at the conclusion of the events Jahhaf narrated. Whereas the initial French trade agreement of 1709 listed only ten general articles, the 1737 revision encompassed twenty-four remarkably specific points.[7] The success of the agreement hinged upon the first article, which required the restitution of the sums that had been unlawfully seized from the French, which constituted the grounds for the attack. Most of the following articles were intended to protect the French from future appropriations of both goods and cash at Mocha and Bayt al-Faqih, as well as guarding them and those whom they employed from personal mistreatment in Yemen. But here as well the material concerns that have been discussed in the previous chapters and that Jahhaf hints at also appear. In the 1709 agreement, the French were given the right to mount their flag on their lodge, but the 1737 update specifies that they may rent one or more houses and set up their flag from the house "where their chief is lodged," thus subtly pointing to the vexed role of the European flag as a delimited commercial privilege. Moreover, in article 9 the language was updated to specify that their goods would be taken "directly" to their house and inspected there, except for those that needed to be weighed. In the later agreement, they also delineate the policies regarding the unloading of their provisions, as opposed to goods for sale, which undoubtedly included the beverages and medical supplies described in chapter 4. The last item requires that the French nation be treated with "honor and distinction" and follows by asserting their right to ride their horses on the "promenade." This enhanced and expanded trade agreement reflects the experience of merchants who had traded at the port for several decades. But as with Jahhaf's short passage above, it also tacitly recognizes the importance of the objects that constitute the subject of this study, most of which were shipped but not always for sale, such as flags, horses, provisions, and medicine, along with the differential privileges they entailed and the varying uses to which they were put in the trading world of eighteenth-century Yemen.

This study was inspired by the swell of recent historical research oriented around the alluring notion of a "world of goods," in which the early modern sphere was inundated by a newly accessible range of global commodities of great aesthetic, culinary, or sensory appeal. While responding to this general arena of interest, but in line with the concerns of historian Pedro Machado, I also critique some of its latent assumptions, in which the East is characterized inevitably as a rich marketplace for these highly sought-after products, but its inhabitants rarely appear as recipients or consumers of foreign goods.[8] By contrast, I have cast Qasimi Yemen as both purveyor of coffee to the world and recipient of many types of imports in return, from Europe, Asia, Africa, and the Americas. Moreover I have argued that the early modern global surge in demand for foreign products always took place on a local level. As such, one must look to the rejection of certain products and the acceptance of others, in addition to the ways domestic products were used and paired with those from abroad. The specificity of this demand, circulation, and reception is worth exploring in great detail. Porcelain coffee cups from Japan were coveted in Yemen not just because they were made of porcelain and from Asia but also because they held coffee, or rather *qishr*, a common Yemeni drink that pointed to the process by which a valuable local good was prepared for sale and export. These cups were used in repetitive ceremonies that took place among Yemen's merchants and officials on a daily basis but occupied a pointed role during rites of commercial initiation. While the English used the gift economy as one channel to market their domestic woolen products in the East, the Dutch gave pieces of cloth from China, India, Persia, and Europe as gifts to Mocha's trade officials and Yemen's imam. The imam could then bring some of these gifts into the ceremonial fold to communicate a set of messages that were deeply embedded in local ritual activity. Horses were not favored simply because of their monetary value but also because of their unique ability to articulate social difference in Mocha, a port where identity and economic power were connected in complicated ways. I argued that these global products were desired (or rejected) in Yemen on the level of the particular rather than the generic, and that in intensely commercial societies, marketplace goods have the potential to far exceed their meanings as economic products.

The related message is that everything that came on boats across seas is worthy of study, whether in the cargo hold or the officers' cabins. By looking beyond the purview of goods that were intended for the overseas marketplace, we can understand the complex enterprise of trade, which was dependent on a range of material objects that were displayed and consumed or given as gifts, official and informal. At stake here as well is the meaning of the import and the construction of the foreign. In Yemen, imported goods were common but played varying roles and may not be read as undifferentiated exotica or emblems of the triumph of foreign modes of consumption. Locals commonly sought some items, such as porcelain coffee cups, Indian muslin, and spices and spiced products, but also European medicine. By contrast, they had little interest in raised chairs and tables and quills made of goose feathers. Certain goods, such as wine and Batavian arrack, developed a following, but primarily along the coastal fringe. It is fitting to reiterate Thomas' statement: "Western commodities cannot be seen to embody some irresistible attraction that is given the status of an inexorable historical force. Indigenous people's interests in goods, strangers, and contact were variable and in some cases were extremely constrained."[9]

Europeans in Indian Ocean Ports

These inquiries help us understand the complex place that European merchants occupied in Indian Ocean ports, an issue scholars are still grappling with, although I suggest that this quandary should be treated on a case-by-case basis rather than in sweeping or generalized terms. In Yemen, an elite cross-section of merchants from Europe, India, and the Arab lands constituted a class of "major overseas merchants," a designation that has been assigned not based on the volume of their trade or a comparison of their profits over time, figures that are unattainable for all of these communities. Rather it has been assessed according to their social engagements, the rituals and routines they were invited to engage in, and the ties they initiated through gift-giving and letter writing. To this end, a purely transactional or economic model for understanding merchant status has been wholly rejected.

It may seem strange to group the merchants associated with the Dutch, English, and French East India companies so seamlessly with the Sunni Bohra merchant Mulla Muhammad 'Ali of Surat or Sidi Yaqut Khan of Danda-Rajpuri with his African roots, for these various groups are often situated in opposition to one another as they competed for economic or maritime dominance within the Indian Ocean arena. Yet European merchants clearly shared more with those major merchants than they did with other religious minorities in Yemen, such as the Jewish residents of Mocha who lived in an extramural quarter, sometimes referred to as a ghetto, to the south of the city. The Baniyans, also *dhimmi*s, occupied a more liminal space. They lived within the safety of the walls of Mocha but were not granted many of the core privileges of other major merchants. Nor did they engage in gift exchange with Yemen's imam or his trade officials. Rather they tendered a yearly poll tax and were duly charged for both their entry into and exit from Yemen, instead of receiving the elaborate ceremonies of reception and dispatch at the port that were described in chapters 1 and 3.

It is also worth noting that the European merchants of Yemen appear to have been the only ones governed by written trade agreements, which they placed a great deal of value upon, as with the French treaties of 1709 and 1737. By contrast, the major merchants from India, who were mostly Muslim, did not rely upon written trade agreements or contracts with the imam of Yemen, as their right to trade there was never contested or called into question.[10] The Baniyan merchants of Mocha were bound by the well-known conventions of the Pact of 'Umar, which governed religious minority communities throughout the Muslim world without specificity to trade interactions and were enforced with varying levels of stringency.

Even with these written agreements, European merchants were still expected to engage in the commercial rites of social interaction in line with the customs and routines that were in acceptance for major traders in Yemen. Most of these expectations were wholly missing from their formalized contracts or indicated only in a cursory fashion.[11] Of course, the European merchants would balk at some of these requirements, particularly the overriding responsibility to give gifts, as arbitrary additions to their yearly commitments. Although they expressed ambivalence and sometimes even outrage at them, their actual practices reveal a tacit acceptance of these rituals and observances, as well as their growing deftness at meeting these demands, indicating that they understood how essential these practices were to the functioning of their commercial enterprises in Yemen. It also appears that the local authorities in Yemen, the imam and his provincial governors, were happy to enter into agreements with European trading companies, but they never saw these documents as self-sustaining, freestanding, or all-inclusive. Rather trade agreements were incomplete and contingent accords that had to be reaffirmed in tangible and visible ways and on a yearly basis, through ceremonial observances and the regular exchange of gifts.

While relying heavily upon the corpus of VOC and EIC trade documents, I have offered various suggestions for dealing with their omnipresent presumptions of Oriental despotism and underlying fears of accusations of malfeasance. In order to understand these sources and their implicit limitations, we must read across a wide corpus of letters, registers, inventories, and requests rather than cherry-picking single quotes or useful references. I have not cast the Dutch and English as crude proto-colonizers or as bumbling merchants who were unable to recognize the mechanics of the local system of trade, but rather as residents of Yemen who became accustomed to these expectations, even if they were unable to represent the depth of that understanding fully to their superiors back in home offices. Moreover while duly acknowledging the copious critiques of these records that have underpinned the historical study of early modern maritime Asia, I insist that they are useful for the historian, but more so when we combine perspectives across different groups, such as those written in Dutch, English, French, and Arabic, thus moving beyond the single company perspective that still dominates, but also hinders, the analytical scope of Indian Ocean studies. By conceiving of these records as material objects in their own right, with their own history of inscription, we are afforded a critical perch from which to think about the project of commercial documentation in the western Indian Ocean and to grapple with the perennial imbalance of its available source material.

Even with this clear interest in European traders and a deep reliance on their perspectives, this study has homed in upon the world of intra-Asian commerce, which the Dutch called the "country trade" and were extremely invested in. Yet we know much more about the transit of ships and their goods from Amsterdam to Batavia, for instance, than we do about those that plied western Indian Ocean waters. Yemen, of course, has always been an outlier in the study of the Indian Ocean trade, as opposed to the much more thoroughly examined ports of the subcontinent, which were also connected to it. This study attempts to remedy some of these imbalances.

The Performance of Trade

Philip Stern, Adam Clulow, Bhawan Ruangsilp, and other historians have written of the avid participation of European merchants in local rituals, ceremonial activities, and materially oriented official protocols in India, Japan, and Thailand in the seventeenth and eighteenth centuries. Stern describes "the use of ceremony and display" by the English in India as a means "to represent and constitute stateliness and political power."[12] Clulow has examined closely the ways VOC merchants engaged in the "theatrical demonstration" of authority, but also fealty and loyalty in Tokugawa Japan, and Ruangsilp sketches the growing Dutch aptitude in local ceremonial rites and social engagement in Ayutthaya as a reflection of their "pragmatism" in all matters related to the trade.[13] I suggest that the engagement of European merchants with these practices represents far more than the rote absorption of Asian ritual modes or the blind adoption of undifferentiated status symbols: these performative material displays and repetitive social rites were deeply embedded in commercial systems. And the goods that were featured prominently in them did not simply reflect the fixed status and position of those involved; these mobile items were bestowed to represent official approval but also closely examined to vet one's identity. They could affirm the solidity of a merchant's maritime enterprises and, by doing so, tacitly suggest his continuing suitability to engage in the long-distance trade. As such, they possessed a great deal of effective agency and were active tools in a dynamic cognitive world where untested merchants needed to be evaluated seriously and even established merchants could be subject to reconsideration.

By engaging directly with these social and material practices, we can begin to approach answers to certain outstanding questions. In his study of the longevity of merchant wealth in Gujarat, Nadri argues that, contrary to prevailing opinion, certain trading families in India sustained enduring financial legacies that crossed generations.[14] It is no surprise that the family of Mulla Muhammad 'Ali serves as one of his key examples. Although Nadri does not suggest this, we can be certain that Muhammad 'Ali's long-term economic resilience hinged upon more than his wise economic transactions and smart investments in a trading system that was subject to political unrest, pirate attacks, and weather-induced shipwrecks. I have suggested that this Gujarati merchant was an exemplar in socially navigating the Yemen trade and that he passed these principles down to the next generation as well. As shown in chapter 1, his *nakhudha* and son refused to accept a snub to his status upon entry into the port of Mocha in 1730, presumably because it would signify or inspire a downgrade of his profile. Moreover, through his son and other proxies, Muhammad 'Ali strategically engaged in gift exchange with Yemen's imam on a regular basis, in sharp contrast to his European cohorts, who tried to resist such distributions. In the case of Mocha, Muhammad 'Ali was greatly proficient in these social aspects of the trade, which may help us understand, at least in part, why his maritime empire maintained its stability even after his premature death.

This book focuses on trade but deals little with actual financial transactions. I suggest a very different orientation for our study of long-distance wholesale maritime commerce than that which is normally proposed. In this model, the economic historian is called upon to read company sources with an eye to social engagements. At the same time, the art historian is asked to look beyond the world of the precious and extant goods that can be found in the halls of modern museums and to turn to masses of relatively undifferentiated objects, described in slight and incomplete written references and almost never pictured. In order to do so, the tools of the archaeologist and the theoretical frameworks of the anthropologist provide significant leverage. I suggest that interdisciplinary lenses and methods can help to open up a new set of questions that Indian Ocean studies, with its long-standing quantitative inclinations, has long avoided.

Notes

Introduction

Epigraph. Nicholas Thomas, *Entangled Objects: Exchange, Material Culture, and Colonialism in the Pacific* (Cambridge, MA: Harvard University Press, 1991), 123–124.

1. William Gervase Clarence-Smith and Steven Topik, eds., *The Global Coffee Economy in Africa, Asia, and Latin America, 1500–1989* (Cambridge, UK: Cambridge University Press, 2003).

2. John Carswell, *Blue and White: Chinese Porcelain around the World* (London: British Museum Press, 2000); Robert Finlay, *A Pilgrim Art: Cultures of Porcelain in World History* (Berkeley: University of California Press, 2010).

3. Beverly Lemire and Giorgio Riello, "East and West: Textiles and Fashion in Early Modern Europe," *Journal of Social History* 41:4 (Summer 2008): 887–916; Giorgio Riello and Tirthankar Roy, eds., *How India Clothed the World: The World of South Asian Textiles, 1500–1800* (Leiden: Brill, 2009).

4. Of particular interest is James Grehan, *Everyday Life and Consumer Culture in Eighteenth-Century Damascus* (Seattle: University of Washington Press, 2007).

5. Michel Tuchscherer, "Coffee in the Red Sea Area from the Sixteenth to the Nineteenth Century," in Clarence-Smith and Topik, *The Global Coffee Economy,* 52.

6. For coffee to Iran and the Gulf area, see Rudi Matthee, "Coffee in Safavid Iran: Commerce and Consumption," *Journal of the Economic and Social History of the Orient* 37 (1994): 1–32.

7. R. B. Serjeant, "The Yemeni Coast in 1005/1597; An Anonymous Note on the Flyleaf of Ibn al-Mujawir's *Tarikh al-Mustabsir,*" *Arabian Studies* 7 (1985): 187–191.

8. There are some exceptions to this general perception of isolation, particularly concerning the diplomatic relations sustained during the era of Imam al-Mutawakkil Isma'il and his successor. E. van Donzel, *Foreign Relations of Ethiopia, 1642–1700: Documents relating to Khodja Murad,* Uitgaven van het Nederlands Historisch-Archaeologisch Instituut te Istanbul XLVI (Leiden: Nederlands Historisch-Archaeologisch Instituut te Istanbul, 1979); E. van Donzel, *A Yemenite Embassy to Ethiopia 1647–49* (Stuttgart: F. Steiner, 1986); François Blucasz, "Les relations entre le Yémen et l'Inde au XVIIème siècle: Extraits de la correspondance entre l'imam zaidite al-Mutawakkil 'ala Allah Isma'il b. al-Qasim et le sultan moghol Awrangzib," master's thesis, Université de Paris-Sorbonne (Paris IV), 1992.

9. From 1718 to 1722, before the official establishment of the Generale Indische Compagnie (Ostend Company), private traders dispatched six ships to Mocha from Ostend, making the southern Arabian Peninsula one of the earliest areas of interest for this short-lived company that was dissolved in 1735. Jan Parmentier, "The Ostend Trade to Moka and India (1714–1735): The Merchants and Supercargos," *Mariner's Mirror* 73:2 (1987): 123, 137.

10. Kristof Glamann, *Dutch-Asiatic Trade, 1620–1740* (The Hague: Martinus Nijhoff, 1958), 191.

11. G. J. Knaap, "The Dutch East India Company and the Expansion of Coffee Cultivation in Java, Ambon, and Ceylon 1700–1730," in *Trading Companies in Asia, 1600–1830,* edited by J. van Goor (Utrecht: Hes Uitgevers, 1986), 36.

12. Gilbert Buti, "Marseille entre Moka et café des îles: Espaces, flux, réseaux, XVIIe–XVIIIe siècles," in *Le commerce du café avant l'ère des plantations coloniales: Espaces, réseaux, sociétés (XVe–XIXe siècle),* edited by Michel Tuchscherer (Cairo: Institut français d'archéologie orientale, 2001), 213–244.

13. In fact, these sources are considered so valuable for local history that some seventeenth-century VOC records were translated into Arabic. C. G. Brouwer and A. Kaplanian, *Al-yaman fi awa'il al-qarn al-saba' 'ashar: Muqtatafat min al-watha'iq al-hulandiyah al-muta'alliqah bi-al-tarikh al-iqtisadi li-janub al-jazirah al-'arabiyah, 1614–1630* (Amsterdam: D'Fluyte Rarob, 1989).

14. Nancy Um, "1636 and 1726: Yemen after the First Ottoman Era," in *Asia Inside Out: Changing Times,* edited by Eric Tagliacozzo, Helen Siu, and Peter Perdue (Cambridge, MA: Harvard University Press, 2015), 112–134.

15. See Pierre François Guyot Desfontaines, *Relation de l'expédition de Moka en l'année 1737 sous les ordres de M. de la Garde-Jazier, de Saint-Malo* (Paris: Imprimerie Joseph Bullot, 1739); Mocha *dagregister,* VOC 2447, January 25–April 6, 1737, 156–238, VOC Records, National Archives, The Hague.

16. One can gain an understanding of these positions from European records, but the titles and their associated responsibilities were not the same from port to port. For instance, the term *shahbandar,* which was used widely in the eastern Indian Ocean to describe a port official, was used in the western Indian Ocean and Red Sea to specify the head of a group of foreign merchants. Nagashima's article on the *shahbandar* of Surat illustrates the difficulties in understanding the precise responsibilities of any port position over time. Hiromu Nagashima, "The *Shahbandar* at Surat in the Mughal Empire," *Nagasaki Prefectural University Review* 29:4 (1996): 1–28.

17. Private trade among both the French and English had escalated during this period. But because private supercargos did not leave systematic records, their activities are much more difficult to explore than those of the companies. For that reason, the emphasis here is on company trade and practices.

18. Although it is quite general, the definition of the term *tajir* that I offer is more precise than the one provided by the *Encyclopedia of Islam,* which only specifies someone who buys and sells commodities. M. A. J. Beg, "Tajir," *Encyclopedia of Islam,* new edition (Leiden: Brill, 1960), 10:67.

19. André Raymond, "Une famille de grands negociants en café au Caire dans la première moitié du XVIIIe siècle: Les Sharaybi," in Tuchscherer, *Le commerce du café,* 111–124; Jessica Goldberg, *Trade and Institutions in the Medieval Mediterranean: The Geniza Merchants and Their Business World* (Cambridge, UK: Cambridge University Press, 2012); Gagan D. S. Sood, "'Correspondence Is Equal to Half a Meeting': The Composition and Comprehension of Letters in Eighteenth-Century Islamic Eurasia," *Journal of the Economic and Social History of the Orient* 50:2–3 (2007): 177.

20. As an example, see the biographical entry for Sa'd al-Din al-'Udayni, a merchant who started his career as a humble coffee husker. The passage emphasizes his piety and generosity to the poor. In terms of his trade profile, only his great wealth is mentioned repeatedly, along with the pronouncement that he could turn a profit from selling dust.

Muhammad Zabara, *Nashr al-'arf li-nubla' al-yaman ba'd al-alf,* 3 vols. (Sanaa: Markaz al-dirasat wa al-buhuth al-yamani, 1985), 2:725–728.

21. 'Abbas b. 'Ali al-Musawi al-Makki, *Nuzhat al-jalis wa munyat al-adib al-anis,* 2 vols., edited by Muhammad Mahdi Khurasan (Al-Najaf, Iraq: al-Matba'a al-Haydariyya, 1967), 2:262.

22. Goldberg, *Trade,* 47.

23. Letter to Batavia, from Abraham Pantzer, G. Schoeten, and H. Burggraaf, Mocha, August 22, 1716, VOC 9057, 24–25, VOC Records.

24. In 1719 he was still described as one of six merchants who had dominated the trade that season. Memorie en berigt navolgens der hoogen en veel g'agtens ordre van den hoog Edelen Ho. A. Heer Christoffel van Zwoll gouverneur generall, from Abraham Pantzer, Mocha, August 15, 1719, VOC 1964, 105, VOC Records.

25. Ibid.

26. Qasimi Yemen presents a relatively unique case in which Hindus and Jains were considered *dhimmi*s, comparable to Mughal India in the same era. Technically neither could be granted this status because the Baniyans were not *ahl-al kitab* (people of the book).

27. Nancy Um, *The Merchant Houses of Mocha: Trade and Architecture in an Indian Ocean Port* (Seattle: University of Washington Press, 2009), 166–167.

28. Natasha Glaisyer, *The Culture of Commerce in England, 1660–1720* (Woodbridge, UK: Boydell Press, 2006), 9.

29. There is no mention of 'Abd al-Ghafur travelling to the Red Sea coast during the height of his trading empire, although his name and reputation were widespread throughout the city of Mocha. We have evidence that his grandson Muhammad 'Ali visited Mocha only once, in 1727 en route to Mecca and Madina. However, it is possible that both Muhammad 'Ali and his grandfather had travelled to Mocha as *nakhudha*s earlier in their careers. For instance, Muhammad 'Ali sent his son, Muhammad Husayn, as his *nakhudha* to Yemen in 1730. Mocha *dagregister,* March 30 and May 22, 1730, VOC 2202, 273, 291, VOC Records.

30. Sood, "'Correspondence'."

31. Jane Hathaway, "The Mawza' Exile at the Juncture of Zaydi and Ottoman Messianism," *AJS Review* 29:1 (April 2005): 117.

32. Bernard Haykel, *Revival and Reform in Islam: The Legacy of Muhammad al-Shawkani* (Cambridge, UK: Cambridge University Press, 2003), 115–126.

33. As one of the privileges, the Yemenite Salim al-'Iraqi was appointed head of the Sanaa mint in the mid-eighteenth century.

34. Francesca Trivellato, *The Familiarity of Strangers: The Sephardic Diaspora, Livorno, and Cross-Cultural Trade in the Early Modern Period* (New Haven, CT: Yale University Press, 2009); Sebouh David Aslanian, *From the Indian Ocean to the Mediterranean: The Global Trade Networks of Armenian Merchants from New Julfa* (Berkeley: University of California Press, 2011); Goldberg, *Trade.*

35. Avner Greif, "Reputations and Coalitions in Medieval Trade: Evidence on the Maghribi Traders," *Journal of Economic History* 49:4 (December 1989): 857–882; Trivellato, *Familiarity;* Aslanian, *From the Indian Ocean;* John Smail, "Credit, Risk, and Honor in Eighteenth-Century Commerce," *Journal of British Studies* 44:3 (July 2005): 439–456.

36. Greif, "Reputations," 866–867.

37. Woodruff Smith argues that material objects were used to convey abstract concepts of individual character, such as trust and reputation, in early modern Europe, but outside of the maritime context of trade. Woodruff D. Smith, *Consumption and the Making of Respectability, 1600–1800* (London: Routledge, 2002).

38. Aslanian, *From the Indian Ocean,* 180.

39. Robert Ross, "Sumptuary Laws in Europe, the Netherlands and the Dutch Colonies," in *Contingent Lives: Social Identity and Material Culture in the VOC World,* edited by Nigel Worden (Cape Town: ABC Press, 2007), 382–390.

40. Robert Ross, *Status and Respectability in the Cape Colony, 1750–1870: A Tragedy of Manners* (Cambridge, UK: Cambridge University Press, 1999), 3.

41. Gerald Groenewald, "A Class Apart: Symbolic Capital, Consumption and Identity among the Alcohol Entrepreneurs of Cape Town, 1680–1795," *S. A. Tydskrif vir Kultuurgeskiedenis* 26:1 (June 2012): 14–32.

42. As a useful example, Leor Halevi has demonstrated the utility of these frameworks for thinking about medieval trade in the Islamic world. Leor Halevi, "Religion and Cross-Cultural Trade: A Framework for Interdisciplinary Inquiry," in *Religion and Trade: Cross-Cultural Exchanges in World History, 1000–1900,* edited by Francesca Trivellato, Leor Halevi, and Catia Antunes (Oxford: Oxford University Press, 2014), 24–61.

43. Arjun Appadurai, "Introduction: Commodities and the Politics of Value," in *The Social Life of Things: Commodities in Cultural Perspective,* edited by A. Appadurai (Cambridge, UK: Cambridge University Press, 1989), 6–16.

44. Pierre Bourdieu, *The Logic of Practice,* translated by Richard Nice (Stanford: Stanford University Press, 1990), 111–121.

45. Annette Weiner, *Inalienable Possessions: The Paradox of Keeping-While-Giving* (Berkeley: University of California Press, 1992), 39.

46. Thomas, *Entangled Objects*, 52.

47. Ibid., 84.

48. Ibid., 4.

49. Zabara, *Nashr,* 1:303.

50. Sanjay Subrahmanyam, *Explorations in Connected History: Mughals and Franks* (New Delhi: Oxford University Press, 2005), 15, and 1–20 for a critique of the use of European and local sources in early modern South Asian history.

51. Ann Laura Stoler, *Along the Archival Grain: Epistemic Anxieties and Colonial Common Sense* (Princeton, NJ: Princeton University Press, 2010), 1.

52. Ibid., 20.

53. Toby L. Ditz, "Formative Ventures: Eighteenth-Century Commercial Letters and the Articulation of Experience," in *Epistolary Selves: Letters and Letter-Writers, 1600–1945,* edited by Rebecca Earle (Aldershot, UK: Ashgate, 1999), 61.

54. Paula Sanders, *Ritual, Politics, and the City in Fatimid Cairo* (Albany, NY: SUNY Press, 1994).

55. Trivellato, *Familiarity,* 7.

Chapter 1: Rites of Entry at the Maritime Threshold

1. All quotes and citations are from the 1732 English edition of the text, based on the 2004 facsimile, unless otherwise marked. When my translations differ, I cite the 1716 French edition published by A. Cailleau. Jean de la Roque, *A Voyage to Arabia Felix (1708–10),* introduction and bibliographies by Carl Phillips (1732; New York: Oleander Press, 2004), 75–81.

2. In addition to these firsthand accounts, some sections were penned directly by the author, an Orientalist scholar who was otherwise occupied with the translation of Arabic texts. Based on interviews with those who had travelled, he interpreted many aspects of

their Yemen journey and also provided an extended study of the coffee plant, its history, and trade. As such, this was one of the first texts to provide a glimpse of Yemen, which had achieved new visibility because of the rising interest in coffee across Europe. *Voyage de l'Arabie Heureuse* was first published in French (Paris: Huguier, 1715; Paris: A. Cailleau and Amsterdam: Steenhouwer et Uytwerf, 1716) and soon after translated into Italian (Venice: Presso Sebastian Coleti, 1721), English (London: G. Strahan and R. Williamson, 1726); under the title *A Voyage to Arabia Foelix* (Cornhill: E Symon, 1732; London: James Hodges, 1742), and German (Leipzig: Braun, 1740).

3. Generally the Dutch mention that they were brought into the port according to "the tradition of the land" and make reference to the crowds, musicians, and horses and their visit to the governor's house. For an example, see Mocha *dagregister,* February 20, 1731, VOC 2252, 328, VOC Records, National Archives, The Hague.

4. James Hevia, *Cherishing Men from Afar: Qing Guest Ritual and the Macartney Embassy of 1793* (Durham, NC: Duke University Press, 1995), 74.

5. Mocha *dagregister,* February 10 and 12, 1730, VOC 2202, 250–251, VOC Records.

6. In the *dagregister,* Sidi Yaqut Khan II is referred to as "landlord of Danda-Rajpuri [*landheer van den deragiepour*]." He was born in 1706 and died in either 1732 or 1734. The *dagregister* mentions ships associated with him in the years 1729–1731 and then again in 1736–1737, after he died. John McLeod, "The Later History of Janjira," in *Habshi Amarat: African Elites in India,* edited by Kenneth X. Robbins and John McLeod (Ocean Township, NJ: Mapin, 2006), 188. According to Jasdanwalla, he was a prolific builder in India and clearly had access to personal funds, likely obtained through the trade. Faaeza Jasdanwalla, "African Settlers on the West Coast of India: The Sidi Elite of Janjira," *African and Asian Studies* 10 (2011): 48–49.

7. His name, 'Anbar, is mentioned only in reference to his visit to the imam's court, which followed in the same year. Mocha *dagregister,* July 20, 1730, VOC 2252, 201, VOC Records.

8. Mocha *dagregister,* May 13–14, 1730, VOC 2202, 288–290, VOC Records.

9. Ashin Das Gupta speaks about the "considerable deference" paid to the Mughal imperial ships in Yemen, but without any detail. Ashin Das Gupta, *Indian Merchants and the Decline of Surat, c. 1700–1750* (1979; Delhi: Manohar, 1994), 287. When the imam's *nakhudha* appeared in Mocha from Surat in March 1723, he was welcomed in "a splendid fashion by the whole government with riders (who jousted in front of our loge) and the whole garrison of soldiers." Mocha *dagregister,* March 19, 1723, VOC 9117, 88, VOC Records.

10. Mocha *dagregister,* January 25, 1737, VOC 2447, 156–157, VOC Records.

11. Mocha *dagregister,* April 25, 1729, VOC 9123, 283, VOC Records.

12. On his arrival in the city, see Mocha *dagregister,* February 5, 1730, VOC 2202, 246–247, VOC Records. A complete biographical sketch of Khazindar can be found in Um, *The Merchant Houses,* 68–76.

13. At this time, he also tried to introduce other controversial innovations, such as charging the Europeans a higher tax rate on goods from Surat, which Francis Dickinson, the EIC factor, contested by leaving his goods in front of the governor's house and refusing to move them, similar to Muhammad Husayn's mode of protest. Mocha *dagregister,* March 21, 1730, VOC 2202, 269–270, VOC Records.

14. Letter to the General Directors, Bombay, from William Phipps, Thomas Rammell, and Henry Albert, Mocha, July 20, 1721, IOR/G/17/1 pt. 1, 52r-52v, Mocha Factory Records, British Library, London.

15. In 1734 and 1735 the English provided small tips to the governor's drummers and horse keepers for helping to welcome the captains on shore, suggesting that they were willing to pay for appropriate acknowledgment of their status. Account Particulars of Presents given to the Governour etc Officers of Mocha as Customary for Ship Princess Louisa Capt Richard Pinnell Comm., July 1734, IOR/G/17/2, pt. 1, 315r; Account of Presents given the Governour and Officers of Mocha for Ship King William, July 25, 1735, IOR/G/17/2, pt. 1, 322r, both in Mocha Factory Records.

16. Mocha *dagregister,* March 30, 1735, VOC 2356, 146, VOC Records.

17. Sanders, *Ritual,* 8, 14.

18. As examples, see the Eid al-Adha celebration held in Mocha in 1708 and the arrival of an ambassador from the Hijaz in 1709. Mocha *dagregister,* December 14, 1708, and July 2, 1709, VOC 1784, 1888–1889, 2188–2189, VOC Records.

19. Haykel, *Revival,* 55. The Ottoman origin of these rites of entry is suggested by Henry Middleton's 1610 account, which mentions the gathering of the city's notables and music at the jetty, leading to a lavish visit at the Ottoman governor's house. "An Account of the Captivity of Sir Henry Middleton," in Roque, *Voyage to Arabia,* 252.

20. Ross, *Status,* 19. Similarly, but in regard to diplomatic missions, historian Adam Clulow refers to "the moment of transfer from ship to shore" as "the first stage on which to mark out their authority," which also "needed to set the right tone for the subsequent embassy." Adam Clulow, *The Company and the Shogun: The Dutch Encounter with Tokugawa Japan* (New York: Columbia University Press, 2013), 76–77.

21. Thomas, *Entangled Objects,* 119.

22. Markus Rediker, *Villains of All Nations: Atlantic Pirates in the Golden Age* (Boston: Beacon Press, 2004), 164.

23. For instance, one evening the French claimed they saw a ship waving a Dutch flag, which was confirmed by another observer. The Dutch saw no blue, only red, so they believed it was actually a "Moorish" flag. Mocha *dagregister,* April 21, 1723, VOC 9117, 98, VOC Records.

24. Rediker, *Villains,* 8.

25. R. B. Serjeant, *The Portuguese off the South Arabian Coast* (Oxford: Clarendon Press, 1963), 117, 127.

26. Rediker, *Villains,* 8.

27. Ibid., 164.

28. According to Lauren Benton, trading ships often carried "multiple flags and passes" as well. Lauren Benton, *A Search for Sovereignty: Law and Geography in European Empires, 1400–1900* (Cambridge, UK: Cambridge University Press, 2010), 117. Aslanian describes how English private merchants would fly Armenian colors to get past Spanish restrictions on their trade in Manila in the second half of the seventeenth century (*From the Indian Ocean,* 59).

29. Philippe Rault, *Les drapeaux bretons de 1188 à nos jours* (Spézet, France: Coop Breizh, 1998), 34, figs. 47, 48. It is also possible that they flew the colors of the Compagnie des Indes, which, at this time, was white with a French coat of arms in the center.

30. For instance, they used the English flag off the coast of Abyssinia (Roque, *Voyage to Arabia,* 35).

31. They had initially set off from Brest in two ships in addition to a small supply vessel, which they eventually discarded along the way.

32. It was only later that the Dutch in Mocha realized that the third ship, which they referred to as *De Overwinnaar,* was one of their own, inspiring anger at the new arrivals.

This escalated when the French tried to sell the ship to Governor al-Huraybi. Mocha *dagregister*, June 14, 1709, VOC 1784, 2144r-v, VOC Records.

33. Roque, *Voyage de l'Arabie*, 90. Grandpré also observed this flag in 1790, saying that it was hoisted on Fridays. He disparagingly said it was "miserably delineated" and "instead of [a] sword, one might take it for a pair of breeches." Louis de Grandpré, *A voyage in the Indian Ocean and to Bengal Undertaken in the Year 1790: containing an account of the Sechelles Islands and Trincomale. To which is added, A voyage in the Red Sea; including a description of Mocha* (1801; Boston: David Carlisle, 1803), 214. All of the following quotes and textual references from Grandpré come from the 1803 Boston translation of this narrative, unless otherwise marked. References to images are drawn from the various early nineteenth-century editions, including Paris (1801) and London (1803).

34. In fact, the French had planted their own flag on the southern fort when they took it briefly, and this may have been what was intended in this triumphal representation from 1737. However, it is difficult to discern the details of the minuscule flags in this panoramic image.

35. Apparently the flag of the Ostenders was displayed for the first time in 1723, only after the GIC was officially chartered. Mocha *dagregister*, May 23, 1723, VOC 9117, 206v, VOC Records.

36. As further evidence of this point, in the 1849 Ottoman manuscript left by Mustafa Hami, several but not all of the forts depicted in Mocha, al-Hudayda, and al-Luhayya display flags, but none of the houses is shown with a flag hoisted. Klaus Kreiser, "An Unpublished Ottoman Manuscript on the Yemen in 1849: Mustafa Hami's *Sevku 'l-asker 'l-cedid der 'ahd-i Sultan Mecid*," *Arabian Studies* 7 (1985): 169–182.

37. Roque, *Voyage to Arabia*, 84.

38. Mocha *dagregister*, January 22, 1723, VOC 9117, 56v-57v, VOC Records.

39. For more on Ottoman interventions into Qasimi dealings with foreign merchants, see Um, "1636 and 1726," 112–134.

40. Jane Hathaway, "The Ottomans and the Yemeni Coffee Trade," *Oriento Moderno* 26:1 (2006): 168.

41. Um, "1636 and 1726," 128.

42. Haykel, *Revival*, 115–117.

43. Berigt ingevolge het g'ordonneerde door den E. E. agtb. Heer Pieter Phoonsen directeur benevens den Raad tot Souratta, from A. Domburg, Surat, May 15, 1740, VOC 2509, 1462; Mocha *dagregister*, August 20 and 21, 1739, VOC 2509, 1609, both in VOC Records.

44. Carsten Niebuhr, *Reisebeschreibung nach Arabien und andern umliegenden ländern* (Copenhagen: Nicolaus Möller, 1774), 1:429.

45. Martha Mundy, "San'a' Dress, 1920–75," in *San'a': An Arabian Islamic City*, edited by R. B. Serjeant and R. Lewcock (London: World of Islam Trust, 1983), 533.

46. In addition, Niebuhr's flowered overrobe pictured in figure 1.2 is certainly foreign, perhaps of silk brocade from Iran or even printed cotton from India.

47. John Irwin and Margaret Hall, *Indian Embroideries* (Ahmedabad, India: Textile Museum, 1973), pls. 11A and 11B.

48. Igor Kopytoff, "The Cultural Biography of Things: Commodification as a Process," in Appadurai, *The Social Life of Things*, 73–74.

49. Grandpré included an engraving of the informal Baniyan dress in his publication, but it appears to be a mere copy of Niebuhr's, which he was surely familiar with. Louis de Grandpré, *Voyage dans l'Inde et au Bengale: fait dans les années 1789 et 1790* (Paris: Dentu,

1801), 2:184. It has been suggested that even Niebuhr's image of the Baniyan (Figure 1.4) borrowed from a previous source dated 1630. However, the dress appears differently in the two illustrations, so one cannot dismiss the later image as lacking "direct empirical observation." Niebuhr had a great deal of experience with Baniyans in Yemen and India, and would have been able to correct any misrepresentations of their dress. Moreover, with its mention of Baurenfeind as the artist at the bottom, we cannot assume that the image was wholly imagined in Copenhagen. Anne Haslund Hansen, "Niebuhr and the Visual Documentation of the Arabian Voyage, 1761–1767," in *Early Scientific Expeditions and Local Encounters: New Perspectives on Carsten Niebuhr and "The Arabian Journey,"* edited by Ib Friis, Michael Harbsmeier, and Jørgen Bœk Simonsen, Scientia Danica Series H, Humanistica, 4, vol. 2 (Viborg, Denmark: Det Kongelige Danske Videnskabernes Selskab, 2013), 130.

50. It is notable that the long robe represents the tradition of stitched garments, and the everyday wear can be associated with draped and unsewn garments, a significant opposition in Indian dress codes. Emma Tarlo, *Clothing Matters: Dress and Identity in India* (Chicago: University of Chicago Press, 1996), 26–33; Finbarr B. Flood, *Objects of Translation: Material Culture and the Medieval "Hindu-Muslim" Encounter* (Princeton, NJ: Princeton University Press, 2009), 64.

51. Grandpré, *A voyage,* 240.

52. Roque, *Voyage to Arabia,* 78.

53. R. B. Serjeant, "The Hindu, Baniyan, Merchants and Traders," in Serjeant and Lewcock, *San'a',* 434; Haykel, *Revival,* 125.

54. The same can be said about dress codes among different classes. Lower-class Yemenis could, and apparently sometimes did, adopt the dress of their wealthier counterparts, which was seen as a social disruption. Mundy, "San'a' Dress," 529–530.

55. Mocha *dagregister,* January 4, 1709, VOC 1784, 1903v, VOC Records.

56. Ann Rosalind Jones and Peter Stallybrass, *Renaissance Clothing and the Materials of Memory* (Cambridge, UK: Cambridge University Press, 2000), 5. Emma Tarlo has made the same point in regard to colonial and contemporary India in *Clothing Matters.*

57. Valentin Groebner, *Who Are You? Identification, Deception, and Surveillance in Early Modern Europe,* translated by M. Kyburz and J. Peck (Brooklyn, NY: Zone Books, 2007), 11.

58. Alan Mikhail, *The Animal in Ottoman Egypt* (Oxford: Oxford University Press, 2013); Sandra Swart, "Riding High—Horses, Power, and Settler Society, c. 1654–1840," *Kronos* 29 (November 2003): 47–63; Donna Landry, *Noble Brutes: How Eastern Horses Transformed English Culture* (Baltimore: Johns Hopkins University Press, 2009).

59. As described by Elizabeth Lambourn, "horsemania" in India emerged from a circular set of exchanges, commercial and intellectual, between the Middle East and the subcontinent. Although the surge in demand for imported horses is evidenced only beginning in the thirteenth century, it likely represents a much longer set of preoccupations. Elizabeth Lambourn, "Towards a Connected History of Equine Cultures in South Asia: Bahri (Sea) Horses and 'Horsemania' in Thirteenth-Century South India," *Medieval Globe* 2:1 (2016): 57–100.

60. In general the literature has highlighted horses coming from the Gulf rather than the Red Sea. But, as the figures show, a large number were also transported through the Red Sea to India after the medieval period. Simon Digby, *War-Horse and Elephant in the Delhi Sultanate: A Study of Military Supplies* (Oxford: Orient Monographs, 1971), 29–33; Lambourn, "Towards a Connected History"; Elizabeth Lambourn, "Of Jewels and Horses: The Career and Patronage of an Iranian Merchant under Shah Jahan," *Iranian Studies* 36:2 (June 2003): 222.

61. Mocha *dagregister,* August 13 and 15, 1731, VOC 2252, 164–165, VOC Records.

62. Landry, *Noble Brutes,* 3, 9.

63. Rapport door den mochase opperhoofden, from Dirck Clercq and Cornelius Snoeck, aboard the *Nieuwburg*, September 22, 1701, VOC 1660, 777, VOC Records.

64. Dagelijkse aantekening gehouden bij de ondercoopluijden Joan Josua Ketelaar en Joan van der Needen op de reijse p[r] schip *Oostersteijn* na Mocha, December 21, 1705, VOC 9115, 27–28, VOC Records.

65. Swart, "Riding High," 53.

66. Mocha *dagregister*, May 22, 1724, VOC 9118, 120–121, VOC Records.

67. They were also sometimes restricted from moving through the eastern gate on foot. Grandpré, *A voyage*, 214.

68. Several months earlier, the imam had informed the three European groups that they could travel to the inland town of Mawza' as a privilege. At this point, they asked if the ban on riding freely in the city was still in place: The May edict may have been a belated response to that earlier query. Mocha *dagregister*, November 4, 1723, VOC 9118, 63–64, VOC Records.

69. Mocha *dagregister*, January 17, 1735, VOC 2356, 127–128, VOC Records. This restriction was still in place at the end of the eighteenth century, as attested to by Cloupet, who visited Mocha in 1788. M. Cloupet, "New Travels in Arabia Felix (1788)," in Roque, *Voyage to Arabia*, 392.

70. He was offered the horse as a gift the next day, which he refused. Mocha *dagregister*, February 17–18, 1737, VOC 2447, 193–194, VOC Records.

71. Niebuhr, *Reisebeschreibung*, 1:368.

72. Carsten Niebuhr, *Description de l'Arabie, faite sur des observations propres et des avis recueillis dans les lieux mêmes* (Amsterdam: S. J. Baalde, 1774), 51–52.

73. The Dutch were so used to these ceremonies that they wrote about them with great familiarity but little detail. For instance, when the new VOC resident, Jan van den Sturk, disembarked at Mocha in January 1730, he was celebrated at the governor's house "as usual with coffee, rosewater, and agarwood incense." Mocha *dagregister*, January 10, 1730, VOC 2202, 230–232, VOC Records.

74. Early seventeenth-century sources, such as Pieter van den Broecke's 1616 account from Mocha, describe coffee as a hot dark beverage. But by the early eighteenth century, *qishr* appears to have replaced *bunn* as the local drink of choice.

75. Apparently *qishr* was in limited demand outside of Yemen in the early period of coffee consumption. It was exported to the Sinai in the late fifteenth century, along with *bunn*. But after the sixteenth century, only *bunn* was sent. Mutsuo Kawatuoko, "Coffee Trade in the al-Tur Port, South Sinai," in Tuchscherer, *Le commerce du café*, 54.

76. For instance, the Dutch mention tobacco coming to Mocha from Calicut (Mocha *dagregister*, April 30, 1735, VOC 2356, 153) and from Basra via the Gulf (Mocha *dagregister*, January 21, 1727, VOC 9121, 120, both in VOC Records).

77. R. B. Serjeant, "The Market, Business Life, Occupations, and the Legality and Sale of Stimulants," in Serjeant and Lewcock, *San'a'*, 175.

78. C. G. Brouwer, "A Hazardous Item: The International Tobacco Trade of the Red Sea Port of al-Mukha, Reflected in Seventeenth-Century Dutch Records," *Itinerario* 32:2 (July 2008): 43; Mocha *dagregister*, January 25, 1728, VOC 9122, 91, and August 22, 1728, VOC 9123, 50, VOC Records.

79. For the debates about the legality of coffee, see Ralph Hattox, *Coffee and Coffeehouses: The Origins of a Social Beverage in the Medieval Near East* (Seattle: University of Washington Press, 1985).

80. Dinah Jung, *An Ethnography of Fragrance: The Perfumery Arts of 'Adan/Lahj* (Leiden: Brill, 2011), 203.

81. Joachim Meyer, *Sensual Delights: Incense Burners and Rosewater Sprinklers from the World of Islam* (Copenhagen: David Collection, 2015), 7.

82. Rendement van alle soorten van Goederen als er sederd primo medio Julij A° pass° bij 't sluijten der negotieboekjes sijn vercogt geworden, from J. v. Steenwijk, J. E. v. Mijlendonk, David Sommans Junior, Mocha, August 27, 1723, VOC 9104, 88–89, VOC Records.

83. Meyer, *Sensual Delights,* 7. However, evidence drawn from ancient Arabian altars suggests that frankincense was not often consumed domestically even in the pre-Islamic period. Nigel Groom, "Trade, Incense, and Perfume," in *Caravan Kingdoms: Yemen and the Ancient Incense Trade,* edited by Ann C. Gunter (Washington, DC: Arthur M. Sackler Gallery, Smithsonian Institution, 2005), 112.

84. Although he mentions them, he failed to include the tobacco pipe and the embroidered napkin in this image.

85. Edward J. Keall, "The Evolution of the First Coffee Cups in Yemen," in Tuchscherer, *Le commerce du café,* 43, 50. A few modern examples of this type of coffee pot are in the collection of the British Museum.

86. Sarah Posey, *Yemeni Pottery* (London: British Museum Press, 1994), 43.

87. Axelle Rouguelle and Hardy-Gulbert also found traces of Thai celadon in the Mocha survey. Claire Hardy-Guilbert and Axelle Rougeulle, "Ports islamiques du Yémen: Prospections archéologiques sur les côtes yéménites (1993–1995)," *Archéologie islamique* 7 (1997): 154–156.

88. Ibid., 154–155.

89. Timothy Power, "A First Ceramic Chronology for the Late Islamic Arabian Gulf," *Journal of Islamic Archaeology* 2:1 (2015): 19.

90. VOC records confirm that "chinese bruijne copjes" were available in Mocha in 1719, when the Dutch bought three corgies from a certain Captain Louis "Esqer." Extract der Schenkagien gedaan, August 19, 1719, VOC 1964, 197, VOC Records. Chinese and Japanese gilded cups appear on multiple lists, primarily for gifts. Waer in 't afgedwongene present aen den jman bestaan heeft en dies beloop, from J. v. Alderwereld, J. v. Steenwijk, Jacobus Augier, Ge. Duijk, Mocha, August 26, 1722, VOC 9104, 73, VOC Records.

91. Keall, "The Evolution."

92. Claire Hardy-Guilbert and Axelle Rougeulle, "Archaeological Research into the Islamic Period in Yemen: Preliminary Notes on the French Expedition, 1993," *Proceedings of the Seminar for Arabian Studies* 25 (1994): 40.

93. Meyer, *Sensual Delights,* cats. 28, 29, 72–75.

94. The type pictured by Niebuhr, with a round foot and no handle, was not included in Sterenn Le Mageur's typology of incense burners from the port of al-Shihr. However, it is clear that this type in wood and reed would not have survived in the archaeological context. Le Mageur's examples are made of more durable materials, such as stone or metal. Sterenn Le Mageur, "Typology of Incense-Burners of the Islamic Period," *Proceedings of the Seminar for Arabian Studies* 41 (2011): 173–186.

95. Meyer, *Sensual Delights,* cat. 11, 38–39.

96. Hardy-Guilbert and Rougeulle note the predominance of imported over local wares in their intramuros site survey of Mocha, whereas local wares were found in greater quantities outside of the walls ("Ports," 156). This imbalance adds evidence for Niebuhr's contention that the elite merchants who lived inside the walls used imported wares more frequently than the more middling locals (mostly living outside the walls). At the same time, his discussion makes clear that local objects were always paired with those from

abroad, even in well-to-do households. A full excavation is needed to come to further conclusions.

97. Um, *The Merchant Houses,* 135–138; Nancy Um, "Spatial Negotiations in a Commercial City: The Red Sea Port of Mocha, Yemen during the First Half of the Eighteenth Century," *Journal of the Society of Architectural Historians* 62:2 (June 2003): 178–193.

98. The Baniyan Mathura had owned the Dutch residence before it was sold to Hasan Hasusa in 1735. The Baniyans lived within the walls and were not relegated to a single quarter, unlike the Jewish and Somali communities, which resided in separate enclaves outside of the city walls. Um, *The Merchant Houses,* 173–177.

99. It also specifies that they could sleep at the Daké, an undefined term, at night. It may refer to the gate at the jetty or possibly the *khan.* Roque, *Voyage to Arabia,* 84; Roque, *Voyage de l'Arabie*, 104.

100. For an incident when an English sailor went on shore at night, see Mocha *dagregister,* May 5, 1730, VOC 2202, 285–286, VOC Records.

101. Mocha *dagregister,* February 14, 1725, VOC 9119, 127, VOC Records.

102. Dagelijkse aantekening, February 19, 1706, VOC 9115, 98–100; Mocha *dagregister,* May 13, 1731, VOC 2252, 395, both in VOC Records.

103. Mocha *dagregister,* July 21, 1724, VOC 9118, 2, VOC Records.

104. There are few references to these common travellers, but some *faqir*s (paupers) from India were said to have come on shore quite freely in February 1737. Mocha *dagregister,* February 10, 11, and 13, 1737, VOC 2447, 184–186, VOC Records.

105. Both practices were noted in the early nineteenth century, when some Malay pilgrims arrived in Mocha. "Caroline" Journal, 1821, Log 656 1821C, Phillips Library, Peabody Essex Museum, Salem, MA.

106. Roque, *Voyage to Arabia,* 84.

107. Goldberg, *Trade,* 172–173.

108. Olivia Remie Constable, *Housing the Stranger in the Mediterranean World: Lodging, Trade, and Travel in Late Antiquity and the Middle Ages* (Cambridge, UK: Cambridge University Press, 2003), 103–104.

109. Letter to General Directors, July 20, 1721, IOR/G/17/1, pt. 1, 67r, Mocha Factory Records.

110. Nancy Um, "Reflections on the Red Sea Style: Beyond the Surface of Coastal Architecture," *Northeast African Studies* 12:1 (2012): 260–264.

111. This assumption derives largely from commonly circulated knowledge, but very few wood samples have been tested. Of those that have, local woods such as ficus and acacia have also appeared. It is clear that we need to test more samples in order to better understand what types of wood were used in local building. Michael Mallinson, Laurence Smith, Colin Breen, Wes Forsythe, and Jacke Phillips, "Ottoman Suakin 1541–1865: Lost and Found," in "The Frontiers of the Ottoman World," special issue of *Proceedings of the British Academy* 156 (2009): 490.

112. After they left Istanbul heading for Egypt, they assumed these long robes. While in Yemen, Niebuhr and his companions modified their dress many times. He donned Yemeni dress when he went on an expedition to Ghalayfiqa. But when the group went to the highlands, they claimed that they were from "al-Sham," or Syria. Niebuhr, *Reisebeschreibung,* 1:34, 322, 338, 345.

113. Although he does not concentrate on trade, Sood provides a compelling model for exploring cognitive patterns and social interactions that were mutually understood around a vast sphere that included Mocha. Gagan D. S. Sood, "Circulation and Exchange

in Islamicate Eurasia: A Regional Approach to the Early Modern World," *Past and Present* 212 (2011): 113–162, doi: 10.1093/pastj/gtr001.

114. By contrast, Sood has suggested that the ceremonies that concluded the sealing of trade negotiations are of central importance. Those terminal receptions are treated in chapter 3. Ibid., section V.

115. Groebner, *Who Are You?*

Chapter 2: European Merchant Tribute in Yemen

1. Leonard Blussé, "Amongst Feigned Friends and Declared Enemies," in *Making Sense of Global History*, edited by Solvi Sogner (Oslo: Universitetsforlaget, 2001), 155.

2. Cynthia Viallé, "In Aid of Trade: Dutch Gift-giving in Tokugawa Japan," *Daigaku shiryohensanjo kenkyu kiyo* 16 (2006): 57–78; Cynthia Viallé, "'To Capture Their Favor': On Gift-Giving by the VOC," in *Mediating Netherlandish Art and Material Culture in Asia*, edited by Thomas DaCosta Kauffman and Michael North (Amsterdam: Amsterdam University Press, 2014), 291–320; Bhawan Ruangsilp, *Dutch East India Company Merchants at the Court of Ayutthaya: Dutch Perceptions of the Thai Kingdom, ca. 1604–1765* (Leiden: Brill, 2007); Clulow, *The Company;* Martha Chaiklin, *Cultural Commerce and Dutch Commercial Culture: The Influence of European Material Culture on Japan, 1700–1850* (Leiden: CNWS, 2003).

3. For a useful summation of this interdisciplinary revival, see John Watkins, "Toward a New Diplomatic History of Medieval and Early Modern Europe," *Journal of Medieval & Early Modern Studies* 38 (2008): 1–14. Blussé's invocation toward a "new diplomatic history" was, by contrast, delivered in response to the "new military history" rather than the old diplomatic history, which Watkins critiques as methodologically outdated and resistant to theoretical engagement.

4. Jurrien van Goor, *Prelude to Colonialism: The Dutch in Asia* (Hilversum, Netherlands: Uitgeverij Verloren, 2004), 29.

5. Blussé, "Amongst Feigned Friends," 155.

6. Sanjay Subrahmanyam, *The Career and Legend of Vasco da Gama* (Cambridge, UK: Cambridge University Press, 1998), 136–138.

7. Chaiklin, *Cultural Commerce,* 33.

8. Georges Bataille, "The Notion of Expenditure," in *Visions of Excess: Selected Writings, 1927–1939,* edited by Allan Stoekl (Minneapolis: University of Minnesota Press, 1985), 118, 123.

9. Cecily Hilsdale, *Byzantine Art and Diplomacy in an Age of Decline* (Cambridge, UK: Cambridge University Press, 2014), 18.

10. A recent study about Mamluk diplomatic gifts is a useful springboard, in that it takes patterns of giving seriously while also recognizing the difficulties in identifying gifts based on lengthy but relatively undifferentiated rosters and lists. Doris Behrens-Abouseif, *Practising Diplomacy in the Mamluk Sultanate: Gifts and Material Culture in the Medieval Islamic World* (London: I. B. Tauris, 2014).

11. Thomas, *Entangled Objects,* 100.

12. By comparison, see the case of Siam or Japan. Ruangsilp, *Dutch,* 57–70; Clulow, *The Company,* 25–94.

13. Clulow, *The Company,* 253.

14. C. G. Brouwer, *Al-Mukha: Profile of a Yemeni Seaport as Sketched by Servants of the Dutch East India Company* (Amsterdam: D'Fluyte Rarob, 1997), 270–273.

15. The Dutch use phrases such as "*par usantie*" (as usual), "*gewoonlijke jaarlijxe schenkagie*" (ordinary yearly presents), and "*schenkagie volgens jaarlijkse gewoonte*" (gifts according to the yearly practice). For instance, see Mocha *dagregister,* August 14, 1725, VOC 9105, 305, VOC Records, National Archives, The Hague.

16. This contrasts the VOC situation in Japan, where their gifts were, at least initially, delivered in lieu of taxes or fees, but then later were used to offset them. Chaiklin, *Cultural Commerce,* 38.

17. Extract van de Schenkagie goederen, VOC 9057, 1717, 46–50, VOC Records.

18. The first extant gift register from the period under consideration dates from 1706 and documents gifts to the governor of Bayt al-Faqih. It included spices, candied spices, Chinese silk, a piece of *perpetuana* (wool twill fabric), and a jug of spirits. Dagelijkse aantekening, May 9, 1706, VOC 9115, 144, VOC Records.

19. One ell = approximately 69 centimeters. Beginning in the 1630s, Leiden became the center of the *laken* industry. Brouwer translates the term *laken* as "brocade" and lists varieties in wool and silk for seventeenth-century Mocha. In the case of eighteenth-century Yemen, woolen fabrics appear almost exclusively, and very few examples were woven with metallic threads. W. O. Dijk, "The VOC's Trade in Indian Textiles with Burma, 1634–90," *Journal of Southeast Asian Studies* 33:3 (October 2002): 497; C. G. Brouwer, *Al-Mukha: The Transoceanic Trade of a Yemeni Staple Town as Mapped by Merchants of the VOC, 1614–1650: Coffee, Spices, and Textiles* (Amsterdam: D'Fluyte Rarob, 2006), 232.

20. This list of port workers also included "maccadores," who may have been translators.

21. According to John Guy, the bafta was Surat's most frequently exported textile. Its quality could range from coarse to fine, and it was usually dyed red or blue and undecorated. John Guy, *Woven Cargoes: Indian Textiles in the East* (New York: Thames and Hudson, 1998), 50.

22. Extract, August 19, 1719, VOC 1964, 197–200; Specificatie der gedaene schenkagien, 1722, VOC 9104, 21–23; Letter to Batavia, from J. v. Steenwijk, J. E. v. Mijlendonk, D. Sommans, Mocha, August 27, 1723, VOC 9104, 37–40, all in VOC Records.

23. In some cases, the spiced oils are described in general terms as *oliteiten,* but in others, unspecified types of *oliteiten* are differentiated from the specifically named spiced oils.

24. Viallé, "'To Capture,'" 293.

25. Ibid., 294.

26. Clulow, *The Company,* 246–254.

27. When values are documented in guilders, I have converted them to Spanish reals using the rate of 1 Spanish real = 48 stuivers. Brouwer, *Al-Mukha: Transoceanic,* 399.

28. For instance, in 1719 the VOC sent 1,626,748 pounds of coffee (6,461 bales) to Batavia on two ships. But 1729 was a particularly poor year for the coffee intake; their single ship left Mocha with only 301.5 bales. Mocha *dagregister,* August 19, 1719, VOC 9116, 15, and August 20, 1729, VOC 2202, 181–190, VOC Records.

29. Although the earlier gift had included two more pounds of cloves and nutmeg, those relatively inexpensive spices had little effect on the overall value of the gift.

30. Sonia Ashmore, *Muslin* (London: V&A, 2012), 24.

31. The word cossae comes from *khas,* or "special," a term used to suggest high quality. Malmals made for imperial use were sometimes specified by the term *khas* as well. Yet historian Om Prakash refers to the cossaes exported by the VOC as a "staple variety of muslin." Ultimately, all of these types of piece goods came in varying levels of quality that are hard to differentiate based on sparse textual references. Ashmore, *Muslin,* 17, 158; Om

Prakash, "From Negotiation to Coercion: Textile Manufacturing in India in the Eighteenth Century," *Modern Asian Studies* 41:6 (November 2007): 1335; Extract, August 19, 1719, VOC 1964, 197, VOC Records.

32. Jung, *Ethnography,* 16.

33. Extract, August 19, 1719, VOC 1964, 197, VOC Records.

34. These candied products were made of spices such as nutmeg, cloves, and ginger but could also be produced from other aromatic substances and fruit, such as licorice, mango, blimbing, lemon, apricot, and quince. Only the candied spices were offered in Yemen. Cynthia Viallé, "Tot schenkagie daar het te pas comen sal," *Aziatische Kunst* 23: (1993): 8–11.

35. Arne Hoff, *Dutch Firearms,* edited by Walter A. Stryker (London: Sotheby Parke Bernet, 1978), 222.

36. For instance, specimens from the late seventeenth and early eighteenth centuries feature a representation of the Buddha, a winged dragon, and other decorative forms. Ibid., 135, 223.

37. Behrens-Abouseif suggests that this was also the case in Egypt, where well-known Mamluk manufactures, such as enameled glassware and carpets, were rarely given as diplomatic gifts (*Practising,* 171).

38. They were specified as rough, ordinary, or bleached. Rendement van alle soo danige goederen, August 25, 1722, VOC 9104, 60–61, VOC Records.

39. Willem Floor, *The Persian Textile Industry in Historical Perspective, 1500–1925* (Paris: Harmattan, 1999), 74.

40. Els M. Jacobs, *Merchant in Asia: The Trade of the Dutch East India Company during the Eighteenth Century* (Leiden: CNWS, 2006), 58–60.

41. Ibid., 277.

42. Letter to Batavia, from W. v.d. Bergh, J. Akersloot, Ras Macquet, en J. A. de Cailliou, Mocha, August 15, 1735, VOC 9111, 50, VOC Records.

43. Mehmet Bulut, "The Role of the Ottomans and Dutch in the Commercial Integration between the Levant and Atlantic in the Seventeenth Century," *Journal of the Economic and Social History of the Orient* 45:2 (2002): 224. According to Floor, both Dutch and English woolens were worn by the middle class in eighteenth-century Iran (*Persian,* 220).

44. On *eisen* as a common practice across Asia, see Viallé, "'To Capture,'" 296.

45. It should be noted that the mundane and usually quite generic *eis* lists that the VOC factors generated in Mocha diverge starkly from the unique *eisboeken* from Japan, through which gift recipients could request specific and sometimes unusual objects. Viallé, "In Aid," 65–68; Minoru Omori, "Eisch Boek in Dutch-Japanese Trade," in *Asian Trade Routes, Continental and Maritime,* Studies on Asian Topics, 13, edited by K. R. Haellquist and Scandinavian Institute of Asian Studies (London: Routledge, 2013), 199–208; Chaiklin, *Cultural Commerce,* 49–70.

46. Extract, 1719, VOC 1964, 198, VOC Records.

47. These shawls were usually from Surat and sometimes referred to as *pomerijs.* Extract, 1719, VOC 1964, 197, VOC Records. *Pomerijs* probably derived from *pamri,* a Marathi term that signified a long narrow cloth of three ells by one ell that could be draped over the shoulders or wrapped as a turban. *Henry Yule Hobson-Jobson: A Glossary of Anglo-Indian Colloquial Words and Phrases,* Digital Dictionaries of South Asia, accessed January 20, 2016, http://dsal.uchicago.edu/dictionaries/hobsonjobson/. The *pomerijs* was costly and associated with robes of honor. *VOC-Glossarium: Verklaringen van Termen, Verzameld uit de Rijks Geschiedenis Publicatiën die Betrekking hebben op de Verenigde Oost-Indische Compagnie* (The Hague: Instituut voor Nederlandse Geschiedenis, 2000), 93.

48. Specificatie, 1722, VOC 9104, 23, VOC Records.

49. Chaiklin, *Cultural Commerce,* 33.

50. Ruangsilp, *Dutch,* 140–141.

51. Another study of English gift practices can be found in Nancy Um, "Order in the 'Arbitrary': The Distribution, Content, and Temporal Cycles of English Merchant Tribute in Eighteenth-Century Yemen," *Journal of Early Modern History* 18:3 (2014): 227–253.

52. The only exceptions were two watches that were given to 'Ali bin Amir Rizq, son of the governor at that time, and the merchant Muhammad Yasin in 1718. In the English case, we have four extant gift registers. Acc't of what presented the following persons for two Ships, dated 1718, IOR/G/17/1, pt. 1, 12r-12v; Diary excerpt, dated May 11, 1720, IOR/G/17/1, pt. 1, 8r; List of what Presented the Governours and Officers of Mocha and Beetlefuckee, dated August 1720, IOR/G/17/1, pt. 1, 34r; Account of Presents given the Sundry Officers of Mocha and Beetlefuckee from July 17, 1721 to July 14, 1722, IOR/G/17/1, pt. 1, 134r-136v and its duplicate IOR/G/17/1, pt. 1, 138r-141v, all in Mocha Factory Records, British Library, London.

53. Not all registers provide the exact dates of gifts tendered, but the ones that do suggest these standard dates for bestowal.

54. These coins were minted by the imam and went by the names *harf, kabir, komassi* (from *khumsiyya*), and *buqsha.* They were used widely around the city, particularly in the bazaar.

55. Floor, *Persian,* 70.

56. K. N. Chaudhuri, *The Trading World of Asia and the English East India Company, 1660–1760* (Cambridge, UK: Cambridge University Press, 1978), 222–226.

57. Dimities were cotton cloths that had cords or ribs added for a textured surface. Hummums were a type of muslin that was coarser than the malmal. Cynthia V. A. Schaffner, "Textile Glossary," in *The Interwoven Globe: The Worldwide Textile Trade, 1500–1800,* edited by Amelia Peck (New York: Metropolitan Museum of Art, 2015), 305–306.

58. I thank Sylvia Houghteling for making sense of these embossed cloths and encouraging me to look more closely at European woolen textiles. Chaudhuri describes embossed cloths in India as well (*Trading World,* 223), and Diderot illustrated a fabric embosser in his encyclopedia from this period. "Cloth Cutting and Figuring," in *The Encyclopedia of Diderot and d'Alembert Collaborative Translation Project* (Ann Arbor: Michigan Publishing, University of Michigan Library, 2010), accessed April 3, 2014, http://hdl.handle.net/2027/spo.did2222.0001.434.

59. The shalbofts were likely Deccani, and the hummums were probably from Bengal, although the dimities could have been made in England.

60. The English gift baftas were worth 5 Spanish reals apiece, whereas the ones the Dutch repurposed were purchased from Mocha's market and priced at only 1.5 Spanish reals.

61. Account of Presents, July 17, 1721 to July 14, 1722, IOR/G/17/1, pt. 1, 134r-136v, Mocha Factory Records.

62. Chaudhuri, *Trading World,* 222.

63. Ibid., 223.

64. Floor, *Persian,* 71.

65. Grehan, *Everyday Life,* 213; Gilbert Buti, "Des goûts et des couleurs: Draps du Languedoc pour clientèle levantine au XVIIIe siècle," *Rives nord-méditerranéennes* 29 (2008), accessed November 17, 2015, http://rives.revues.org/1393.

66. Letter to Chief and Factors, Mocha, from Will[em] Phipps, Jno Courtney, Robt Cowan, Robert Newlin, Geo Percivall, John Sarson, Bombay, September 30, 1722, IOR/G/17/1, pt. 2, 188v, Mocha Factory Records.

67. Letter, from William Phipps, Edward Say, Henry Albert, Tho Rammell, Mocha, July 20, 1721, IOR/G/17/1, pt. 1, 55r, Mocha Factory Records.

68. Buti, "Des goûts," lines 22–25.

69. Letter to Court of Directors, from Francis Dickinson, Mocha, April 23, 1729, IOR/G/17/2, 7r, Mocha Factory Records.

70. The same list mentions the need for broadcloth in purple, chocolate, and mulberry, but without swatches. Several types of embossed varieties are requested but not sampled, including those in green with white flowers, green with red flowers, and yellow with red flowers, as well as embossed carpets at various dimensions. Patterns of cloth proper for Mocha Anno 1721, IOR/G/17/1, pt. 1, 119r, Mocha Factory Records.

71. They returned the unsold broadcloth to Bombay in 1722 because of the colors, but merchants in Bombay sent some of the same pieces back to Mocha the next year complaining that it would not sell in India either! Letter to Chief and Factors, September 30, 1722, IOR/G/17/1, pt. 2, 187v, Mocha Factory Records.

72. Niebuhr, *Description,* 190.

73. John Baldry, *Textiles in Yemen: Historical References to Trade and Commerce in Textiles in Yemen from Antiquity to Modern Times,* Occasional Paper 27 (London: British Museum, 1982), 58–63.

74. Resolutie genomen in 'SE Comp[s]. gehuurde wooning ter Stede Mocha, September 28, 1724, VOC 9105, 67–69, VOC Records.

75. These overall sums for cash gifts did not include the alcoholic beverages they doled out throughout the trade season to port workers, costs that were tabulated separately in the VOC account books.

76. In previous years, they had been tendered on varied dates, June 1717 and August 1719, for instance.

77. Letter to Court of Directors, from Robert Cowan, John Gerrard, Thomas Rammell, John Style, and Francis Dickinson, Mocha, August 6, 1725, IOR/G/17/1, pt. 3, 434v, Mocha Factory Records.

78. Behrens-Abouseif, *Practising,* 123.

79. Linda Komaroff, "The Art of the Art of Giving at the Islamic Courts," in *Gifts of the Sultan: The Arts of Giving at the Islamic Courts,* edited by Linda Komaroff (New Haven, CT: Yale University Press, 2011), 20; Anthony Cutler, "Gifts and Gift Exchange as Aspects of the Byzantine, Arab, and Related Economies," *Dumbarton Oaks Papers* 55 (2001): 249–250.

80. John McLane, *Land and Local Kingship in Eighteenth-Century Bengal* (Cambridge, UK: Cambridge University Press, 1993), 96.

81. Sudipta Sen also disagrees with McLane's interpretations of gifts in eighteenth-century Bengal, but based on an entirely different understanding of gift practices and economies. He believes that gifts and patronage "were always regarded above mere money." Sudipta Sen, *Empire of Free Trade: The East India Company and the Making of the Colonial Marketplace* (Philadelphia: University of Pennsylvania Press, 1998), 70.

82. Chaiklin describes a much more structured terminology for Japan, where a specific term was used to describe an official gift, and another a special request (*Cultural Commerce,* 38). In Yemen customary and special gifts are usually collapsed on the same registers, as we see in VOC 1964 from 1719, VOC Records.

83. Letter to Batavia, August 22, 1716, VOC 9057, 10–11, VOC Records.

84. The attack on the Dutch factory in Mocha, described at length by Das Gupta, took place right after this visit was completed in February 1717 (*Indian Merchants,* 162).

85. This imbalance of plates to cups speaks to the particular culinary needs of the recipients, who mainly used metal or metal-plated tableware. By contrast, local elites relied heavily upon imported cups for coffee drinking, as discussed in chapter 1. It is interesting that the Dutch, who had prime access to Japanese porcelain, bought these wares in the bazaar, leading us to wonder who else carried such large quantities of Japanese ceramics to Mocha's market. Niebuhr, *Description,* 46–47; C. J. A. Jörg and Oliver Impey, *Fine and Curious: Japanese Export Porcelain in Dutch Collections* (Amsterdam: Hotei, 2003), 12.

86. According to Gawronski, eyeglasses were greatly desired in Asia and always included in eastbound cargos. Some examples were of high quality, adorned with tortoiseshell, gold, and silver. The ones offered in Yemen were extremely basic, evaluated at only half a florin apiece. Jerzy Gawronski, *De "Equipagie" van de* Hollandia *en de* Amsterdam*: VOC-bedrijvigheid in 18de-eeuws Amsterdam* (Amsterdam: De Bataafsche Leeuw, 1996), 156, 172.

87. This is not the only instance of a foreign doctor treating Imam al-Mahdi, who happened to suffer from various ailments during the latter part of his reign. Nancy Um, "Foreign Doctors at the Imam's Court: Medical Diplomacy in Yemen's Coffee Era," *Genre: Forms of Discourse and Culture* 48:2 (July 2015): 261–288.

88. Roque, *Voyage to Arabia,* 191–192.

89. Mocha *dagregister,* October 8, 1737, VOC 2447, 117, VOC Records.

90. Diary, dated May 11, 1720, IOR/G/17/1, pt. 1, 8r, Mocha Factory Records. We do not have a record of this Dutch gift in the VOC documents. They do mention a gift to the governor of Bayt al-Faqih, given at his departure for the court, not his return, although it was only 10.4 Spanish reals and thus markedly smaller than that given by the English. Reecquening van Extraordinaire ongelden, 1722, VOC 9104, 199, VOC Records.

91. Account of Presents, July 17, 1721 to July 14, 1722, IOR/G/17/1 pt. 1, 135r, Mocha Factory Records.

92. Translate of the Emaums Phirmaund to the English, received Francis Dickinson, 1729, IOR/G/17/2, 19, Mocha Factory Records.

93. Ania Loomba, "Of Gifts, Ambassadors, and Copy-Cats: Diplomacy, Exchange, and Difference in Early Modern India," in *Emissaries in Early Modern Literature and Culture: Mediation, Transmission, and Traffic, 1550–1700,* edited by Brinda Charry and Gitanjali Shahani (Burlington, VT: Ashgate, 2009), 43.

94. Viallé, "'To Capture,'" 294–295.

95. These complaints are encompassed amply in earlier studies on Mocha. See, for instance, Das Gupta, *Indian Merchants,* 163–64.

96. In a few cases, customary gifts were also disputed. In 1717, when VOC merchants offered gifts to Mocha's governor Amir Rizq, he demanded an additional 300 Spanish reals per ship, in addition to gifts for the lower officers. Letter to Batavia, from A. Pantzer and G. Scholten, Mocha, August 29, 1717, VOC 9057, 29, VOC Records.

97. Letter to William Phipps, Bombay, from Henry Albert, John Geckie, Thomas Rammell, and John Style, Mocha, August 11, 1722, IOR/G/17/1 pt. 1, 166r, Mocha Factory Records. The commotion about this demand was significant enough for the Dutch, who were facing similar demands, to hear about it. Mocha *dagregister,* September 15, 1722, VOC 9117, 33, VOC Records.

98. Letter to William Phipps, Bombay, from John Sarson and Francis Dickinson, Mocha, May 31, 1723, IOR/G/17/1 pt. 2, 231r, Mocha Factory Records.

99. Letter to Court of Directors, from Robert Cowan, John Gerrard, Thomas Rammell, John Style, and Francis Dickinson, Mocha, August 6, 1725, IOR/G/17/1 pt. 3, 434v, Mocha Factory Records.

100. Extract of Sundry Minutes taken by the Supercargoes of the Prince Williams Diary at Mocha, IOR/G/17/2, pt. 2, 185, Mocha Factory Records.

101. Ibid., 185, 187v.

102. Letter to Batavia, August 26, 1722, VOC 9104, 73–74, VOC Records.

103. Resolutie genomen in SE Comp[s]. gehuurde wooningh ter Steede Mocha, September 15, 1724, VOC 9105, 62–65, VOC Records.

104. Resolutie genomen in 'SE Comp[s]. gehuurde woning ten Stede Mocha, July 15, 1732, VOC 9108, 100, VOC Records.

105. Letter to the Court of Directors, from Robert Cowan and Francis Dickinson, Mocha, July 12, 1724, IOR/G/17/1, pt. 2, 321v, Mocha Factory Records.

106. As one example, see John Ramsay McCulloch, *A Dictionary, Practical, Theoretical, and Historical of Commerce and Commercial Navigation* (London: Spottiswoods and Shaw, 1849), 863.

107. Loomba, "Of Gifts," 52.

108. The theme of greed is commonly repeated across European records. As a few examples, see Loomba, "Of Gifts," 43; Ruangsilp, *Dutch,* 223; Viallé, "'To Capture,'" 295.

109. Timothy Davies, "British Private Trade Networks in the Arabian Seas, c. 1680–c. 1760," PhD diss., University of Warwick, 2012, 293–295.

110. The case of Mr. Edward Say late Chief of Mocha, received in court May 5, 1722, IOR/G/17/1, pt. 2, 309r -309v, Mocha Factory Records; Chaudhuri, *Trading World,* 369; Davies, "British," 299–300.

111. For instance, see Viallé's quote about gifts given at Tonkin in 1679 ("'To Capture,'" 295).

112. Robert Markley, "Alexander Hamilton, the Mughal War, and the Critique of the East India Company," *Genre: Forms of Discourse and Culture* 48:2 (July 2015): 240.

113. Ruangsilp, *Dutch,* 84, 218.

114. Rudi Matthee, "Gift-giving in the Safavid Period," *Encyclopaedia Iranica,* edited by Ehsan Yarshater (New York: Bibliotheca Persica Press, 2001), 10:612.

115. Grandpré, *A voyage,* 235.

116. Niebuhr, *Reisebeschreibung,* 1:413.

117. Grandpré, *A voyage,* 235.

118. Niebuhr, *Description,* 55–56.

119. Barbier, de la Grelaudiere, and those in their party who actually witnessed these events, conveyed their impressions to Roque, who then committed them to paper in *Voyage to Arabia* (210–211).

120. Baldry stops short of this conclusion but was perplexed by the fact that Mocha port officials wore such sumptuous robes, as described by Roque, while the imports consisted of low-quality cloth (*Textiles,* 46).

121. Grehan, *Everyday Life,* 216.

122. Thomas, *Entangled Objects,* 108.

123. Michelle Maskiell, "Consuming Kashmir: Shawls and Empires, 1500–2000," *Journal of World History* 13:1 (Spring 2002): 33.

124. Thomas, *Entangled Objects,* 29.

125. Weiner, *Inalienable Possessions,* 42.

CHAPTER 3: MERCHANTS FROM INDIA AND THEIR GIFT PRACTICES IN YEMEN

1. Ghada Hijjawi Qaddumi, translator and annotator, *Book of Gifts and Rarities: Kitab Hadaya wa al-Tuhaf* (Cambridge, MA: Harvard University Press, 1996); Linda Komaroff, ed., *Gifts of the Sultan: The Arts of Giving at the Islamic Courts* (New Haven, CT: Yale University Press, 2011). Behrens-Abouseif is unique in devoting an entire subsection to the Rasulids of Yemen in her study, but mostly as gift givers rather than recipients (*Practising*, 37–45).

2. Cutler, "Gifts," 266.

3. Komaroff, "The Art," 25–27.

4. Mocha *dagregister*, March 21 and May 9, 1729, VOC 9123, 175, 185, VOC Records, National Archives, The Hague.

5. "*Gewoonlijke jaarlijxe geschenken voor den Iman en de hoffs groten.*"

6. Even as late as 1725, these *nakhudha*s are still described as those of 'Abd al-Ghafur, who had died in 1718 and whose affairs were already being handled by his successor and grandson, Muhammad 'Ali. Mocha *dagregister*, June 10, 1725, VOC 9119, 182–183; Mocha *dagregister*, March 30 and May 22, 1730, VOC 2202, 273, 291, both in VOC Records.

7. Ghulam Nadri, "The Maritime Merchants of Surat: A Long-Term Perspective," *Journal of the Economic and Social History of the Orient* 50:2 (2007): 250.

8. Das Gupta, *Indian Merchants*, 236.

9. Mocha *dagregister*, July 20, 1730, VOC 2252, 201, VOC Records.

10. On June 22, 1724, at the end of Ramadan, Imam al-Mutawakkil sent two horses to Mocha, one intended for 'Abd al-Ghafur (or rather Muhammad 'Ali) and the other for Chalabi. However, it is uncertain if these were given in the context of yearly gift exchange or for Eid al-Fitr. Mocha *dagregister*, June 22, 1724, VOC 9118, 125, VOC Records.

11. Brouwer, *Al-Mukha: Profile*, 271–272.

12. It is clear that Muhammad 'Ali's gifts were intended to arrive at the court before Ramadan, which began on March 30, 1729. By contrast, in 1730 the *nakhudha* 'Anbar returned from Sanaa on July 20 (his departure date was not recorded), but he had only arrived in Mocha in May, relatively late in the season.

13. As mentioned in the previous chapter, Dutch gifts were tendered at various times, but after the year 1724, with the institution of cash gifts, they were always given on July 15, when they closed their yearly account books, close to the end of the high trading season.

14. It was commonly the ruler's responsibility to host traveling embassies generously. Behrens-Abouseif, *Practising*, 11.

15. With their relatively generic names, these representatives could have been local or foreign. Mocha *dagregister*, May 22, 1730, VOC 2202, 291, VOC Records.

16. Mocha *dagregister*, June 10, 1725, VOC 9119, 182–183, VOC Records.

17. But at the same time, they doubted that these gifts ever reached the intended recipient, suspecting that the governor or one of his officials intercepted them along the way. This suspicion was based on past experience. While governor of Mocha, al-Huraybi had withheld foreign presents intended for Imam al-Mahdi Muhammad. He worked with the *wazir* al-Hubayshi, who stored these gifts, including textiles, weapons, gems, and letters, in his house in Ibb, where they were discovered in 1708. Although the governor and the *wazir* were asked to account for their actions, they were both later restored to their positions and continued to wield a great deal of influence in the following decades. Um, *The Merchant Houses*, 67.

18. Muhsin bin al-Hasan (Abu Talib), *Tarikh al-yaman fi 'asr al-istiqlal 'an al-hukm al-'uthmani al-awwal*, edited by 'Abd Allah Muhammad al-Hibshi (Sanaa: Al-Mufaddal

Offset Printers, 1990), 265. I thank Fatima Muhaidat for her assistance in translating some parts of this extended passage on the Persian embassy to Yemen.

19. Hasan, *Tarikh,* 297–298. On June 14, 1701, a Dutch observer wrote that this Persian mission had arrived in Yemen a few months earlier and was at the court at that time. Rapport, 1701, VOC 1660, 784, VOC Records.

20. Hasan, *Tarikh,* 301.

21. Sinem Arcak, "Gifts in Motion: Ottoman-Safavid Cultural Exchange, 1501–1618," PhD diss., University of Minnesota, 2012, 189, 232. Others, such as the Mamluks, rarely gave or received Qur'an manuscripts as gifts. Behrens-Abouseif, *Practising,* 151.

22. W.569, Walters Art Museum and Garrett no. 31G, Department of Rare Books and Special Collections, Islamic Manuscripts Collection, Princeton University Library. The Yemeni example is held in the collection of Hasan Muhammad Zayd of Sanaa. I thank Michele Lamprakos for providing photographs of the manuscript from her visit in 2005.

23. He gave this dagger to a certain Ahmad Agha, an envoy of Salim Pasha. Hasan, *Tarikh,* 305.

24. Alexey Konstantinovich Levykin, ed., *The Tsars and the East: Gifts from Turkey and Iran in the Moscow Kremlin* (Washington, DC: Smithsonian Institution, 2009), cat. 15.

25. Based on the craftsmanship of the mounts and their arrangements, it has been proposed that these ruby-, turquoise-, and pearl-encrusted objects with golden surfaces were made in a single Safavid workshop. Inna Isidorovna Vishnevskaya, "Eastern Treasures of the Russian Tsars," in Levykin, *The Tsars,* 5–6.

26. For more on these Ottoman ambassadors, see Um, "1636 and 1726."

27. Roque, *Voyage to Arabia,* 219–220.

28. Otto Kurz, *European Clocks and Watches in the Near East* (Leiden: Brill, 1975); Peter Burschel, "A Clock for the Sultan: Diplomatic Gift-Giving from an Intercultural Perspective," *Medieval History Journal* 16:2 (2013): 547–563; Behrens-Abouseif, *Practising,* 126. EIC merchants gave two watches "with Arabian characters" as gifts to Mocha merchants Sidi 'Ali bin Amir Rizq and Muhammad Yasin in 1718, very rare examples of nontextile and noncash bestowals from the English. Acc't, 1718, IOR/G/17/1, pt. 1, 12r, Mocha Factory Records, British Library, London.

29. Mikhail, *Animal,* 109–130; Matthee, "Gift-giving," 609.

30. Arcak, "Gifts," 226; Komaroff, "The Art," 20; Behrens-Abouseif, *Practising,* 31; Hedda Reindl-Kiel, "No Horses for the Enemy: Ottoman Trade Regulations and Horse Gifting," in *Pferde in Asien: Geschichte, Handel und Kultur,* edited by R. Kauz, R. Ptak, and A. Schottenhammer (Vienna: Austrian Academy of Sciences Press, 2009), 47.

31. Weiner, *Inalienable Possessions,* 33.

32. Viallé, "'To Capture,'" 309.

33. The most complete study on official tribute practices in the Islamic world focuses on Iran and almost entirely on etymology. It pays little attention to the material components of these gifts. Ann Lambton, "*Pishkash,* Present or Tribute?," *Bulletin of the School of Oriental and African Studies* 57:1 (February 1994): 145–158.

34. George Annesley (Viscount Valentia), *Voyages and Travels to India, Ceylon, the Red Sea, Abyssinia, and Egypt* (London: W. Miller, 1809), 2:336.

35. Letter to William Phipps, Bombay, from Robert Cowan, Mocha, July 12, 1724, IOR/G/17/1, pt. 1, 325v, Mocha Factory Records.

36. Khazindar was not the only governor to transmit unsatisfactory gifts to the imam that year. The governor of Bayt al-Faqih sent more than 50,000 Spanish reals' worth of gifts

to the imam and was then asked to send another 20,000 reals. Mocha *dagregister,* September 17, 1724, VOC 9119, 54–55, VOC Records.

37. Mocha *dagregister,* September 4–6, 1730, VOC 2252, 221, VOC Records.

38. Mocha *dagregister,* September 22, 1730, VOC 2252, 224–225, VOC Records.

39. Mocha *dagregister,* August 25–31, 1732, VOC 2252, 168, VOC Records.

40. Mocha *dagregister,* June 25, 1736, VOC 2415, 341, VOC Records.

41. Mocha *dagregister,* September 30, 1729, VOC 2202, 199–201, VOC Records.

42. Mocha *dagregister,* October 30, 1725, VOC 9120, 31, VOC Records.

43. Mocha *dagregister,* December 16, 1731, VOC 2252, 217–218, VOC Records.

44. A turban is mentioned only once, in the case of ʻAnbar in 1730, and vests are mentioned occasionally as well, but never as often as the more ubiquitous robe.

45. Behrens-Abouseif, *Practising,* 23.

46. Stewart Gordon, "Introduction: Ibn Battuta and a Region of Robing," in *Robes of Honour:* Khilʻat *in Precolonial and Colonial India,* edited by Stewart Gordon (New Delhi: Oxford University Press, 2003), 2.

47. Gavin R. G. Hambly, "The Emperor's Clothes: Robing and 'Robes of Honour' in Mughal India," in Gordon, *Robes of Honour,* 43.

48. Gordon, "Introduction," 4, 6.

49. Hasan, *Tarikh,* 297–301.

50. Flood, *Objects,* 77. Gail Minault describes *nazr* as distinct from *pishkash* in that *nazr* was delivered in person. These distinctions may have been germane in the Yemeni context as well. Gail Minault, "The Emperor's Old Clothes: Robing and Sovereignty in Late Mughal and Early British India," in Gordon, *Robes of Honour,* 127.

51. Mocha *dagregister,* March 30, 31, and April 9, 1727, VOC 9121, 156–157, 166, VOC Records.

52. Mocha *dagregister,* July 7, 1731, VOC 2252, 421–422, VOC Records.

53. Governor al-Huraybi then tried to convince the Dutch to leave at least one of the horses behind for him rather than sending them all on the eastbound ship. After advice from their broker and Qasim al-Turbati, the Dutch decided to give two of the horses to al-Huraybi as a gift. They warned that al-Huraybi could interfere in their future trade if they did not oblige his demand. Rapport aan den Hoog Ed[len] agtbaren gestrengen Heer Joan van Hoorn gouverneur generaal, signed Joan Josua Ketelaar and Joan van der Needen, on board the *Oostersteijn,* November 13, 1706, VOC 9115, 46–47, VOC Records.

54. "*Cirrepauw of eeren kleed.*" Dagelijkse aantekening, July 4, 1706, VOC 9115, 217, VOC Records.

55. Ketelaar had served as the chief of the VOC outpost in Agra before travelling to Mocha. He was a skilled linguist and even penned a Hindi-Urdu and Persian grammar, which exists in manuscript form today. "The Earliest Hindustani Grammar," Universiteitsbibliotheek Utrecht, Bijzondere Collecties, accessed June 2, 2014, http://bc.library.uu.nl/node/180.

56. The later VOC *dagregisters* from the 1720s and 1730s give fewer details about exit ceremonies, but in 1726 the Dutch referred to the *khilʻa* as "*een araabise rok*" (an Arab robe). Mocha *dagregister,* August 17, 1726, VOC 9121, 21, VOC Records. In 1734 the English mention the cloak given upon leaving the port, but only in regard to a tip of 7 Spanish reals paid to the governor's servant who offered it to them. Account, July 1734, IOR/G/17/2, pt. 1, 315r, Mocha Factory Records.

57. Dagelijkse aantekening, July 29, 1706, VOC 9115, 237–240, VOC Records.

58. Apparently they were then "re-claimed from the Asian captains—though probably not from their European colleagues—on their departure from the port city, together

with a 'gratuity.'" Brouwer, *Al-Mukha: Profile,* 259. In 1610 the English captain Sir Henry Middleton also noted this Ottoman practice of awarding robes upon arrival at Mocha rather than departure, describing the garment as "a vest of crimson silk and silver." "An Account of the Captivity of Sir Henry Middleton," in Roque, *Voyage to Arabia,* 252.

59. Mocha *dagregister,* August 29, 1709, VOC 1784, 2224–2225, VOC Records.

60. Grandpré, *A voyage,* 221.

61. Roque, *Voyage to Arabia,* 225.

62. The wool could have been obtained through Mediterranean channels or perhaps from India or Persia. See Buti, "Des goûts"; Rudi Matthee, "The East India Company Trade in Kerman Wool, 1658–1730," in *Etudes Safavides,* edited by Jean Calmard (Paris: Institut français de recherche en Iran, 1993), 343–383.

63. Brouwer, *Al-Mukha: Profile,* 259–260; Nurhan Atasoy, Walter B. Denny, Louise W. Mackie, and Hülya Tezcan, *Ipek: The Crescent and the Rose, Imperial Ottoman Silks and Velvets* (London: Azimuth, 2001), 32.

64. Gordon, "Introduction," 14. In one unique case, the imam awarded a French merchant who had visited him in the highlands with a horse, a mule, and two rare mountain sheep. Mocha *dagregister,* June 9, 1730, VOC 2202, 298–299, VOC Records.

65. Behrens-Abouseif, *Practising,* 125.

66. Niebuhr, *Description,* 144.

67. Reindl-Kiel, "No Horses," 45.

68. Jagjeet Lally, "Empires and Equines: The Horse in Art and Exchange in South Asia, ca. 1600–ca. 1850," *Comparative Studies of South Asia, Africa, and the Middle East* 35:1 (May 2015): 99.

69. Reindl-Kiel, "No Horses," 48.

70. Mocha *dagregister,* June 10, 1725, VOC 9119, 182–183, VOC Records.

71. Mocha *dagregister,* May 22, 1730, VOC 2202, 291, VOC Records.

72. Reindl-Kiel, "No Horses," 49.

73. Grandpré, *A voyage,* 226.

74. Mocha *dagregister,* August 18, 1729, VOC 2202, 179–181, VOC Records.

75. Davies, "British," 126–130.

76. Even gifts received personally by VOC envoys were considered to be the property of the company. Viallé, "'To Capture,'" 309.

77. Letter to Batavia, August 22, 1717, VOC 9057, 12, VOC Records.

78. Some of these horses may have been regifted, for the VOC sent many Arabian horses to Japan and Siam in this era. Martha Chaiklin, "The Merchant's Ark: Live Animal Gifts in Early Modern Dutch-Japanese Relations," *World History Connected,* 9: 1 (February 2012), accessed March 23, 2015, http://worldhistoryconnected.press.illinois.edu/9.1/index.html; Ruangsilp, *Dutch,* 171.

79. Servants Wages Viz't, by Thomas Rammell, May 31, 1720, IOR/G17/1, pt. 1, 27r, Mocha Factory Records.

80. An Abstract of Expenses in Mocha Factory, signed Edward Say and Thomas Rammell, Mocha, May 31, 1720, IOR/G/17/1, pt. 1, 38, Mocha Factory Records.

81. Letter to Chief and Factors, September 30, 1722, IOR/G/17/1, pt. 2, 193r, Mocha Factory Records.

82. Avinoam Shalem, "Performance of the Object," in Komaroff, *Gifts of the Sultan,* 111; Behrens-Abouseif, *Practising,* 13.

83. Arcak, "Gifts," 41–49.

84. Shalem, "Performance," 111.

85. Letter to the Court of Directors, July 12, 1724, IOR/G/17/1, pt. 1, 325r, Mocha Factory Records.

86. Mocha *dagregister*, May 9, 1729, VOC 9123, 185, VOC Records.

87. Dagelijkse aantekening, May 23, June 17, and July 4, 1706, VOC 9115, 184–185, 217–218; Rapport, November 13, 1706, VOC 9115, 45–48, both in VOC Records.

88. Mocha *dagregister*, January 20, 1709, VOC 1784, 1919v-1920r, VOC Records.

89. For instance, see Komaroff, *Gifts of the Sultan,* figs. 83, 103, pp. 88, 112.

90. Shalem, "Performance," 111–112.

91. Extract, August 19, 1719, VOC 1964, 197, VOC Records.

92. Jan van Campen and Ebeltje Hartkamp-Jonxis, *Asian Splendour: Company Art in the Rijksmuseum* (Zutphen, Netherlands: Walberg Pers, 2011), 17–18.

93. Letter to Batavia, August 15, 1735, VOC 9111, 50, VOC Records.

94. A box given to King Phetracha of Siam in 1688 was made of sandalwood and contained eleven and a half ounces of sandalwood oil, among other types. Another given to the Ethiopian ambassador Khoja Murad in 1691 was also made of sandalwood, with sixteen ounces of the same oil within. Viallé, "Tot schenkagie," 14–15.

Chapter 4: Everyday Objects and Tools of the Trade

1. Franck Goddio, "Search and Excavation," in *Treasures of the San Diego,* edited by Jean-Paul Desroches (New York: Elf, 1994), 78.

2. Jerzy Gawronski, Bas Kist, and Odilia Stokvis-van Boetselaer, *Hollandia Compendium: A Contribution to the History, Archeology, Classification and Lexicography of a 150 Ft Dutch East Indiaman (1740–1750)* (Amsterdam: Rijksmuseum, 1992).

3. The EIC factory in Mocha was founded in 1618 and operated into the nineteenth century, although it was pulled and reestablished several times during that period. The first decades of the eighteenth century are notable because of the relatively consistent documentation that has been preserved from this factory.

4. An inventory of the Dead Stock, Mocha, January 7, 1722, IOR/G/17/1, pt. 2, 198r-201v, Mocha Factory Records, British Library, London.

5. Letter to Chief and Factors, September 30, 1722, IOR/G/17/1, pt. 2, 193r, Mocha Factory Records.

6. Inventory of the Warehouse Remains and Dead Stock, Mocha, January 9, 1723, IOR/G/17/1, pt. 2, 282r-285v; Inventory of the Sundries, Mocha, August 13, 1740, IOR/G/17/2, pt. 1, 470r, both in Mocha Factory Records.

7. De volgende goederen resteeren tot gebruyk, signed Willem van den Sturk, Mocha, August 15, 1734, VOC 9110, 180v, VOC Records, National Archives, The Hague. Another inventory was taken in 1739, when the establishment was being shut down, and is similar in content. Berigt, VOC 2509, 1479–1480, VOC Records.

8. Giorgio Riello, "'Things Seen and Unseen': The Material Culture of Early Modern Inventories and Their Representation of Domestic Interiors," in *Early Modern Things: Objects and Their Histories, 1500–1800,* edited by Paula Findlen (London: Routledge, 2013), 136.

9. Inventory, January 9, 1723, IOR/G/17/1, pt. 2, 283r, Mocha Factory Records.

10. However, certain provisions at Mocha were quite expensive, so some may have been shipped to the port to avoid costly local purchases. Letter to Mocha, from William Phipps, Bombay, August 19, 1721, IOR/G/17/1, pt. 1, 79r, Mocha Factory Records.

11. Eijsch van d'onderstonde coopmanschappen, provisien, goederen tot geschenk en gebruijk, Mocha, 1735, VOC 9111, 217r-219r, VOC Records.

12. In place of the Dutch term *brandewijn,* I use *jenever* throughout, whereas *franse brandewijn* is translated as "brandy." *Gedistilleerde water,* which was produced in both Holland and Batavia and prepared with various herbs and spices, including scurvy grass, anise, and caraway seeds, is translated as "spirits." Henriette De Bruyn Kops, *A Spirited Exchange: The Wine and Brandy Trade between France and the Dutch Republic in Its Atlantic Framework, 1600–1650* (Cambridge, UK: Cambridge University Press, 2007), 238, 319; Gawronski, *De "Equipagie,"* 199–200.

13. Gawronski et al., *Hollandia Compendium,* 212.

14. The 1712 *eis* grouped together all of the requested goods for sale, gifts, and company use, without specification, thus leaving a few uncertainties about the intended use of some objects. De goederen en coopmansz. die wij verweijnen alhier, Mocha, VOC 1843, pt. 1, 20–21; Eijsch, Mocha, VOC 1843, pt. 2, 17–18, both in VOC Records.

15. List of necessarys wanting for the use of the factory, signed Edward Say and Thomas Rammell, Mocha, July 28, 1720, IOR/G/17/1, pt. 1, 33v, Mocha Factory Records.

16. John Baldry, "The English East India Company's Settlement at al-Mukha, 1719–1739," *Arab Gulf* (University of Basra) 13:2 (1981): 19; List of stores wanting in the Rt Honble Companys Factory at Mocha, August 1722, IOR/G/17/1, pt. 2, 179r, Mocha Factory Records.

17. This number escalated during the high trade season, when the supercargos and senior crewmen could sleep on shore.

18. Joji Nozawa, "Wine as a Luxury at the Dutch Factory in Japan during the Second Half of the Eighteenth Century," in *Luxury in the Low Countries,* edited by R. C. Rittersma (Brussels: Pharo, 2010), 88.

19. Berigt, 1739, VOC 2509, 1480, VOC Records.

20. Stewards Account of Disbursements for the Month of January 1722, signed Francis Dickinson, Mocha, January 31, 1722, IOR/G/17/1, pt., 1, 388r, Mocha Factory Records.

21. Two items that appear consistently on stewards' registers but could not be identified are "kella flower" and "temper."

22. Gawronski, *De "Equipagie,"* 264.

23. Ibid., 242.

24. The English purchased a large water jar for 2.4 Spanish reals in 1721. Stewards Account of Disbursement for the Mocha Factory, February 1721, signed Francis Dickinson, March 7, 1721, IOR/G/17/1, pt. 1, 43r, Mocha Factory Records.

25. Similar types were used around the Arabian Peninsula. For Gulf examples, see Power, "A First," 5–6.

26. Jaap R. Bruijn, *Commanders of Dutch East India Company Ships in the Eighteenth Century* (Woodbridge, UK: Boydell Press, 2011), 205; R. J. Yntema, "A Capital Industry: Brewing in Holland, 1500–1800," in *Beer! The Story of Holland's Favourite Drink,* edited by R. E. Kistemaker and V. T. van Vilsteren, translated by Shaffer's English (Amsterdam: De Bataafsche Leeuw, 1994), 79; R. J. Yntema, "Beer in Abundance: Distribution and Consumption in Early Modern Holland," in *Beer!,* 88, 94. By 1748 they were making beer in Asia, as indicated by the export of Flemish hops to the region. Gawronski, *De "Equipagie,"* 174.

27. Diary, 1720, IOR/G/17/1, pt. 1, 7v, Mocha Factory Records.

28. He mentions another type of drink made from fermented grapes that was available in al-Luhayya, which did not suit European tastes either. Niebuhr, *Description,* 50.

29. Extract, 1717, VOC 9057, 50; Extract, 1719, VOC 1964, 200, both in VOC Records.

30. Letter to Batavia, from Willem van den Bergh, Jacob Akersloot, Joan Alfonse du Cailliou, Mocha, August 18, 1736, VOC 2415, 79, VOC Records.

31. Dagelijkse aantekening, April 21, 1706, VOC 9115, 140–146, VOC Records.

32. Memorie, August 19, 1719, VOC 1964, 88, VOC Records.

33. Mocha *dagregister*, January 12, 1720, VOC 9116, 75–76, VOC Records.

34. Nozawa, "Wine," 97.

35. Memorie, August 19, 1719, VOC 1964, 88–89, VOC Records.

36. Niebuhr, *Description*, 49.

37. Derek L. Elliott, *The Voyages of William Ferguson, 1731–1739* (London: Hakluyt Society, forthcoming), fascicle 9.8v. I thank Derek Elliott for generously sharing his edition of the volume with me before it appears in print.

38. Niebuhr, *Description*, 50.

39. Letter to Chief and Factors, September 30, 1722, IOR/G/17/1, pt. 2, 189r, Mocha Factory Records.

40. A. T. Gerritsen, "The Global Life of a Soya Bottle," unpublished lecture delivered at Leiden University, December 12, 2014.

41. David Hancock, *Oceans of Wine: Madeira and the Emergence of American Trade and Taste* (New Haven, CT: Yale University Press, 2009), 97–103, 364–384.

42. Niebuhr, *Description*, 50.

43. Gawronski, *De "Equipagie,"* 262.

44. Viallé, "Tot schenkagie," 6.

45. Similar bottles carry different letters that stood for the personal initials of the owner of the vessel.

46. Specialized wine and beer glasses were provisioned even for the ship's crews on VOC journeys. One would imagine that the same would be the case for the long-established factories. Gawronski, *De "Equipagie,"* 161, 173.

47. Rudi Matthee, "Alcohol in the Islamic Middle East: Ambivalence and Ambiguity," *Past and Present*, suppl. 9 (2014): 100–125.

48. Lodewijk Wagenaar, "The Culture Dimensions of the Dutch East India Company," in Kauffman and North, *Mediating*, 163.

49. Mocha *dagregister*, November 2–13, 1719, VOC 9116, 53–54, VOC Records.

50. When a Dutch soldier died on the mountain road to Sanaa in 1715, the VOC merchant Hendrik Burggraaf had great difficulty finding anyone who would deign to bury the body. Memorie, August 19, 1719, VOC 1964, 80–81, VOC Records. Even the Baniyans had their own separate burial place in Mocha, where cremation was not permitted.

51. Iris Bruijn, *Ships' Surgeons of the Dutch East India Company* (Leiden: Leiden University Press, 2009), 29.

52. By contrast, VOC surgeons were authorized to operate only on board their ships and in foreign lands. They were not allowed to practice in the Republic unless they followed a different certification process. Ibid., 86, 98.

53. In Batavia, for instance, the "city surgeon" was designated specifically to deliver care to the general population outside of company employees. Ibid., 106. The resident surgeon in a small outpost like Mocha had a much broader remit.

54. Although the resident surgeon would not charge those from his own company for services rendered, outsider merchants had to pay. In this case, the VOC covered the cost for Zegens' (unsuccessful) treatment, along with that of others who were sick at the time. In total, it amounted to 40 Spanish reals. Memorie, August 19, 1719, VOC 9103, 72, VOC

Records. However, the company did not cover injuries resulting from a fight or venereal disease. Bruijn, *Ships' Surgeons,* 59.

55. Garcia da Orta, *Colloquies on the Simples and Drugs of India* (London: Henry Sothern, 1913); Bruijn, *Ships' Surgeons,* 54; William Dalrymple, "Personal Encounters: Europeans in South Asia," in *Encounters: The Meeting of Asia and Europe, 1500–1800,* edited by A. Jackson and A. Jaffer (London: V&A, 2004), 160.

56. Niebhur, *Description,* 115.

57. Bruijn, *Ships' Surgeons,* 22.

58. Grandpré describes a German doctor who benefited from this perception. He practiced medicine in Mocha at the end of the eighteenth century but was unskilled and often ended up killing his patients! (*A voyage,* 248).

59. Niebuhr, *Reisebeschreibung,* 1:368.

60. For a fuller record of this imam's foreign medical care, see Um, "Foreign Doctors."

61. Rapport, November 13, 1706, VOC 9115, 45, VOC Records.

62. Letter to Batavia, from Christiaan van Vrijberghen, Mocha, August 20, 1713, VOC 1843, 6, VOC Records.

63. As another example, the French doctor in VOC service, Daniel Broudebouche, served as a major conduit to King Phetracha of Siam in the late seventeenth century. He used his privileged position to provide valuable information to VOC merchants who did not have the same level of access to the court. Ruangsilp, *Dutch,* 156, 158.

64. Roque, *Voyage to Arabia,* 190.

65. Ibid., 228.

66. Letter to William Phipps, Bombay, from Henry Albert, John Geckie, Mocha, April 22, 1722, IOR/G/17/1, pt. 1, 121, Mocha Factory Records.

67. Mocha *dagregister,* June 14, 1701, VOC 1660, 784, VOC Records.

68. Bas Kist and Jan Veenendaal, "Doctor's Cabin," in *The World of Jan Brandes, 1743–1808: Drawings of a Dutch Traveller in Batavia, Ceylon and Southern Africa,* edited by Max de Bruijn and Remco Raben (Amsterdam: Rijksmuseum, 2004), 123.

69. Ibid., 123; Gawronski, *De "Equipagie,"* 211.

70. Bruijn, *Ships' Surgeons,* 98, 103.

71. Gawronski, *De "Equipagie,"* 223–224.

72. A. M. G. Rutten, *Blue Ships: Dutch Ocean Crossing with Multifunctional Drugs and Spices in the Eighteenth Century* (Rotterdam: Erasmus, 2008).

73. Mocha *dagregister,* February 19, 1706, VOC 9115, 99–100, VOC Records.

74. Indent of Medicines Wanting for the Use of Mocha Factorie, signed John Mackenzie, August 5, 1722, IOR/G/17/1, pt. 1, 158r, Mocha Factory Records.

75. Mocha *dagregister,* June 20, 1709, VOC 1784, 2165, VOC Records.

76. Elliott, *The Voyages,* fascicle 10.6r.

77. However, VOC standards and practices for packaging medicines were not uniform until 1769, when the Amsterdam Chamber established guidelines for them, undoubtedly in response to the many complaints that shipments of medicine had been ruined because of improper wrapping and preservation. Rutten, *Blue Ships,* 25.

78. The Dutch had begun to import Japanese wares to Batavia for this purpose as early as 1653. Jörg and Impey, *Fine,* 209.

79. Bruno E. J. S. Werz and Jane E. Klose, "Ceramic Analysis from the VOC Ship Oosterland (1697)," *South African Journal of Science* 90 (October 1994): 525.

80. In Japan some of these medicine jars were repurposed; one was turned into an incense burner and buried with Tokugawa Hidetada. Viallé, "'To Capture,'" 310.

81. The 1722 inventory shows the most complete list of weights and scales at the EIC establishment, whereas those from 1723 and 1740 are much shorter. This probably points to uneven documentation standards rather than the loss of equipment.

82. The English specify theirs as averdupoize (avoirdupois). An inventory, January 7, 1722, IOR/G/17/1, pt. 2, 198v-198r, Mocha Factory Records.

83. Many merchants who passed through Mocha tried to summarize the diverse weights, measures, and coinage systems in the city, indicating that these systems were quite confusing for the visitor. Of many, see Niebuhr, who draws on several sources (*Description,* 191–193).

84. Roque, *Voyage to Arabia,* 105.

85. Letter, July 20, 1721, IOR/G/17/1, pt.1, 66r-66v, Mocha Factory Records.

86. Witold Kula, *Of Measures and Men,* translated by R. Szreter (Princeton, NJ: Princeton University Press, 1986), 3–4.

87. Letter to Edward Say, Mocha, from Phipps, Mocha (part of the letter has been lost), June 26, 1721, IOR/G/17/1, pt. 1, 44r-45r, Mocha Factory Records. Many of the merchants on Ostend vessels were actually British, so they had natural affinities with the EIC merchants in Yemen.

88. Letter, from William Phipps, Mocha, August 19, 1721, IOR/G/17/1, pt. 1, 79r-79v, Mocha Factory Records.

89. Miles Ogborn, *Indian Ink: Script and Print in the Making of the English East India Company* (Chicago: University of Chicago Press, 2008), 50.

90. An account of the Weights, Measures, and Coins in Use at Beetlefuckee, signed John Geckie, June 30, 1722, IOR/G/17/1, pt.1, 127r-128r; A Calculate of the Medium of Beetlefuckee Customs house Weights, signed John Style and Nicholas Goodwin, January 22, 1722, IOR/G/17/1, pt. 2, 202; Account of Weights, Coins, and Measures at Mocha, July 1724, IOR/G/17/1, pt. 2, 341–342, all in Mocha Factory Records.

91. Letter to the Court of Directors, from Edward Say and John Hill, Mocha, August 17, 1719, IOR/G/17/1, pt. 1, 17–20, Mocha Factory Records.

92. These would be drawn from the tens of thousands of quills that were needed by the VOC outposts in Asia each year for bookkeeping purposes. Gawronski, *De "Equipagie,"* 158.

93. For instance, they account for the supplies used by the month in 1720. An Abstract of the Several Charges in Mocha Factory for the Year 1720, IOR/G/17/1, pt. 1, 40v, Mocha Factory Records.

94. Gawronski, *De "Equipagie,"* 172.

95. By the late seventeenth century, paper making had become an important Dutch industry with the establishment of mills in the region of Zaan. Previously paper had been imported from France. Jonathan Israel, *Dutch Primacy in World Trade, 1585–1740* (Oxford: Clarendon Press, 1989), 349–350. According to Gawronski, there were several types and sizes of paper in use by the VOC and shipped from the various *kamer*s to Asia. But in Mocha only three sizes were used (*De "Equipagie,"* 172).

96. Ogborn, *Indian Ink,* 23.

97. Goldberg, *Trade,* 62; Aslanian, *From the Indian Ocean,* 86–96; Trivellato, *Familiarity,* 177–193.

98. Sood, "Correspondence," 176–182.

99. Ogborn, *Indian Ink,* xvii.

100. Mocha *dagregister,* December 24, 1730, VOC 2252, 286–287, VOC Records.

101. Letter to Batavia, from W. van den Bergh, J. Akersloot, A. du Cailliou, Mocha, August 15, 1738, VOC 2447, pt. 2, 3–14, VOC Records.

102. When VOC merchants returned the next year to close down the factory formally, they found the *dagregister,* continued it, and eventually brought it back to Surat.

103. Ashin Das Gupta, "Pieter Phoonsen of Surat, c. 1730–1740," *Modern Asian Studies* 22:3 (1988): 552.

104. According to Ogborn, the format for EIC records and letters was standardized in the mid-seventeenth century (*Indian Ink,* 76–103).

105. For comparable examples, see Clulow's discussion of the VOC encounter with scribal practices in early modern Japan (*The Company,* 81) or Ogborn's discussion of the uneven adoption of European scribal and print modes in India (*Indian Ink,* 16–18).

106. Aslanian, *From the Indian Ocean,* 82–120; Sood, "Correspondence."

107. Mocha *dagregister,* October 9, 1731, VOC 2252, 184–185, VOC Records.

108. This is why the imam appointed individuals directly to this coastal position, which could lead to further promotions for the enterprising official. Um, *The Merchant Houses,* 52.

109. Sood, "Correspondence," 177–179.

110. This translator was sometimes recognized with a yearly gift. Account, July 17, 1721 to July 14, 1722, IOR/G/17/1, pt. 1, 136r, Mocha Factory Records.

111. VOC merchants note that Courbesatre, with his perfect knowledge of Arabic, was always called upon to translate missives from Arabic into European languages. Mocha *dagregister,* April 14, 1732, VOC 2252, 260, VOC Records. He was even sent to the imam's court on a French mission in 1730. Mocha *dagregister,* June 9, 1730, VOC 2202, 298–299, VOC Records.

112. Sood, "Correspondence," 179.

113. Mocha *dagregister,* September 12, 1731, VOC 2252, 172–174, VOC Records.

114. Viallé, "'To Capture,'" 298.

115. Although the Yemeni city of Zabid had a paper-making industry, examples of watermarked paper from Venice and the Ottoman Empire have been found in local manuscripts dating from the late eighteenth to the middle of the twentieth century. Anne Regourd, "Les routes commerciales entre Zabid et l'Europe: Les papiers filigranés de fonds manuscrits de Zabid (Yémen, fin 18e—milieu 20e s.)," in *Convegno storia e cultura dello Yemen in età islamica con particolare riferimento al periodo rasûlide (Roma, 30–31 octobre 2003),* edited by R. Traini (Rome: Bardi, 2006), 175.

116. Even when they did send the original in Arabic, they would always include its translation, as in 1719. Letter to Batavia, August 19, 1719, VOC 9103, 63, VOC Records.

117. Rapport, November 13, 1706, VOC 9115, 46, VOC Records; Donzel, *Foreign Relations,* 49.

118. Resolutie, signed David Kelly and Evert Sypesteyn, July 15, 1739, VOC 2509, 1456, 1481, VOC Records.

119. For instance, if their request to have twelve chairs sent over in 1712 was honored, then we may have to reconsider the rather low later number of only six chairs.

120. However, the modifier "China" or "Japan" does not always mean that the item was produced in that place. See, for instance, the discussion of "China escritorios" in Nancy Um, "Chairs, Writing Tables, and Chests: Indian Ocean Furniture and the Postures of Commercial Documentation in Yemen, 1700–1750," *Art History* 38:4 (September 2015): 723. By contrast, few pieces were brought from Europe. With the exception of tables of marble with gilded feet, which were a special order for the "King of Ceylon," large pieces of furniture did not figure prominently in Gawronski's rosters of items shipped to Batavia from Amsterdam in the 1740s (*De "Equipagie,"* 174).

121. Pedro Moura Caravalho, "Goa's Pioneering Role in Transmitting European Traditions to the Mughal and Safavid Courts," in *Exotica: The Portuguese Discoveries and the Renaissance Kunstkammer* (Lisbon: Calouste Gulbenkian Foundation, 2001); Amin Jaffer, *Luxury Goods from India: The Art of the Indian Cabinet-Maker* (London: V&A, 2002); Amin Jaffer, *Furniture from British India and Ceylon: A Catalogue of the Collections in the Victoria and Albert Museum and the Peabody Essex Museum* (Salem, MA: Peabody Essex Museum, 2001); Jan Veenendaal, *Domestic Interiors at the Cape and in Batavia, 1602–1795* (Zwolle, Netherlands: Waanders, 2002).

122. Clive Wainwright, "Only the True Black Blood," *Furniture History* 21 (1985): 250–257.

123. Mocha *dagregister,* August 21, 1731, VOC 2252, 166–167, VOC Records.

124. Mocha *dagregister,* July 26, 1706, VOC 9115, 235, VOC Records.

125. Kist and Veenendaal, "Doctor's Cabin," 123.

126. Richard John Guy, "First Spaces of Colonialism: The Architecture of Dutch East India Company Ships," PhD diss., Cornell University, 2012, 74.

127. Stewards Account, January 31, 1722, IOR/G/17/1, pt. 2, 204, Mocha Factory Records.

128. Grandpré, *A voyage,* 231.

129. Mocha *dagregister,* May 16, 1719, VOC 9116, 96–97, VOC Records; Diary, IOR/G/17/1 pt. 1, 7v, Mocha Factory Records.

130. No local pipes or hookahs or imported clay pipes from Gouda are mentioned. Yet Gawronski describes these as "indispensible" for VOC servants abroad (*De "Equipagie,"* 161).

131. Grandpré, *A voyage,* 218.

132. On the link between writing and upright furniture, see Um, "Chairs."

133. A model for tying together the material and textual is represented capably in Gawronski, *De "Equipagie."*

134. Thomas, *Entangled Objects,* 184.

Conclusion

1. Ogborn, *Indian Ink,* 26.

2. The name of the fort was Qal'at 'Abd al-Ra'uf, after the son of the city's patron saint. It is interesting that Jahhaf mistakenly used the name of one of Mocha's major merchants, 'Abd al-Ghafur, instead.

3. This episode was drawn from Jahhaf by the twentieth-century biographer Muhammad Zabara (*Nashr al-'arf,* 1:303).

4. Desfontaines, *Relation;* Mocha *dagregister,* January 25–April 6, 1737, VOC 2447, 156–238, VOC Records, National Archives, The Hague.

5. Al-Makki, *Nuzhat al-jalis,* 2:262.

6. For an example of the widespread use of these tropes, particularly the loose sexual proclivities of Europeans, see al-Jabarti's response to the Napoleonic invasion of Egypt in 1798. 'Abd al-Rahman al-Jabarti, *Napoleon in Egypt: Al-Jabarti's Chronicle of the French Occupation, 1798,* translated by Samuel Moreh, introduction by Robert L. Tignor (Princeton, NJ: Markus Weiner, 2005), 29.

7. Roque, *Voyage to Arabia,* 84–86; Desfontaines, *Relation,* 90–101.

8. Pedro Machado, *Oceans of Trade: South Asian Merchants, Africa and the Indian Ocean,* c. *1750–1850* (Cambridge, UK: Cambridge University Press, 2014). For an example of these overriding assumptions, see Jerry Brotton, *The Renaissance Bazaar: From the Silk*

Road to Michelangelo (Oxford: Oxford University Press, 2003). The persistence of this paradigm is reflected in the recent exhibition organized by the Rijksmuseum and the Peabody Essex Museum. Karina Corrigan, Jan van Campen, and Femke Diercks, eds., with Janet C. Blyberg, *Asia in Amsterdam: The Culture of Luxury in the Golden Age* (New Haven, CT: Yale University Press, 2015).

9. Thomas, *Entangled Objects,* 103.

10. Trade partnerships in the Islamic world were often supported by written contracts, but there were also many cases of unwritten trade agreements, as described by Goldberg for the merchants of the Cairo Geniza (*Trade,* 133). But it is important to differentiate between those agreements that were forged between merchants and their agents and brokers and those that were forged between merchants and polities.

11. The 1729 renegotiated trade agreement between the EIC and Imam al-Mansur Husayn is the only one that specifically mentions gifts, but only customary ones to Mocha's governors and officials. Translate of the Emaums Phirmaund, 1729, IOR/G/17/2, 19, Mocha Factory Records, British Library, London.

12. Philip J. Stern, *The Company-State: Corporate Sovereignty and the Early Modern Foundations of the British Empire in India* (Oxford: Oxford University Press, 2011), 29.

13. Clulow, *The Company,* 76; Ruangsilp, *Dutch,* 221.

14. Nadri, "Maritime Merchants."

Bibliography

Archival Sources

"Caroline" Journal, 1821, Phillips Library, Peabody Essex Museum, Salem, MA.
Mocha Factory Records, British Library, London.
VOC Records, National Archives, The Hague.

Works Cited

Annesley, George (Viscount Valentia). *Voyages and Travels to India, Ceylon, the Red Sea, Abyssinia, and Egypt.* 3 vols. London: W. Miller, 1809.

Appadurai, Arjun. "Introduction: Commodities and the Politics of Value." In *The Social Life of Things: Commodities in Cultural Perspective*, edited by A. Appadurai, 3–63. Cambridge, UK: Cambridge University Press, 1989.

Arcak, Sinem. "Gifts in Motion: Ottoman-Safavid Cultural Exchange, 1501–1618." PhD diss., University of Minnesota, 2012.

Ashmore, Sonia. *Muslin.* London: V&A, 2012.

Aslanian, Sebouh David. *From the Indian Ocean to the Mediterranean: The Global Trade Networks of Armenian Merchants from New Julfa.* Berkeley: University of California Press, 2011.

Atasoy, Nurhan, Walter B. Denny, Louise W. Mackie, and Hülya Tezcan. *Ipek: The Crescent and the Rose, Imperial Ottoman Silks and Velvets.* London: Azimuth, 2001.

Baldry, John. "The English East India Company's Settlement at al-Mukha, 1719–1739." *Arab Gulf* (University of Basra) 13:2 (1981): 13–38.

———. *Textiles in Yemen: Historical References to Trade and Commerce in Textiles in Yemen from Antiquity to Modern Times.* Occasional Paper 27. London: British Museum, 1982.

Bataille, Georges. "The Notion of Expenditure." In *Visions of Excess: Selected Writings, 1927–1939*, edited by Allan Stoekl, 116–129. Minneapolis: University of Minnesota Press, 1985.

Beg, M. A. J. "Tajir." In *Encyclopedia of Islam.* New edition. Leiden: Brill, 1960.

Behrens-Abouseif, Doris. *Practising Diplomacy in the Mamluk Sultanate: Gifts and Material Culture in the Medieval Islamic World.* London: I. B. Tauris, 2014.

Benton, Lauren. *A Search for Sovereignty: Law and Geography in European Empires, 1400–1900.* Cambridge, UK: Cambridge University Press, 2010.

Blucasz, François. "Les relations entre le Yémen et l'Inde au XVIIème siècle: Extraits de la correspondance entre l'imam zaidite al-Mutawakkil 'ala Allah Ismail b. al-Qasim et le sultan moghol Awrangzib." Master's thesis, Université de Paris-Sorbonne (Paris IV), 1992.

Blussé, Leonard. "Amongst Feigned Friends and Declared Enemies." In *Making Sense of Global History*, edited by Solvi Sanger, 154–168. Oslo: Universitetsforlaget, 2002.

Bourdieu, Pierre. *The Logic of Practice*. Translated by Richard Nice. Stanford: Stanford University Press, 1990.

Brotton, Jerry. *The Renaissance Bazaar: From the Silk Road to Michelangelo*. Oxford: Oxford University Press, 2003.

Brouwer, C. G. *Al-Mukha: Profile of a Yemeni Seaport as Sketched by Servants of the Dutch East India Company*. Amsterdam: D'Fluyte Rarob, 1997.

———. *Al-Mukha: The Transoceanic Trade of a Yemeni Staple Town as Mapped by Merchants of the VOC, 1614–1650: Coffee, Spices, and Textiles*. Amsterdam: D'Fluyte Rarob, 2006.

———. "A Hazardous Item: The International Tobacco Trade of the Red Sea Port of al-Mukha, Reflected in Seventeenth-Century Dutch Records." *Itinerario* 32:2 (July 2008): 39–66.

Brouwer, C. G., and A. Kaplanian, eds. *Al-yaman fi awa'il al-qarn al-saba' 'ashar: Muqtatafat min al-watha'iq al-hulandiyah al-muta'alliqah bi-al-tarikh al-iqtisadi li-janub al-jazirah al-'arabiyah, 1614–1630*. Amsterdam: D'Fluyte Rarob, 1989.

Bruijn, Iris. *Ships' Surgeons of the Dutch East India Company*. Leiden: Leiden University Press, 2009.

Bruijn, Jaap R. *Commanders of Dutch East India Company Ships in the Eighteenth Century*. Woodbridge, UK: Boydell Press, 2011.

Bulut, Mehmet. "The Role of the Ottomans and Dutch in the Commercial Integration between the Levant and Atlantic in the Seventeenth Century." *Journal of the Economic and Social History of the Orient* 45:2 (2002): 197–230.

Burschel, Peter. "A Clock for the Sultan: Diplomatic Gift-Giving from an Intercultural Perspective." *Medieval History Journal* 16:2 (2013): 547–563.

Buti, Gilbert. "Des goûts et des couleurs: Draps du Languedoc pour clientèle levantine au XVIIIe siècle." *Rives nord-méditerranéennes* 29 (2008). Accessed November 17, 2015. http://rives.revues.org/1393.

———. "Marseille entre Moka et café des îles: Espaces, flux, réseaux, XVIIe–XVIIIe siècles." In *Le commerce du café avant l'ère des plantations coloniales: Espaces, réseaux, sociétés (XVe–XIXe siècle)*, edited by Michel Tuchscherer, 213–244. Cairo: Institut français d'archéologie orientale, 2001.

Campen, Jan van, and Ebeltje Hartkamp-Jonxis. *Asian Splendour: Company Art in the Rijksmuseum*. Zutphen, Netherlands: Walberg Pers, 2011.

Caravalho, Pedro Moura. "Goa's Pioneering Role in Transmitting European Traditions to the Mughal and Safavid Courts." In *Exotica: The Portuguese Discoveries and the Renaissance Kunstkammer*, 69–79. Lisbon: Calouste Gulbenkian Foundation, 2001.

Carswell, John. *Blue and White: Chinese Porcelain around the World*. London: British Museum Press, 2000.

Chaiklin, Martha. *Cultural Commerce and Dutch Commercial Culture: The Influence of European Material Culture on Japan, 1700–1850*. Leiden: CNWS, 2003.

———. "The Merchant's Ark: Live Animal Gifts in Early Modern Dutch-Japanese Relations." *World History Connected* 9:1 (February 2012). Accessed March 23, 2015. http://worldhistoryconnected.press.illinois.edu/9.1/index.html.

Chaudhuri, K. N. *The Trading World of Asia and the English East India Company, 1660–1760*. Cambridge, UK: Cambridge University Press, 1978.

Clarence-Smith, William Gervase, and Steven Topik, eds. *The Global Coffee Economy in Africa, Asia, and Latin America, 1500–1989.* Cambridge, UK: Cambridge University Press, 2003.

"Cloth Cutting and Figuring." In *The Encyclopedia of Diderot and d'Alembert Collaborative Translation Project.* Ann Arbor: Michigan Publishing, University of Michigan Library, 2010. Accessed April 3, 2014. http://hdl.handle.net/2027/spo.did2222.0001.434.

Clulow, Adam. *The Company and the Shogun: The Dutch Encounter with Tokugawa Japan.* New York: Columbia University Press, 2013.

Constable, Olivia Remie. *Housing the Stranger in the Mediterranean World: Lodging, Trade, and Travel in Late Antiquity and the Middle Ages.* Cambridge, UK: Cambridge University Press, 2003.

Corrigan, Karina, Jan van Campen, and Femke Diercks, eds., with Janet C. Blyberg. *Asia in Amsterdam: The Culture of Luxury in the Golden Age.* New Haven, CT: Yale University Press, 2015.

Cutler, Anthony. "Gifts and Gift Exchange as Aspects of the Byzantine, Arab, and Related Economies." *Dumbarton Oaks Papers* 55 (2001): 247–278.

Dalrymple, William. "Personal Encounters: Europeans in South Asia." In *Encounters: The Meeting of Asia and Europe, 1500–1800,* edited by A. Jackson and A. Jaffer, 156–169. London: V&A, 2004.

Das Gupta, Ashin. *Indian Merchants and the Decline of Surat, c. 1700–1750.* 1979; Delhi: Manohar, 1994.

———. "Pieter Phoonsen of Surat, c. 1730–1740." *Modern Asian Studies* 22:3 (1988): 551–560.

Davies, Timothy. "British Private Trade Networks in the Arabian Seas, c. 1680–c. 1760." PhD diss., University of Warwick, 2012.

Desfontaines, Pierre François Guyot. *Relation de l'expédition de Moka en l'année 1737 sous les ordres de M. de la Garde-Jazier, de Saint-Malo.* Paris: Imprimerie Joseph Bullot, 1739.

Digby, Simon. *War-Horse and Elephant in the Delhi Sultanate: A Study of Military Supplies.* Oxford: Orient Monographs, 1971.

Dijk, W. O. "The VOC's Trade in Indian Textiles with Burma, 1634–90." *Journal of Southeast Asian Studies* 33:3 (October 2002): 495–515.

Ditz, Toby L. "Formative Ventures: Eighteenth-Century Commercial Letters and the Articulation of Experience." In *Epistolary Selves: Letters and Letter-Writers, 1600–1945,* edited by Rebecca Earle, 57–78. Aldershot, UK: Ashgate, 1999.

Donzel, E. van. *Foreign Relations of Ethiopia, 1642–1700: Documents relating to Khodja Murad.* Uitgaven van het Nederlands Historisch-Archaeologisch Instituut te Istanbul XLVI. Leiden: Nederlands Historisch-Archaeologisch Instituut te Istanbul, 1979.

———. *A Yemenite Embassy to Ethiopia 1647–49.* Stuttgart: F. Steiner, 1986.

"The Earliest Hindustani Grammar." Universiteitsbibliotheek Utrecht, Bijzondere Collecties. Accessed June 2, 2014. http://bc.library.uu.nl/node/180.

Elliott, Derek L. *The Voyages of William Ferguson, 1731–1739.* London: Hakluyt Society, forthcoming.

Finlay, Robert. *A Pilgrim Art: Cultures of Porcelain in World History.* Berkeley: University of California Press, 2010.

Flood, Finbarr B. *Objects of Translation: Material Culture and the Medieval "Hindu-Muslim" Encounter.* Princeton, NJ: Princeton University Press, 2009.

Floor, Willem. *The Persian Textile Industry in Historical Perspective, 1500–1925.* Paris: Harmattan, 1999.

Gawronski, Jerzy. *De "Equipagie" van de* Hollandia *en de* Amsterdam*: VOC-bedrijvigheid in 18de-eeuws Amsterdam*. Amsterdam: De Bataafsche Leeuw, 1996.

Gawronski, Jerzy, Bas Kist, and Odilia Stokvis-van Boetselaer. *Hollandia Compendium: A Contribution to the History, Archeology, Classification and Lexicography of a 150 Ft Dutch East Indiaman (1740–1750)*. Amsterdam: Rijksmuseum, 1992.

Gerritsen, A. T. "The Global Life of a Soya Bottle." Unpublished lecture delivered at Leiden University, December 12, 2014.

Glaisyer, Natasha. *The Culture of Commerce in England, 1660–1720*. Woodbridge, UK: Boydell Press, 2006.

Glamann, Kristof. *Dutch-Asiatic Trade, 1620–1740*. The Hague: Martinus Nijhoff, 1958.

Goddio, Franck. "Search and Excavation." In *Treasures of the San Diego*, edited by Jean-Paul Desroches, 72–117. New York: Elf, 1994.

Goldberg, Jessica. *Trade and Institutions in the Medieval Mediterranean: The Geniza Merchants and Their Business World*. Cambridge, UK: Cambridge University Press, 2012.

Goor, Jurrien van. *Prelude to Colonialism: The Dutch in Asia*. Hilversum, Netherlands: Uitgeverij Verloren, 2004.

Gordon, Stewart. "Introduction: Ibn Battuta and a Region of Robing." In *Robes of Honour:* Khil'at *in Precolonial and Colonial India*, edited by Stewart Gordon, 1–30. New Delhi: Oxford University Press, 2003.

Grandpré, Louis de. *Voyage dans l'Inde et au Bengale: Fait dans les années 1789 et 1790*. 2 vols. Paris: Dentu, 1801.

———. *A voyage in the Indian Ocean and to Bengal Undertaken in the Year 1790: containing an account of the Sechelles Islands and Trincomale. To which is added, A voyage in the Red Sea; including a description of Mocha*. 1801; Boston: David Carlisle, 1803.

Grehan, James. *Everyday Life and Consumer Culture in Eighteenth-Century Damascus*. Seattle: University of Washington Press, 2007.

Greif, Avner. "Reputations and Coalitions in Medieval Trade: Evidence on the Maghribi Traders." *Journal of Economic History* 49:4 (December 1989): 857–882.

Groebner, Valentin. *Who Are You? Identification, Deception, and Surveillance in Early Modern Europe*. Translated by M. Kyburz and J. Peck. Brooklyn, NY: Zone Books, 2007.

Groenewald, Gerald. "A Class Apart: Symbolic Capital, Consumption and Identity among the Alcohol Entrepreneurs of Cape Town, 1680–1795." *S. A. Tydskrif vir Kultuurgeskiedenis* 26:1 (June 2012): 14–32.

Groom, Nigel. "Trade, Incense, and Perfume." In *Caravan Kingdoms: Yemen and the Ancient Incense Trade*, edited by Ann C. Gunter, 104–113. Washington, DC: Arthur M. Sackler Gallery, Smithsonian Institution, 2005.

Guy, John. *Woven Cargoes: Indian Textiles in the East*. New York: Thames and Hudson, 1998.

Guy, Richard John. "First Spaces of Colonialism: The Architecture of Dutch East India Company Ships." PhD diss., Cornell University, 2012.

Halevi, Leor. "Religion and Cross-Cultural Trade: A Framework for Interdisciplinary Inquiry." In *Religion and Trade: Cross-Cultural Exchanges in World History, 1000–1900*, edited by Francesca Trivellato, Leor Halevi, and Catia Antunes, 24–61. Oxford: Oxford University Press, 2014.

Hambly, Gavin R. G. "The Emperor's Clothes: Robing and 'Robes of Honour' in Mughal India." In *Robes of Honour:* Khil'at *in Precolonial and Colonial India*, edited by Stewart Gordon, 31–49. New Delhi: Oxford University Press, 2003.

Hancock, David. *Oceans of Wine: Madeira and the Emergence of American Trade and Taste*. New Haven, CT: Yale University Press, 2009.

Hansen, Anne Haslund. "Niebuhr and the Visual Documentation of the Arabian Voyage, 1761–1767." In *Early Scientific Expeditions and Local Encounters: New Perspectives on Carsten Niebuhr and "The Arabian Journey,"* edited by Ib Friis, Michael Harbsmeier, and Jørgen Bœk Simonsen, 119–144. Scientia Danica Series H, Humanistica, 4, vol. 2. Viborg, Denmark: Det Kongelige Danske Videnskabernes Selskab, 2013.

Hardy-Guilbert, Claire, and Axelle Rougeulle. "Archaeological Research into the Islamic Period in Yemen: Preliminary Notes on the French Expedition, 1993." *Proceedings of the Seminar for Arabian Studies* 25 (1994): 29–44.

———. "Ports islamiques du Yémen: Prospections archéologiques sur les côtes yéménites (1993–1995)." *Archéologie islamique* 7 (1997): 147–196.

Hasan, Muhsin bin al- (Abu Talib). *Tarikh al-yaman fi 'asr al-istiqlal 'an al-hukm al-'uthmani al-awwal.* Edited by 'Abd Allah Muhammad al-Hibshi. Sanaa: Al-Mufaddal Offset Printers, 1990.

Hathaway, Jane. "The Mawza' Exile at the Juncture of Zaydi and Ottoman Messianism." *AJS Review* 29:1 (April 2005): 111–128.

———. "The Ottomans and the Yemeni Coffee Trade." *Oriento Moderno* 26:1 (2006): 161–171.

Hattox, Ralph. *Coffee and Coffeehouses: The Origins of a Social Beverage in the Medieval Near East.* Seattle: University of Washington Press, 1985.

Haykel, Bernard. *Revival and Reform in Islam: The Legacy of Muhammad al-Shawkani.* Cambridge, UK: Cambridge University Press, 2003.

Henry Yule Hobson-Jobson: A Glossary of Anglo-Indian Colloquial Words and Phrases. Digital Dictionaries of South Asia. Accessed January 20, 2016. http://dsal.uchicago.edu/dictionaries/hobsonjobson/.

Hevia, James. *Cherishing Men from Afar: Qing Guest Ritual and the Macartney Embassy of 1793.* Durham, NC: Duke University Press, 1995.

Hilsdale, Cecily. *Byzantine Art and Diplomacy in an Age of Decline.* Cambridge, UK: Cambridge University Press, 2014.

Hoff, Arne. *Dutch Firearms.* Edited by Walter A. Stryker. London: Sotheby Parke Bernet, 1978.

Irwin, John, and Margaret Hall. *Indian Embroideries.* Ahmedabad, India: Textile Museum, 1973.

Israel, Jonathan. *Dutch Primacy in World Trade, 1585–1740.* Oxford: Clarendon Press, 1989.

Jabarti, 'Abd al-Rahman al-. *Napoleon in Egypt: Al-Jabarti's Chronicle of the French Occupation, 1798.* Translated by Samuel Moreh. Introduction by Robert L. Tignor. Princeton, NJ: Markus Weiner, 2005.

Jacobs, Els M. *Merchant in Asia: The Trade of the Dutch East India Company during the Eighteenth Century.* Leiden: CNWS, 2006.

Jaffer, Amin. *Furniture from British India and Ceylon: A Catalogue of the Collections in the Victoria and Albert Museum and the Peabody Essex Museum.* Salem, MA: Peabody Essex Museum, 2001.

———. *Luxury Goods from India: The Art of the Indian Cabinet-Maker.* London: V&A, 2002.

Jasdanwalla, Faaeza. "African Settlers on the West Coast of India: The Sidi Elite of Janjira." *African and Asian Studies* 10 (2011): 41–58.

Jones, Ann Rosalind, and Peter Stallybrass. *Renaissance Clothing and the Materials of Memory.* Cambridge, UK: Cambridge University Press, 2000.

Jörg, C. J. A., and Oliver Impey. *Fine and Curious: Japanese Export Porcelain in Dutch Collections*. Amsterdam: Hotei, 2003.

Jung, Dinah. *An Ethnography of Fragrance: The Perfumery Arts of 'Adan/Lahj*. Leiden: Brill, 2011.

Kawatuoko, Mutsuo. "Coffee Trade in the al-Tur Port, South Sinai." In *Le commerce du café avant l'ère des plantations coloniales: Espaces, réseaux, sociétés (XVe–XIXe siècle)*, edited by Michel Tuchscherer, 51–65. Cairo: Institut français d'archéologie orientale, 2001.

Keall, Edward J. "The Evolution of the First Coffee Cups in Yemen." In *Le commerce du café avant l'ère des plantations coloniales: Espaces, réseaux, sociétés (XVe–XIXe siècle)*, edited by Michel Tuchscherer, 35–50. Cairo: Institut français d'archéologie orientale, 2001.

Kist, Bas, and Jan Veenendaal. "Doctor's Cabin." In *The World of Jan Brandes, 1743–1808: Drawings of a Dutch Traveller in Batavia, Ceylon and Southern Africa*, edited by Max de Bruijn and Remco Raben, 123–124. Amsterdam: Rijksmuseum, 2004.

Knaap, G. J. "The Dutch East India Company and the Expansion of Coffee Cultivation in Java, Ambon, and Ceylon 1700–1730." In *Trading Companies in Asia, 1600–1830*, edited by J. van Goor, 33–50. Utrecht: Hes Uitgevers, 1986.

Komaroff, Linda. "The Art of the Art of Giving at the Islamic Courts." In *Gifts of the Sultan: The Arts of Giving at the Islamic Courts*, edited by Linda Komaroff, 17–32. New Haven, CT: Yale University Press, 2011.

———, ed. *Gifts of the Sultan: The Arts of Giving at the Islamic Courts*. New Haven, CT: Yale University Press, 2011.

Kops, Henriette De Bruyn. *A Spirited Exchange: The Wine and Brandy Trade between France and the Dutch Republic in Its Atlantic Framework, 1600–1650*. Cambridge, UK: Cambridge University Press, 2007.

Kopytoff, Igor. "The Cultural Biography of Things: Commodification as a Process." In *The Social Life of Things: Commodities in Cultural Perspective*, edited by Arjun Appadurai, 64–94. Cambridge, UK: Cambridge University Press, 1989.

Kreiser, Klaus. "An Unpublished Ottoman Manuscript on the Yemen in 1849: Mustafa Hami's *Sevku 'l-asker 'l-cedid der 'ahd-i Sultan Mecid*." *Arabian Studies* 7 (1985): 161–186.

Kula, Witold. *Of Measures and Men*. Translated by R. Szreter. Princeton, NJ: Princeton University Press, 1986.

Kurz, Otto. *European Clocks and Watches in the Near East*. Leiden: Brill, 1975.

Lally, Jagjeet. "Empires and Equines: The Horse in Art and Exchange in South Asia, ca. 1600–ca. 1850." *Comparative Studies of South Asia, Africa, and the Middle East* 35:1 (May 2015): 96–116.

Lambourn, Elizabeth. "Of Jewels and Horses: The Career and Patronage of an Iranian Merchant under Shah Jahan." *Iranian Studies* 36:2 (June 2003): 213–241.

———. "Towards a Connected History of Equine Cultures in South Asia: Bahri (Sea) Horses and 'Horsemania' in Thirteenth-Century South India." *Medieval Globe* 2:1 (2016): 57–100.

Lambton, Ann. "*Pishkash*, Present or Tribute?" *Bulletin of the School of Oriental and African Studies* 57:1 (February 1994): 145–158.

Landry, Donna. *Noble Brutes: How Eastern Horses Transformed English Culture*. Baltimore: Johns Hopkins University Press, 2009.

Lemire, Beverly, and Giorgio Riello. "East and West: Textiles and Fashion in Early Modern Europe." *Journal of Social History* 41:4 (Summer 2008): 887–916.

Levykin, Alexey Konstantinovich, ed. *The Tsars and the East: Gifts from Turkey and Iran in the Moscow Kremlin*. Washington, DC: Smithsonian Institution, 2009.

Loomba, Ania. "Of Gifts, Ambassadors, and Copy-Cats: Diplomacy, Exchange, and Difference in Early Modern India." In *Emissaries in Early Modern Literature and Culture: Mediation, Transmission, and Traffic, 1550–1700*, edited by Brinda Charry and Gitanjali Shahani, 41–76. Burlington, VT: Ashgate, 2009.
Machado, Pedro. *Oceans of Trade: South Asian Merchants, Africa and the Indian Ocean, c. 1750–1850.* Cambridge, UK: Cambridge University Press, 2014.
Mageur, Sterenn Le. "Typology of Incense-Burners of the Islamic Period." *Proceedings of the Seminar for Arabian Studies* 41 (2011): 173–186.
Makki, 'Abbas b. 'Ali al-Musawi al-. *Nuzhat al-jalis wa munyat al-adib al-anis.* 2 vols. Edited by Muhammad Mahdi Khurasan. Al-Najaf, Iraq: al-Matba'a al-Haydariyya, 1967.
Mallinson, Michael, Laurence Smith, Colin Breen, Wes Forsythe, and Jacke Phillips. "Ottoman Suakin 1541–1865: Lost and Found." In "The Frontiers of the Ottoman World." Special issue of *Proceedings of the British Academy* 156 (2009): 469–462.
Markley, Robert. "Alexander Hamilton, the Mughal War, and the Critique of the East India Company." *Genre: Forms of Discourse and Culture* 48:2 (July 2015): 237–259.
Maskiell, Michelle. "Consuming Kashmir: Shawls and Empires, 1500–2000." *Journal of World History* 13:1 (Spring 2002): 27–65.
Matthee, Rudi. "Alcohol in the Islamic Middle East: Ambivalence and Ambiguity." *Past and Present*, suppl. 9 (2014): 100–125.
———. "Coffee in Safavid Iran: Commerce and Consumption." *Journal of the Economic and Social History of the Orient* 37 (1994): 1–32.
———. "The East India Company Trade in Kerman Wool, 1658–1730." In *Etudes Safavides*, edited by Jean Calmard, 343–383. Paris: Institut français de recherche en Iran, 1993.
———. "Gift-giving in the Safavid Period." In *Encyclopedia Iranica,* edited by Ehsan Yarshater, 10:609–614. New York: Bibliotheca Persica Press, 2001.
McCulloch, John Ramsay. *A Dictionary, Practical, Theoretical, and Historical of Commerce and Commercial Navigation*. London: Spottiswoods and Shaw, 1849.
McLane, John. *Land and Local Kingship in Eighteenth-Century Bengal.* Cambridge, UK: Cambridge University Press, 1993.
McLeod, John. "The Later History of Janjira." In *Habshi Amarat: African Elites in India*, edited by Kenneth X. Robbins and John McLeod, 188–198. Ocean Township, NJ: Mapin, 2006.
Meyer, Joachim. *Sensual Delights: Incense Burners and Rosewater Sprinklers from the World of Islam*. Copenhagen: David Collection, 2015.
Mikhail, Alan. *The Animal in Ottoman Egypt*. Oxford: Oxford University Press, 2013.
Minault, Gail. "The Emperor's Old Clothes: Robing and Sovereignty in Late Mughal and Early British India." In *Robes of Honour:* Khil'at *in Precolonial and Colonial India*, edited by Stewart Gordon, 125–139. New Delhi: Oxford University Press, 2003.
Mundy, Martha. "San'a' Dress, 1920–75." In *San'a': An Arabian Islamic City*, edited by R. B. Serjeant and R. Lewcock, 529–541. London: World of Islam Trust, 1983.
Nadri, Ghulam. "The Maritime Merchants of Surat: A Long-Term Perspective." *Journal of the Economic and Social History of the Orient* 50:2 (2007): 235–258.
Nagashima, Hiromu. "The *Shahbandar* at Surat in the Mughal Empire." *Nagasaki Prefectural University Review* 29:4 (1996): 1–28.
Niebuhr, Carsten. *Description de l'Arabie, faite sur des observations propres et des avis recueillis dans les lieux mêmes*. Amsterdam: S. J. Baalde, 1774.
———. *Reisebeschreibung nach Arabien und andern umliegenden ländern.* 2 vols. Copenhagen: Nicolaus Möller, 1774.

Nozawa, Joji. "Wine as a Luxury at the Dutch Factory in Japan during the Second Half of the Eighteenth Century." In *Luxury in the Low Countries*, edited by R. C. Rittersma, 85–106. Brussels: Pharo, 2010.

Ogborn, Miles. *Indian Ink: Script and Print in the Making of the English East India Company.* Chicago: University of Chicago Press, 2008.

Omori, Minoru. "Eisch Boek in Dutch-Japanese Trade." In *Asian Trade Routes, Continental and Maritime*, Studies on Asian Topics 13, edited by K. R. Haellquist and Scandinavian Institute of Asian Studies, 199–208. London: Routledge, 2013.

Orta, Garcia da. *Colloquies on the Simples and Drugs of India*. London: Henry Sothern, 1913.

Parmentier, Jan. "The Ostend Trade to Moka and India (1714–1735): The Merchants and Supercargos." *Mariner's Mirror* 73:2 (1987): 123–138.

Posey, Sarah. *Yemeni Pottery*. London: British Museum Press, 1994.

Power, Timothy. "A First Ceramic Chronology for the Late Islamic Arabian Gulf." *Journal of Islamic Archaeology* 2:1 (2015): 1–33.

Prakash, Om. "From Negotiation to Coercion: Textile Manufacturing in India in the Eighteenth Century." *Modern Asian Studies* 41:6 (November 2007): 1331–1368.

Qaddumi, Ghada Hijjawi, translator and annotator. *Book of Gifts and Rarities: Kitab Hadaya wa al-Tuhaf.* Cambridge, MA: Harvard University Press, 1996.

Rault, Philippe. *Les drapeaux bretons de 1188 à nos jours*. Spézet, France: Coop Breizh, 1998.

Raymond, André. "Une famille de grands negociants en café au Caire dans la première moitié du XVIIIe siècle: Les Sharaybi." In *Le commerce du café avant l'ère des plantations coloniales: Espaces, réseaux, sociétés (XVe–XIXe siècle)*, edited by Michel Tuchscherer, 111–124. Cairo: Institut français d'archéologie orientale, 2001.

Rediker, Markus. *Villains of All Nations: Atlantic Pirates in the Golden Age*. Boston: Beacon Press, 2004.

Regourd, Anne. "Les routes commerciales entre Zabid et l'Europe: Les papiers filigranés de fonds manuscrits de Zabid (Yémen, fin 18e–milieu 20e s.)." In *Convegno storia e cultura dello Yemen in età islamica con particolare riferimento al periodo rasûlide (Roma, 30–31 octobre 2003),* edited by R. Traini, 177–200. Rome: Bardi, 2006.

Reindl-Kiel, Hedda. "No Horses for the Enemy: Ottoman Trade Regulations and Horse Gifting." In *Pferde in Asien: Geschichte, Handel und Kultur*, edited by R. Kauz, R. Ptak, and A. Schottenhammer, 43–49. Vienna: Austrian Academy of Sciences Press, 2009.

Riello, Giorgio. "'Things Seen and Unseen': The Material Culture of Early Modern Inventories and Their Representation of Domestic Interiors." In *Early Modern Things: Objects and Their Histories, 1500–1800*, edited by Paula Findlen, 125–150. London: Routledge, 2013.

Riello, Giorgio, and Tirthankar Roy, eds. *How India Clothed the World: The World of South Asian Textiles, 1500–1800*. Leiden: Brill, 2009.

Roque, Jean de la. *Voyage de l'Arabie Heureuse*. Paris: A. Cailleau, 1716.

———. *A Voyage to Arabia Felix (1708–10).* Introduction and bibliographies by Carl Phillips. New York: Oleander Press, 2004. Originally published as *A Voyage to Arabia Felix* (Cornhill: E. Symon, 1732).

Ross, Robert. *Status and Respectability in the Cape Colony, 1750–1870: A Tragedy of Manners.* Cambridge, UK: Cambridge University Press, 1999.

———. "Sumptuary Laws in Europe, the Netherlands and the Dutch Colonies." In *Contingent Lives: Social Identity and Material Culture in the VOC World*, edited by Nigel Worden, 382–390. Cape Town: ABC Press, 2007.

Ruangsilp, Bhawan. *Dutch East India Company Merchants at the Court of Ayutthaya: Dutch Perceptions of the Thai Kingdom, ca. 1604–1765*. Leiden: Brill, 2007.

Rutten, A. M. G. *Blue Ships: Dutch Ocean Crossing with Multifunctional Drugs and Spices in the Eighteenth Century*. Rotterdam: Erasmus, 2008.

Sanders, Paula. *Ritual, Politics, and the City in Fatimid Cairo*. Albany, NY: SUNY Press, 1994.

Schaffner, Cynthia V. A. "Textile Glossary." In *The Interwoven Globe: The Worldwide Textile Trade, 1500–1800*, edited by Amelia Peck, 305–306. New York: Metropolitan Museum of Art, 2015.

Sen, Sudipta. *Empire of Free Trade: The East India Company and the Making of the Colonial Marketplace*. Philadelphia: University of Pennsylvania Press, 1998.

Serjeant, R. B. "The Hindu, Baniyan, Merchants and Traders." In *San'a': An Arabian Islamic City*, edited by R. B. Serjeant and R. Lewcock, 432–435. London: World of Islam Trust, 1983.

———. "The Market, Business Life, Occupations, and the Legality and Sale of Stimulants." In *San'a': An Arabian Islamic City*, edited by R. B. Serjeant and R. Lewcock, 159–178. London: World of Islam Trust, 1983.

———. *The Portuguese off the South Arabian Coast*. Oxford: Clarendon Press, 1963.

———. "The Yemeni Coast in 1005/1597: An Anonymous Note on the Flyleaf of Ibn al-Mujawir's *Tarikh al-Mustabsir*." *Arabian Studies* 7 (1985): 187–191.

Shalem, Avinoam. "Performance of the Object." In *Gifts of the Sultan: The Arts of Giving at the Islamic Courts*, edited by Linda Komaroff, 111–115. New Haven, CT: Yale University Press, 2011.

Smail, John. "Credit, Risk, and Honor in Eighteenth-Century Commerce." *Journal of British Studies* 44:3 (July 2005): 439–456.

Smith, Woodruff D. *Consumption and the Making of Respectability, 1600–1800*. London: Routledge, 2002.

Sood, Gagan D. S. "Circulation and Exchange in Islamicate Eurasia: A Regional Approach to the Early Modern World." *Past & Present* 212 (2011): 113–162. doi: 10.1093/pastj/gtr001.

———. "'Correspondence Is Equal to Half a Meeting': The Composition and Comprehension of Letters in Eighteenth-Century Islamic Eurasia." *Journal of the Economic and Social History of the Orient* 50:2–3 (2007): 172–214.

Stern, Philip J. *The Company-State: Corporate Sovereignty and the Early Modern Foundations of the British Empire in India*. Oxford: Oxford University Press, 2011.

Stoler, Ann Laura. *Along the Archival Grain: Epistemic Anxieties and Colonial Common Sense*. Princeton, NJ: Princeton University Press, 2010.

Subrahmanyam, Sanjay. *The Career and Legend of Vasco da Gama*. Cambridge, UK: Cambridge University Press, 1998.

———. *Explorations in Connected History: Mughals and Franks*. New Delhi: Oxford University Press, 2005.

Swart, Sandra. "Riding High—Horses, Power, and Settler Society, c. 1654–1840." *Kronos* 29 (November 2003): 47–63.

Tarlo, Emma. *Clothing Matters: Dress and Identity in India*. Chicago: University of Chicago Press, 1996.

Thomas, Nicholas. *Entangled Objects: Exchange, Material Culture, and Colonialism in the Pacific*. Cambridge, MA: Harvard University Press, 1991.

Trivellato, Francesca. *The Familiarity of Strangers: The Sephardic Diaspora, Livorno, and Cross-Cultural Trade in the Early Modern Period.* New Haven, CT: Yale University Press, 2009.

Tuchscherer, Michel. "Coffee in the Red Sea Area from the Sixteenth to the Nineteenth Century." In *The Global Coffee Economy in Africa, Asia, and Latin America, 1500–1989*, edited by William Gervase Clarence-Smith and Steven Topik, 50–66. Cambridge, UK: Cambridge University Press, 2003.

Um, Nancy. "1636 and 1726: Yemen after the First Ottoman Era." In *Asia Inside Out: Changing Times*, edited by Eric Tagliacozzo, Helen Siu, and Peter Perdue, 112–134. Cambridge, MA: Harvard University Press, 2015.

———. "Chairs, Writing Tables, and Chests: Indian Ocean Furniture and the Postures of Commercial Documentation in Yemen, 1700–1750." *Art History* 38:4 (September 2015): 718–731.

———. "Foreign Doctors at the Imam's Court: Medical Diplomacy in Yemen's Coffee Era." *Genre: Forms of Discourse and Culture* 48:2 (July 2015): 261–288.

———. *The Merchant Houses of Mocha: Trade and Architecture in an Indian Ocean Port.* Seattle: University of Washington Press, 2009.

———. "Order in the 'Arbitrary': The Distribution, Content, and Temporal Cycles of English Merchant Tribute in Eighteenth-Century Yemen." *Journal of Early Modern History* 18:3 (2014): 227–253.

———. "Reflections on the Red Sea Style: Beyond the Surface of Coastal Architecture." *Northeast African Studies* 12:1 (2012): 243–271.

———. "Spatial Negotiations in a Commercial City: The Red Sea Port of Mocha, Yemen during the First Half of the Eighteenth Century." *Journal of the Society of Architectural Historians* 62:2 (June 2003): 178–193.

Veenendaal, Jan. *Domestic Interiors at the Cape and in Batavia, 1602–1795.* Zwolle, Netherlands: Waanders, 2002.

Viallé, Cynthia. "In Aid of Trade: Dutch Gift-giving in Tokugawa Japan." *Daigaku shiryohensanjo kenkyu kiyo* 16 (2006): 57–78.

———. "'To Capture Their Favor': On Gift-Giving by the VOC." In *Mediating Netherlandish Art and Material Culture in Asia*, edited by Thomas DaCosta Kauffman and Michael North, 291–320. Amsterdam: Amsterdam University Press, 2014.

———. "Tot schenkagie daar het te pas comen sal." *Aziatische Kunst* 23 (1993): 2–21.

Vishnevskaya, Inna Isidorovna. "Eastern Treasures of the Russian Tsars." In *The Tsars and the East: Gifts from Turkey and Iran in the Moscow Kremlin*, edited by Alexey Konstantinovich Levykin, 1–13. Washington, DC: Smithsonian Institution, 2009.

VOC-Glossarium: Verklaringen van Termen, Verzameld uit de Rijks Geschiedenis Publicatiën die Betrekking hebben op de Verenigde Oost-Indische Compagnie. The Hague: Instituut voor Nederlandse Geschiedenis, 2000.

Wagenaar, Lodewijk. "The Culture Dimensions of the Dutch East India Company." In *Mediating Netherlandish Art and Material Culture in Asia*, edited by Thomas DaCosta Kauffman and Michael North, 141–176. Amsterdam: Amsterdam University Press, 2014.

Wainwright, Clive. "Only the True Black Blood." *Furniture History* 21 (1985): 250–257.

Watkins, John. "Toward a New Diplomatic History of Medieval and Early Modern Europe." *Journal of Medieval & Early Modern Studies* 38 (2008): 1–14.

Weiner, Annette. *Inalienable Possessions: The Paradox of Keeping-While-Giving.* Berkeley: University of California Press, 1992.

Werz, Bruno E. J. S., and Jane E. Klose. "Ceramic Analysis from the VOC Ship Oosterland (1697)." *South African Journal of Science* 90 (October 1994): 522–526.

Yntema, R. J. "Beer in Abundance: Distribution and Consumption in Early Modern Holland." In *Beer! The Story of Holland's Favourite Drink*, edited by R. E. Kistemaker and V. T. van Vilsteren, translated by Shaffer's English, 82–95. Amsterdam: De Bataafsche Leeuw, 1994.

———. "A Capital Industry: Brewing in Holland, 1500–1800." In *Beer! The Story of Holland's Favourite Drink*, edited by R. E. Kistemaker and V. T. van Vilsteren, translated by Shaffer's English, 72–81. Amsterdam: De Bataafsche Leeuw, 1994.

Zabara, Muhammad. *Nashr al-ʿarf li-nubla' al-yaman baʿd al-alf.* 3 vols. Sanaa: Markaz al-dirasat wa al-buhuth al-yamani, 1985.

Index

Page numbers in **boldface** type refer to illustrations.

About the Author

Nancy Um is an associate professor in the Department of Art History at Binghamton University. Her research explores the Islamic world from the perspective of the coast, with a focus on material, visual, and built culture on the Arabian Peninsula and around the rims of the Red Sea and western Indian Ocean from 1500 to 1800. She is the author of *The Merchant Houses of Mocha: Trade and Architecture in an Indian Ocean Port* (University of Washington Press, 2009) and articles in the *Journal of the Society of Architectural Historians, African Arts, Northeast African Studies, Journal of Early Modern History, Genre: Forms of Discourse and Culture, Art History,* and *Getty Research Journal.* She has received research fellowships from the Fulbright program, the National Endowment for the Humanities, the Getty Foundation, and the American Institute for Yemeni Studies.

Perspectives on the Global Past

Anand A. Yang and Kieko Matteson
SERIES EDITORS

Interactions: Transregional Perspectives on World History
Edited by Jerry H. Bentley, Renate Bridenthal, and Anand A. Yang

Contact and Exchange in the Ancient World
Edited by Victor H. Mair

Seascapes: Maritime Histories, Littoral Cultures, and Transoceanic Exchanges
Edited by Jerry H. Bentley, Renate Bridenthal, and Kären Wigen

Anthropology's Global Histories: The Ethnographic Frontier in German New Guinea, 1870–1935
Rainer F. Buschmann

Creating the New Man: From Enlightenment Ideals to Socialist Realities
Yinghong Cheng

Glamour in the Pacific: Cultural Internationalism and Race Politics in the Women's Pan-Pacific
Fiona Paisley

The Qing Opening to the Ocean: Chinese Maritime Policies, 1684–1757
Gang Zhao

Navigating the Spanish Lake: The Pacific in the Iberian World, 1521–1898
Rainer F. Buschmann, Edward R. Slack Jr., and James B. Tueller

Nomads as Agents of Cultural Change: The Mongols and Their Eurasian Predecessors
Edited by Reuven Amitai and Michal Biran

Sea Rovers, Silver, and Samurai: Maritime East Asia in Global History, 1550–1700
Edited by Tonio Andrade and Xing Hang

Exile in Colonial Asia: Kings, Convicts, Commemoration
Edited by Ronit Ricci

Burnt by the Sun: The Koreans of the Russian Far East
Jon K. Chang

Encounters Old and New in World History: Essays Inspired by Jerry H. Bentley
Edited by Alan Karras and Laura J. Mitchell

Shipped but Not Sold: Material Culture and the Social Protocols of Trade during Yemen's Age of Coffee
Nancy Um